What people say abo

A book full of practical experience and genuine interest in the personal growth of people. Worth reading, worth digesting, worth passing on.

Axel Zundler
President, AWZ EVENTS GmbH, Germany

Imagine you are reading this book with an open mind. You're intrigued by it, drawn to the richness of it, and excited by it. Weeks later you notice you've changed the way you are. You're modelling a deeper integrity, walking your talk, behaving in a way you admire – and becoming a trustworthy adviser. 'Trust Me' is passionate, practical and loaded with powerful insight you can use straight away. It comes from a man well versed in life, a man who has combined business success with compassion, and personal power with wisdom. We're proud to have Ken Buist associated with our company. I'm confident you will be too.

Andrew Sercombe
Executive Director, Powerchange, United Kingdom

For those who want to be exceptionally successful, whatever their walk of life, Ken has combined the sound teaching of behavioural analysis along with the personal development of emotional maturity. Aligned with all the elements of trust, this book provides a blueprint for elevating status to that of a trustworthy adviser, whatever journey you are on.

Matthew L Bonnstetter
President & CEO, DISCovering Positive Changes, Inc. USA

This is good. Ken writes from his rich experience as a businessman and as a management consultant. He is a pragmatist, not an academic. Yet the book is firmly grounded in well-attested behavioural theory. Although he rarely cites the specific psychological principles that underpin his work, they should not be hard to find in textbooks on occupational psychology and social psychology. This is a book for busy people who want the facts, ideas and reflections without the psychobabble.

Dr Gordon Lickfold
Business Psychologist

What People Say About This Book

Trust Me' is packed with practical and actionable wisdom for life and work and a handbook for those aspiring to provide the highest standard of professional service. In a punchy fast-moving style, Ken Buist opens up the components of trust and then the values and behaviours that build trust to improve personal and professional performance. 'Trust Me' compactly captures the benefits of focusing on others in business and provides intelligent insight into the consequences of integrity and credibility gaps. Here is a business book, aptly illustrated, that will sharpen self awareness and develop interpersonal relationships in all aspects of life and work.

Dr Mike Thomson
Managing Director, The Goodbrand Works

The workshop Ken carried out with my management team proved to be very enlightening. By facilitating us individually to recognise our unique characteristics and behaviour patterns it enabled each of us to better understand how to relate more effectively with each other based on knowing what communication style worked and did not work when interacting with different personalities. The net result is that team spirit has improved, and projects get implemented more successfully because the level of trust between individuals is now that much greater.

Ken's trusted adviser programme is a must for management teams looking to work more effectively and also for business development teams who want to build better working relationships with clients.

Tim Donovan
Managing Director – Trend Consulting

As we move into an increasingly complex world where change is the norm and sophisticated solutions replace simple products, the need for trust in our relationships with our customers and partners is paramount. But what is trust, how can we quantify it, and more importantly, how can we become more trustworthy?

'Trust Me' is a unique text which not only provides answers to these key questions but also acts as an invaluable guide book for anyone trying to build real trust into their relationships with others. Ken has many years of hard earned experience in the real commercial world from which he draws extensively in this book. This spans many companies and cultures around the globe. He offers real practical advice and valuable insights from which all of us can benefit. I highly recommend this to anyone who is serious about building really productive relationships in today's world.

Chris Coggrave
Managing Principal, Compaq Global Services, EMEA

What People Say About This Book

Ken Buist is one of the rare few who knows the truth -- that in business, interpersonal dynamics are what matters most. Helping others build successful business relationships through listening, creating trust and living authentically, is not only his mission, but his special gift.

Marina Ashanin
Director of Public Affairs, Dow Europe

You've heard the phrase, 'Great salespeople are born not taught', but Ken Buist's methods can help everyone. By increasing your self-awareness and understanding of key personal traits, it is possible to get breakthrough results from trust-based personal relationships. Compared to any sales skills training, he offers a holistic methodology that will benefit both your personal and professional lives. I've seen even the most experienced sales professionals apply Ken's method's and establish enhanced client relationships to great success.

Jerry Coffey
Director Business Critical Services, Compaq Global Services, USA

Being a professional adviser is about being both trusted and trustworthy. Ken Buist's book explains how to be both. So if you are either an adviser or advised, there is something here for you.

Geoffrey Kitt
Client Business Consulting Leader, IBM Global Services

At Reuters we needed to put together a large, global team to implement our internal Information Systems. This needed a blend of IS people, business people and some hybrids of the two from a number of different countries. In order to blend this group together and make them a team with a common goal the essential ingredient was TRUST. Naturally the business people were suspicious, wary and to a certain extent insecure with the IT people and vice versa. Add to that the international element and you can see that we had a difficult situation to manage. Using the approach developed by Ken we were able to get together, draw out the concerns and start to trust each other and understand and appreciate each other's strengths and weaknesses. We moved from an environment of internal strife to a environment of external customer focus which produced great results in a short space of time.'

Roger Newman
IS Applications Director, Reuters

What People Say About This Book

Ken has an extraordinary ability and technique to expose sensitive personal issues, long held beliefs and behaviour patterns which directly effect not only personal performance in and out of the work place but also the performance of others.

Without trusting yourself and your manager, you or your team will not take the chances and risks essential for success in today's business world.

Iain S. Burgess
Reuters PLC, Group Manager
Global Deployment and Customer Service

The importance of good corporate governance lies in its contribution to business prosperity and to accountability. 'Trust Me' is essential reading for the professional looking to improve both elements.

Tim Rose, Chartered Director

Many of the elements contained within 'Trust Me' were instrumental in the successful implementation, improved communication, deepening relationships and the building of trust within a new global senior management team.

Martin Pugh
Managing Director, Linatex Ltd

Imagine the business world as a Christmas tree. Ken just showed us how to turn on the lights.

Karen Arazim
ING Private Bank

I have worked closely with Ken Buist to implement a customized version of the 'Trusted Adviser' Programme within a large, Fortune 50 High Technology Corporation. The principles on which this programme is based, and the techniques for practical application in the sales and marketing environment, are outstanding. Helping individual sales people gain insight into their own temperament strengths and weaknesses is a huge contributor to successful relationship oriented selling. Using the principles of behvioural selling, our sales teams were much better equipped to identify and implement specific strategies to build important trust-based relationships with key clients. They began to understand why some customers viewed them as trusted advisers, and why other's only viewed them as a supplier trying to sell them something. This understanding was transformational to our sales process; the sales teams began to value trust

What People Say About This Book

based customer relationships in a whole new way, and design specific tactical pathways to build deeper client relationships. Selling became more personal and engaging for many sales people, bored with the traditional feature/ benefit product sell. Instead of the product or offering being at the center of their sales effort, the customer was! The real payoff, however, came in the programme's effect on the bottom line. Customers with whom we invested the effort to build deeper, trust based relationships not only purchased MORE products and services from us, but more MISSION CRITICAL products and services. We became a true 'business partner' to our key customers, a competitive advantage of enormous financial and strategic value.'

Bruce Davidson
Director of Sales Programs

TRUST ME –
Becoming a Trustworthy Adviser

For a complete list of Management Books 2000 titles,
visit our web-site on http://www.mb2000.com

TRUST ME – Becoming a Trustworthy Adviser

Ken Buist
with Chris Smith

This book is dedicated to my sister Ola,
who for all my life has been my trustworthy adviser.

Copyright © Ken Buist 2002/2006

All rights reserved. No part of this publication may be reproduced, stored in a retrieval system, or transmitted in any form or by any means, electronic, mechanical, photocopying, recording, or otherwise without the prior permission of the publishers.

First published in 2002 by Management Books 2000 Ltd
This reprint edition published in 2006 by Management Books 2000 Ltd
Forge House, Limes Road
Kemble, Cirencester
Gloucestershire, GL7 6AD, UK
Tel: 0044 (0) 1285 771441
Fax: 0044 (0) 1285 771055
E-mail: info@mb2000.com
Website: www.mb2000.com

Printed and bound in Great Britain by 4edge Ltd of Hockley, Essex
www.4edge.co.uk

This book is sold subject to the condition that it shall not, by way of trade or otherwise, be lent, resold, hired out, or otherwise circulated without the publisher's prior consent in any form of binding or cover other than that in which it is published and without a similar condition including this condition being imposed upon the subsequent purchaser.

British Library Cataloguing in Publication Data is available

ISBN 1-85252-413-8

Contents

Introduction		**14**
Section 1: TRUST AND TRUSTWORTHINESS		**17**
1	Trust Is a Choice	19
2	The Crucial Role	25
3	Becoming a Trustworthy Adviser	33
Section 2: BEHAVIOURAL STYLE		**48**
4	Understanding Temperament	50
5	Temperament and Trustworthiness	64
6	Adapting Our Behaviour	74
7	Communication and Temperament	83
Section 3: EMOTIONAL MATURITY		**93**
8	Can We Really Change?	96
9	Shedding the Snakeskin	122
10	Achieving Personal Growth	144
Section 4: VALUES AND ATTITUDES		**164**
11	Do You See What I See?	166
Section 5: BUILDING RAPPORT		**176**
12	Perceptual Preferences	177
13	Establishing Rapport	192
Section 6: CRUCIAL COMBO		**202**
14	The Crucial Combination	203
15	Know the Wavelength	216
Section 7: INFLUENCE		**232**
16	Empathy, Empathy, Empathy	237
17	Pushing the Buttons	248
18	Concluding Thoughts	257
Other Services		**262**
Index		**263**

Acknowledgments

I usually find that any of my projects is threatened by the lure of alternative activities. I start with high-energy creative enthusiasm, identify a practical application, and then have to resist the temptations caused by the next fifty brilliant ideas that all offer more excitement and greater attraction. It's just the way I'm wired. This work was a typical victim. I succumbed only briefly and wrote a chapter for 'The Influential Leader' which should be the next major project.

I would not have got to the end without my friend and colleague Chris Smith. He helped keep me focused, commenting that my proclivity to take sudden changes of direction was an issue we both had to contend with! Chris took much of my material and translated it from colloquial Scottish into readable English. I appreciate and value his contribution as well as his friendship. Amongst other roles, Chris works as a Leadership Coach and consultant within Personal Transformation Limited.

Much of my valuable learning about how people tick comes from outside the corporate environment. I am indebted to my many private clients; through counselling, therapy and coaching I have been privileged to share in what for them have been very intimate and, on occasions, painful journeys. Their responses have taught me innumerable skills and insights. I am indebted also to the executives of client corporations such as DHL, AIG, Balfour Beatty, LogicaCMG, as well as retailers like Topshop Topman who continue to employ me and my team in order to help to transform their people so that they may bring out the best in them.

I am grateful to the many delegates from these corporations who have enjoyed my workshops, seminars and conferences. Their openness and honesty has at times been overwhelming; their preparedness to trust in order to achieve personal growth continues to be most humbling. I know many have been helped along the way, but that has only been because they were prepared to take responsibility and make changes in their lives.

Finally I would like to acknowledge my long-suffering wife Susi. She is a calm port in the midst of a storm, a continual source of encouragement, and a valuable sounding board for a creative brain that benefits from

Acknowledgements

harnessing what can often be just crazy ideas. Her love and support have made this book possible. I also thank my three children - Lara, Angus and Rosi - three unique individuals who continue to teach me so much. Along with Susi they are often at the centre of examples or anecdotes I use during my presentations and I look forward to many more in the future.

Ken Buist
2006

Introduction

Squatting precariously in an old rowing boat firing flares into the night sky was not the task I had in mind. The fact that the boat was on a river in the Borneo jungle, with the enemy due to arrive on the opposite bank to my unit, was a compelling argument against this proposal. Unfortunately the idea came from my commanding officer in the form of a order.

Facing enemy action is daunting enough; deliberately putting yourself in the crossfire could reasonably be described as somewhere between reckless and suicidal, depending on your sense of adventure. But this was not an adventure; it was my job. Illuminating the jungle sky from a vulnerable old rowing boat might easily have been my last act on earth. My comrades under the stress of fire could easily become responsible for my death.

The challenge at that time was extreme trust. I had to trust my commanding officer that his plan was wise, necessary, and that he cared about my welfare. I also had to trust my comrades to expedite their instructions professionally and at all times be aware that I was still in that boat and depending on them to avoid hitting me with stray bullets.

Writing this book just over thirty years later is a testament to all those men. My trust was not misplaced, their concern for my life came through in their actions and the plan was a success. Our professionalism was proved and eventually our engagement came to an end. However, although my degree of trust was tested to the limit, it has continued to be a challenge in peacetime, albeit in far less threatening situations.

This work is firstly a consummation. The observations and insights shared in this book regarding the motives, style, characteristics, and behaviours that combine to make each of us so unique, are the product of over thirty years of working in the people business.

Secondly, it should prove to be a valuable textbook. Each section contains a thoroughly developed theory derived from combining proven psychological principles with personally evaluated practices, which I have consistently applied in the no-nonsense world of commerce.

Thirdly, it is an equipping tool. The value added to individuals and organisations by training and development modules and team-collaborating

Introduction

processes can be measured both subjectively and objectively. Wherever an individual can testify to personal growth and subsequent business success, there is evidence of value. Most of the material in this book has achieved that goal already; having impacted the lives of thousands of course and conference delegates over the years. In addition, businesses have acknowledged increased sales volumes, enhanced client satisfaction, and greater profitability as directly resulting from the participation of its teams and managers in training workshops that use materials included in this publication. The evidence speaks for itself.

Trust Me guides the reader through stages of understanding and personal development, leading to the place of maturity and effectiveness in the advanced role of a Trustworthy Adviser. Some of the material is accompanied by exercises and questionnaires enabling the reader to make personal assessments of their aptitudes and giving direct applications to areas that might benefit from attention and development.

The pressing commercial need at this time is a professionalism extending beyond mere responsiveness and the provision of good service. Because the role of trusted adviser transcends all professions and industries, there will never be a formal governing body able to set standards, regulate practices, register trained members, and discipline those who wilfully transgress accepted principles. The aim of this publication is to introduce an enquiring professional public to the qualities and characteristics of good practitioners, to provide an education through learning processes, challenges for those developing this role in their career settings, and to accompany training courses offered to commercial organisations. The goals are demanding, but so is the standard I and others in the field are seeking to set. Whether you proceed to develop this as a part of your career or not, it is my sincere wish that in studying the following material, you grow in personal insight and further develop your understanding of others.

Ken Buist

SECTION 1

TRUST AND TRUSTWORTHINESS

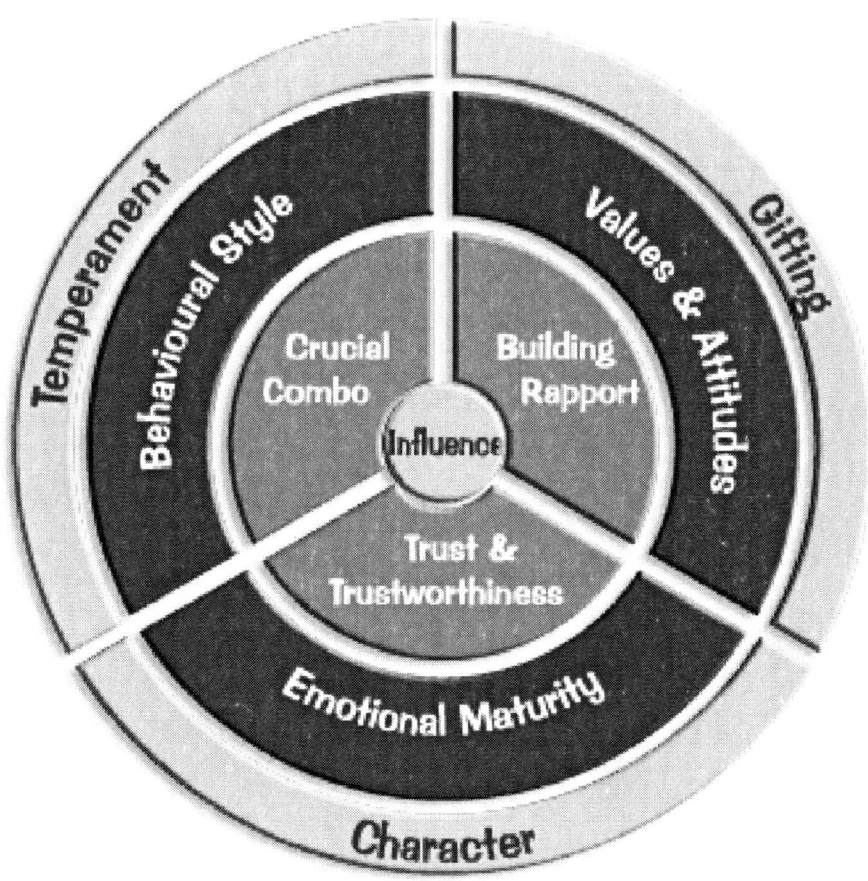

This model demonstrates the components necessary in becoming a Trustworthy Adviser. Each section of the book unpacks this model block by block, examining the Seven Essentials that together create a Trustworthy Adviser. Each section is important in its own right, but should not be viewed in isolation. All Seven Essentials impact one another. They are therefore presented in a sequence that enables the reader to build one upon another.

This section establishes our first building block. We define both the nature of trust and its demands. We look at how to win the trust of others, their expectations and impressions. Trust and trustworthiness will be examined dynamically; how they actually work and find expression. Practical ways of growing in trustworthiness will be provided. We will also explain the ingredients vital to a Trustworthy Adviser relationship and provide guidance to developing oneself in this role.

1

TRUST IS A CHOICE

The cliff-hanger

We've all seen it many times over. The people presenting us with this image also know we've seen it; therefore they try to give us a new and more dramatic version each time. The challenge must be enormous; movie makers just cannot resist the impulse to create a scene where one person's fate is determined by their trust of another.

Central to the drama are four crucial words, usually followed by two others that are clearly implied and not entirely necessary. Let's set the scene. Someone, usually the male hero, but not always, is either on top of a rockface, a tall building, or a secure perch over a fire, chasm, crocodile-filled river, or whatever hazard fits the story. Another person, often a beautiful woman with fantastic legs, is struggling to maintain her hold on a crumbling or slippery surface. He reaches out, attempting to deliver his lines as though no one else has ever formed those four famous words before in the entire history of not just the cinema, but human existence. 'Give me your hand!' Usually a look of uncertainty crosses the face of the one in peril. If it does we might get the other two words, which the first instruction clearly implied: 'Trust me!'

Now, if the person in the safer position is the villain of the story, so much the better. If a woman is saving the murderer of her husband, better still. The aim is to pull us into the psyche of one or both parties and cause us to empathise with them. To ask questions like, 'Would I trust him?' Or; 'She has good reason to hate me, is this her revenge?' Crucial to the drama is the relationship; it takes precedence over the crocodiles, the bubbling lava stream, the sinking ship, the frayed rope bridge, or whatever. Can the person in jeopardy place their trust in the one who purports to be their saviour? That is the issue with which we are to engage and become emotionally involved. Without a personal trust angle, the cliff-hanger is just an overworked device like squealing tyres and kisses in the sunset.

Few of us have ever been in life-threatening situations of the kind we encounter at the cinema, but we all know the challenge to place our trust in another person and how it feels at that moment. Whatever the context, 'Trust me' is a phrase that stirs our emotions, demands our powers of analysis and reasoning, giving rise to comparisons and memories we might prefer to keep to ourselves. Yet generally we would acknowledge that trust makes for better relationships, greater security, and general well being.

Every day we exercise this faculty, most days we expect others to place a degree of trust in us. We approach traffic lights with an implicit trust that they are properly programmed to ensure that when we cross on green; other junctions are held at red. Moreover, we trust complete strangers to stay where they are when the lights are against them. And so our working days continue with varying degrees of trust being invested, exercised, and placed in people, machinery, systems and communications. This vital assumption interlocks businesses with consumers, governments with citizens, professionals with clients, life partners and families. Yet when we stop to examine the subject we realise there are some people we trust not at all, others; 'Only are far as we can throw them', a lot of people; just a little, some a moderate amount, and just a few do we trust implicitly. Fortunately, life involves very few actual cliff hangers.

What are we looking for?

Even if we have never stopped to define it, trust is something we know by intuition. It is more of a feeling than a theoretical concept. Trust is truly an emotional experience, so too is mistrust. Philosophers may make propositions to attempt measuring this faculty but the reality extends far beyond a cerebral exercise. It digs into the fibre of our souls; illuminating how we view others, our self-esteem, personal motivations, whether we have integrated past experiences or failed to come to terms with them. Unless we have been deeply scarred by disappointment or abuse, we still retain a desire to find others in whom we can place our trust and establish some security.

A baby, without vocabulary, can express trust in complete strangers who take it in their arms. Equally, we have all seen babies pull a fearful facial expression, let their lower lip quiver, and yell disapproval until a parent delivers it from the perceived threat. With no language to define trust, a baby just plain knows what it feels. This simple illustration reveals how fundamental to human relationships the issue of trust actually is. The family friend can be made to feel accepted, valued, empathetically connected to the proud parent, and acknowledged by a vulnerable newborn as a safe person to be with. Alternatively, the child is temporarily distressed, the friend is embarrassed, may feel rejected and inadequate, the parent is also embarrassed and the adults have to work out how to express their appreciation of one another and the child when clearly the central person has very fixed views about just who is allowed on their team. The same goes for all the other sorts of teams, relationships, and introductions. Trust is always high on the agenda.

Having said that trust is an emotion, how would you want to define it? Before reading on, take a pencil and jot down a single sentence definition of what you understand it to mean.

Your definition may, or may not, assume mutual trust. It might simply express personal trust. However, if you are to grow professionally your own trustworthiness will need to develop, find expression, be recognised by others, and become part of your reputation. (We all have reputations but rarely get to find out exactly what they are!) Others will need time and opportunity to assess whether you fulfil their expectations, are discreet, wise, prudent, insightful, and operate at all times within the boundaries of a trustworthy individual. This is what colleagues and associates look for, and what business partners so earnestly seek. Qualifications abound and writing C.V's is an art form. Trustworthiness, however, requires more than a good command of dynamic language combined with the ability to study well and choose the best path for career advancement. It cannot be faked and by definition occupies a territory impregnable to short-cuts and episodic incursions.

Bearing in mind the professional need for trust to embrace

trustworthiness and be a dynamic between two or more parties, perhaps you would value making some amendments to your earlier definition by broadening it to include these aspects?

Definitions that challenge

Individual trust has been defined as: *'Being prepared to willingly relinquish control, making oneself vulnerable to another in order to achieve a certain outcome or consequence'*. Does that describe the attitude of the person hanging over the crocodiles?

Trust between two parties is where a 'Win win' attitude replaces the scenario of 'I trust you to help me for my benefit alone'. It has been described as: *'Possessing a shared belief that the parties can depend on one another to achieve a common purpose, to function with the same value system, and to always act so as to maintain and promote the dignity, welfare and interests of each other as absolute equals'*.

Would that adequately describe trust in the context of marriage? Or between business partners?

Looking at these definitions, it is a sobering thought to consider that in business we ask clients to consider us as people who can be trusted. Moreover, if we are to develop our professionalism to embrace the role of a Trusted Adviser, there are many more things to be communicated, understood and agreed to, besides our ability to be punctual, return phone calls, submit estimates and reports on time, give value for money service and scrupulously keep accurate records for our billing and expenses claims. Those things are what begin to build trust. Behind them lies an inner world of integrity and probity.

No one is forced to trust. We may be forced to act as though we trust, such as the murderer having to rely on the widow of his victim to save him from the crocodiles, but that could never be truly described as a trusting relationship; not even an act of trust. Being desperate does not make us trusting; it simply makes us take risks we would prefer to avoid if at all possible. Trust is never coerced. Trust is a choice. We give it entirely, partially, or not at all. My free will is never over-ruled in this matter. In every situation or relationship requiring a degree of trust and dependability, I am in control of my responses. The man about to fall into the jaws of a dozen ferocious reptiles can choose that to be his fate, or can take the risk that his rescuer might be genuine, or can choose to trust implicitly. It is his choice completely.

To sum up, trust is a currency of almost every interpersonal relationship. The deeper the relationship becomes, the more vital the part trust has to play. Trust enables us to collaborate confidently with each other. When we trust, communication becomes more open and frequent. Silences become less threatening, often reassuring. Trust brings freedom from the fear of confronting issues. Conflicts are more speedily resolved. These benefits consequently lead to a deeper, more productive relationship. This is what colleagues, clients, and partners are looking for. Our role is to enable them to make that choice by being what they require.

Fragile yet resilient
It is this combination of qualities that makes trust so demanding and so desirable. Trust can easily be broken. Most broken relationships reflect broken trust in one form or another. It may be due to one huge indiscretion or failure, it could be a series of minor but irritating insensitivities. The issue is the moment trust was deemed to have broken down. At that point the relationship was doomed.

Once broken it may be impossible to repair. An offended client is not too interested in gifts of cigars or perfume. A child who expects his father to turn up to his sports day is not placated by a trip to MacDonald's. Yet once trust is established and proven it makes the parties very forgiving, even defensive of one another.

This seems contradictory but this fragile toughness is at the essence of trust; it means I have come to the conclusion that someone is for me: they want my best, my success, my partnership. That conclusion has led me to a decision; I will favour them with knowledge about me, my goals and plans, I will commit something of my reputation and credibility into their hands, I will choose to work with them in preference to others who may be equally gifted yet lack those qualities that make them trustworthy in my estimation. I have joined my observations and analysis to my emotions and brought them all under the power of my will.

Because we do not suspend our critical faculties when we choose to trust someone, we are still able to discern weaknesses; knowing clearly when trust has been breached, abused, or neglected. However, if it is nurtured and built upon, we stick with that choice and are able to withstand the temptations to doubt the one we trust in, to back away from necessary confrontation and to fall prey to those who try to win our favour with flattery or sycophancy. Trust develops resilience without losing its fragility.

To sum up the ground covered thus far, we can say that:

- Trust is personal.
- Trust is emotional.
- Trust is rational.
- Trust means relinquishing control.
- Mutual trust entails the belief that each party seeks to significantly benefit the other.
- Trust involves our inner world of integrity and probity.
- Trust is organic. It can: grow; suffer from neglect; sustains damage; and experiences recovery.

2

THE CRUCIAL ROLE

Beyond the mundane

A solicitor once told me that there was only one reason why people drew up trust agreements. We were examining one at the time. Expecting either a pithy legal insight, or perhaps some spiritual observation about human collaboration, I waited a few seconds, realised he was withholding his revelation pending my enquiry, and provided the requisite question. 'What's that?' I asked. The answer was simple, obvious and apparently cynical: 'Lack of trust', he announced. 'Nobody really trusts anyone. If they did, verbal agreements would suffice. Trusts abound because trust is absent. Even among charitable organisations. That's what keeps me in business.'

Yet in many areas trust does abound. Every activity that depends on the reliability of a person, procedure, or product is built on assumptions that we take for granted. The moment a doctor is found guilty of negligence, an accountant of malpractice, a safety system is proved faulty, a child's toy is dangerous, or a legal loophole fails to prevent fraud, the public howls with disgust. Partly our outrage is to do with an expectation of justice, mostly it is to do with our faith being breached by those persons or systems which should be affirming and rewarding that faith. We get angry when our trust is abused. Yet we often find ourselves trusting without any better reason than the need to get things done.

In the daily routines of life, trust is implicit in western civilisation. We book tickets on the internet, and by telephone, without thinking twice about revealing credit card details. The mechanic has fixed the car, because he charged me for doing so – therefore I assume my journey will be safe. I book my baggage onto my flight, fully convinced it will be at the other end when I wait at the carousel to collect it. (Have you ever experienced it being sent to another continent? If so, your reaction was probably a mixture of inconvenience, travel weariness and broken trust.)

We expect the software to produce the graphics for our reports and presentations because the techies are very gifted and they promised it would be glitch-free and ready on time. This medicine the doctor prescribed for my throat infection is safe, properly tested, and will not produce damaging side effects. Our team will work late tonight, at a moment's notice, because they know we wouldn't ask if it could be avoided, and besides, we all aim to be the best unit in the company. The caterers will make certain not to offer pork products to our Jewish and Muslim customers.

The above lists are all examples of daily trust involving assumptions about competence, professionalism and care. They affect our careers, our health, our financial security, even our personal safety. Yet they lack the substance that makes life special. There is no real emotional interaction (except perhaps with a cogently synergistic work team). The trust is real, yet it fails to convey any sense of depth or spirituality. It seems to lack cost, beyond an agreed fee or rate per hour.

Fulfilment, however, arises when we successfully place our trust in someone personally, not because we must, but because we choose to do so, having had the opportunity to build a relationship in which he or she has proved reliable and demonstrated his or her commitment. Even more fulfilling is the experience of self worth we derive from people acknowledging that they perceive us to be trustworthy, dependable, loyal and credible: a person safe with confidences, able to offer judicious advice and one whose services they recommend to fellow professionals. This is one of the rewards of the Trusted Adviser.

The territory trust occupies – Six key facts about trust:

- Trust exceeds contractual obligations.
- Trust goes beyond promises.
- Trust is not limited to formal agreements.
- Trust believes the best.
- Trust is flexible.
- Trust has to be nurtured.

1. Trust exceeds contractual obligations
Contractual obligations may be the starting place; they may not. Clearly, a failure to fulfil contractual obligations will never lead to a place of trust but the reverse does not necessarily apply. Many professionals and skilled workers do exactly the job we require but our relationship is formal, it terminates once the job specified is complete.

Trust focuses on the invisible yet measurable attributes of human character. It is a response to an often unstated invitation to go beyond the written, legal framework. Genuine trust can remain intact even when contractual requirements have not been met because we know that the other party would only fail us if there was an unavoidable and totally unforeseeable reason. We trust them.

2. Trust goes beyond promises
Adolph Hitler promised peace but Churchill advised his political contemporaries not to trust him. Anyone can make a promise. When someone we deem trustworthy makes a commitment, however, we exercise trust. It is a form of faith in the other person.

Sometimes promises are impossible to keep. None of us control events sufficiently to be able to guarantee our promises but we make them as declarations of intent. I cannot keep an appointment if my train is delayed or the roads are blocked because of an accident. Your production quota will not be met if the plant catches fire or a foreign government imposes an embargo on the raw material supply.

Trust extends beyond the spoken word. It assumes the best of intentions and the strenuous efforts of the other party to fulfil their word. Trust exists when we are persuaded by something in the character of the one we rely upon. That is far more than a belief that this person will keep his or her word and honour promises because the business depends on it.

3. Trust is not limited to formal agreements
Agreements usually satisfy all parties for two reasons. Firstly, we feel that our goals and requirements have been properly stated and cannot be subject to misunderstanding or misinterpretation. Secondly, we are satisfied that the other party has adequately expressed their commitments and obligations. Agreements often follow a period of negotiation and bargaining, which give way to a process of drafting and revision.

Our trust at this stage is in our ability to state what we want, to obtain unequivocal commitments from the other party, and to assess their intention and capability to fulfil their obligations. Our expectations are not based on genuine trust but on what we perceive to be a sufficiently compatible business ethic, their desire for a good reputation, plus their fear of litigation and costly compensation clauses written into the text and without which we would refuse to proceed. It is all about winning and controlling.

A formal agreement contains all the points on which we have won and all those on which the other party has won. Where they coincide, we declare it a 'win-win'. We have also agreed to trust what we can control, what they can control, and how we will control each other. Unfortunately failure occurs in those areas that neither of us can control and consequently all parties definitely lose. World events can wreck agreements overnight. Economic downturns can veer us off course despite everybody working hard to succeed. Accidents ruin our estimated progress plans and the loss of key players puts our schedules behind. The challenge is what chemistry remains between the parties when formal agreements fail through no fault of those involved?

4. Trust believes the best

Genuine trust is expressed when we hear a bad report and respond with phrases like; 'That doesn't sound like the Bill I know. He isn't like that.' We believe the best and dismiss rumours and gossip.

Trust triumphs in uncertainty. Because it has emotional roots as well as evidence to support the logic of our attitude, we can continue to believe in the other party's character and behaviour even when our faith in them is challenged, or when lack of communication results in feeling we are left in the dark. We trust their integrity and we trust their intentions.

5. Trust is flexible

Agreements are fine and often necessary but trust can save us the need to negotiate. Partners with high levels of trust can resolve the details as they proceed because each knows that the other wants him or her to succeed. This mutuality obviates the need to agree every point, to pause for new definitions when external changes impact the plans, to renegotiate the commitments every time an unforeseen eventuality poses the 'What if... now that...' questions.

It enables us to be responsive because the goals haven't changed and the players are still on the same side. Difficulties usually cause suspicious parties to separate and trusting parties to grow stronger. Trust allows others to act with initiative and this flexibility produces new activities in which we see our trust rewarded and choose to extend it further.

6. Trust has to be nurtured

This is not a trophy to be won and placed in a cabinet, occasionally to be removed for inspection and admiration. Nurture involves continuous contact, interaction, taking small yet thoughtful actions. It requires repeating our statements of commitment, demonstrating the priority of our thinking. That way, when circumstances contrive to keep us from communicating, such as going on holiday at the time of a major upheaval in the organisation, trust does not wither or die. It has been nurtured.

In the same way that coming home late without prior warning can stretch the credibility of our marriage vows, we have to ensure that any relationship founded on trust is protected by vigilant attention. Bad punctuality, not being adequately prepared for a meeting, failing to return calls; these may not eventually prevent us from doing a professional job because we know how to pull out the stops and complete the task. However, if the basis of the task was trust, our inattention to these issues could well lead the other party to terminate the relationship abruptly, despite our meeting the final deadline on time, within budget, and with success.

Trust requires careful maintenance and it needs enhancement as well. Nothing in relationships is static. People mature, expectations change, business cycles occur and social values shift. If I am aware of changes, either in my clients or the world in which they live and work, I can consider their impact, allow for the effects, ask appropriate questions and take the necessary actions. To enhance trust requires awareness, pausing for consideration, analysing thoughtfully, and acting wisely. Just as rushing into relationships often fails to allow for trust to develop, failure to recognise the time needed for enhancement can cause trust to be eroded and become mechanical.

What are the benefits of becoming a Trusted Adviser?

Clients will:

- involve you earlier in the sales cycle
- invite you to their strategy table
- actively seek your advice
- trust your responses and judgements
- provide you with opportunities
- recommend you to other potential clients
- share confidential information
- provide testimonials
- be inclined to accept and act on your recommendations
- warn you of any potential downsides or dangers
- treat you more like a friend than a business associate
- pay your bills on time
- attempt to make interactions enjoyable
- give you the benefit of the doubt
- allow you to learn from your mistakes
- look out for you
- take pride in your abilities and outcomes
- want to keep working with you again & again.

Conclusion

The personal investment in going that extra mile is more than repaid in the long term. Lasting success belongs to those who take the trouble to develop empathy towards clients and colleagues, learn how to guard themselves from indiscreet remarks, and acquire the skills of Exemplary Listening™ and Socratic questioning (more of this later on). When these 'soft skills' are combined with genuine strength of character by which individuals, teams or companies become renowned for their scrupulous honesty, probity, and integrity, the word spreads very fast in the business community. Firstly, we have to apply ourselves to becoming mature individuals: reliable, flexible, self-controlled and displaying genuine humility. This will pay dividends not only in commercial terms, but in every area of our lives.

Becoming a Trustworthy Adviser is to enter a crucial role in the business community. The demands of an ever shrinking, yet increasingly impersonal, world place a higher premium on the quality of a person's character than on the calibre of their expertise which can often be matched elsewhere. Organisations are increasingly aware of the need to attract and retain personnel whose value lies beyond their capabilities and compatibility with colleagues. The search is for those upon whom they and their clients can depend in all circumstances: the foreseen and the unpredictable.

Summary

- The Trustworthy Adviser exceeds routine assumptions.
- This role operates beyond duty, promises, obligations, and legal demands.
- Trust involves both faith and flexibility.
- Nurture ensures continuance.

Before proceeding, can I invite you to return to the Benefits list? It might be helpful to consider this list and place a tick against the three items you most want to achieve in your business relationships. These will give you a continued focus for achievement as we proceed.

Once you have done this, you might find it helpful to categorise all the listed items according to where in the relationship you see them occurring: short, medium, or long-term. Entering 1, 2, or 3, to denote each anticipated stage, you should be able to construct a progress strategy by which you can asses how far along the journey a relationship has travelled, or needs to travel in order for your priorities to be achieved. The boxes below are for your entries.

BOX 1 SHORT TERM	BOX 2 MEDIUM TERM	BOX 3 LONG TERM

3

BECOMING A TRUSTWORTHY ADVISER

This chapter examines a number of challenging factors, offering practical guidance on the personal development involved in becoming a trustworthy adviser.

The essential qualities

- Accountability
- Interdependency
- Vulnerability
- Overcoming self-disqualification by self-forgiveness
- The Trustworthiness Quotient™ (TTQ)
- Advice and guidance on improving your TTQ

Beginning with bedrock

No tall building depends on foundations and design alone. If that were the case the Netherlands would have plenty. Dutch engineers have devoted their attention to what lies beneath the surface; the height of their buildings is not determined by their ability to design structures or dig foundations. The governing factor is that there just isn't the bedrock to begin with! Driving poles into the ground provides the platform on which a foundation screed can be laid, but that only permits a few stories to be built on top. The Shell building in Amsterdam only has seven floors for this reason.

The issue of bedrock has a direct bearing on our character development as well. If solid characteristics are not present, our behaviours will be erratic and inconsistent with those seeking to be trusted by others.

Here are the qualities of successful trusted advisers. If you start to feel uncomfortable, or wish you had picked up another book, don't stop yet! This list is a signpost pointing to where this book and its related development programme are designed to take you, so please don't feel condemned. An attractive holiday brochure describing your destination is sometimes what you need to get through the long winter nights. Those pictures also provide motivation when exercising patience at the check-in desk. Treat this list as that sort of encouragement; it tells you where we are going and what you will be like at the end of the journey.

Trustworthy advisers:

- are totally dependable in all that they do
- bring correction with grace
- work hard and play hard
- are honest and trustworthy
- give clients support to come to their own conclusions
- always keep their word
- are not self centred or conceited
- tell the whole truth at the appropriate time
- make clients feel comfortable
- think of long term relationships rather than a quick fix
- continually bring fresh perspectives
- won't take advantage of clients
- don't try to impose what they think is right
- don't use people for their own ends
- sensitively challenge to make clients think
- promote sensitivity and kindness
- don't let people down

- are good stewards of time and talent
- stay calm and don't lose their cool
- help clients to be analytical and objective, not emotional
- recognise and respect authority
- give clients options and allow them to choose
- hang in there and persevere
- are prepared to admit when they are wrong
- continually put others' interests first
- allow people to be experts in their fields
- don't have a martyr complex
- have a sense of humour and can laugh at themselves
- are teachable and eager to learn
- have a mature attitude
- are adaptive & flexible
- are responsible and responsive
- have right connections - not in a vacuum
- do not hide the commercial aspect of a relationship
- stick to commitments - time & money.

Three key words

To establish the bedrock of trustworthiness in our lives and begin to fulfil this daunting list of attributes, there are three principles needing to be considered, embraced, and put into practice. To varying degrees you will be exercising these already but we need to examine their significance in this context. They are accountability, interdependency and vulnerability.

☑ Accountability

'Trust me, I'm a doctor.' These five words, when spoken into the ear of an accident victim, are intended to bring about co-operation and calm. Our society has encouraged us to place implicit trust in those who wear uniforms; a stiff white coat and stethoscope have always been regarded as symbols of trustworthiness and a kind of unofficial medical uniform. Harold Shipman wrecked that image.

For readers not acquainted with this UK tragedy, Shipman was a doctor practicing in his local community. He was convicted in 2000 of being responsible for terminating the lives of many of his patients by lethal injection. The full scale of his murderous career may never be known. Estimates reached as high as three hundred, but have settled around two hundred at the time of writing.

One of the components making Shipman's crimes so easy to commit and cover up was the complete independence and lack of accountability he enjoyed for so many years. He was never called to account for the abnormally high number of deaths within his practice, at his surgery, or on days when he visited those elderly patients. His previous problems of drug addiction were also outside any realm of supervision or monitoring; they could have easily occurred again without anyone being any the wiser. Worse still, this ex-addict's medical practice had far beyond the average turnover of morphine and no one called him to account or explain for this. Accountability was absent and tragedy was the result.

If someone considers you to be trustworthy, acceptance of that trust makes you accountable for a satisfactory outcome. You also accept the responsibility that accompanies it. Being accountable is an expression of that responsibility, a recognition that you are to deliver as expected, to explain your actions and decisions, to allow another person to question and examine your performance, achievements, standards, and behaviours. It is a means of honouring the trust that has been placed in us.

☑ Interdependency

The traditional back-room boffin – with wild hair, an unkempt beard, seriously unfashionable glasses, zero social skills, and a wardrobe supplied by charity shops – has been largely replaced by team-working, technical staff with a developed sense of self-esteem. The archetype may be largely a feature of cartoons but he represents more than just a single-agenda social misfit. The boffin was always wildly independent.

The modern working environment now demands interdependent teams; groups of employees whose success requires that they depend on one another's skills and contributions. Marriage is the classic social relationship where interdependency benefits the goals of both partners, enabling them to find the best in one another and themselves individually. The concept is not new, but its application and development in the workplace is relatively recent.

A Trusted Adviser is mature in the skills of interdependency, even if by nature a leader or innovator. The later section on Emotional Maturity develops this theme with regard to our basic temperament types. What has to be said at this point is that a client and Trusted Adviser relationship is one of mutuality. Mutual respect, mutual concern, and mutual comfort are essential aspects of a trusting relationship. Both parties, whether individuals or teams, are clearly there for each other. It is this commitment to each other's total welfare that has engendered the relational atmosphere to produce trust in the first place.

☑ Vulnerability

By putting their trust in you, clients are making themselves vulnerable. They relinquish some, or even all, of their control. Only the very naive do this lightly. Even those areas of society in which we used to exercise trust easily have been brought into question. The BCCI scandal robbed banking of its air of respectability, the nurse whose personal mental illness led to harming, even killing, her hospital patients, prosecution of corrupt police officers, the crisis among Lloyds' names in the 1990s insurance scandal, all these and other controversies have made trust even rarer and therefore trustworthiness more valuable.

Most adults can recall incidents of broken trust and the disappointment, anger and frustration that accompanied the experience. National scandals and personal hurts form a strong inner resistance to trusting others and the decision to do so is consequently one involving risk assessment, character analysis and persuading our self-preserving emotions of fear and detachment that this is a worthwhile case for relinquishing some control. The greater the trust, the greater the vulnerability.

This has to be borne in mind when seeking to be trusted. Different temperament types enter trusting relationships quicker than others – generally the more extroverted ones – and experiences temper most of our natural proclivities in some way. Asking for trust is asking for vulnerability; the capacity to get hurt, be let down, made to look foolish, possibly loss of reputation and money. The role of the potential Trusted Adviser is to develop characteristics that communicate dependability. It is not the cultivation of superficial behaviours that sell a persona. Two of those characteristics are patience and understanding. They will both be vital at the early stages of client trust development.

Did you forgive yourself?

You may have found the list of trustworthy attributes more than a little challenging. It may have evoked feelings of guilt. Most of us would scan such a list and be able to recognise failings that have impacted our personal and professional relationships. We usually have a footnote in our minds about those events such as 'I was under a lot of pressure at the time', or; 'I'll never allow myself to offer such unreasonable expectations in the future', or; 'We both failed to communicate adequately and got badly burned as a result'.

The issue we have to resolve before progressing towards Trusted Adviser status is whether or not we have faced our failings, forgiven ourselves and found closure on the event. The first stage is simply a useful exercise in humility that enables us to learn from our failings and turn bad experiences into good lessons. Forgiveness, however, may be the key issue in re-establishing our self-confidence.

If something we did or said caused another person to feel disappointed in us, and knowing that is a source of personal irritation, the solution lies in a form of apology. A bunch of flowers is as effective a peace offering as it is an expression of appreciation between a man and his partner. Sometimes simple gifts accompanied by apologies can bring healing to both parties. At the very least, we should always attempt to resolve grievances quickly and it might be helpful to make a note to yourself about someone you need to contact in order to obtain closure on what is still a painful, or uncomfortable memory. Feeling guilty is a spiritual condition needing spiritual medicine.

The other crucial aspect is self-forgiveness. When we allow our standards to be compromised, or look back on behaviours we now regard as deplorable, the impact of such memories can be a disabling of our self-esteem. We say the right words and smile at the right times but our influence over others often causes them to doubt our sincerity rather than be convinced of it. If that is the case, we need to take a little time to re-visit the event in our imagination, consider how we would have acted or spoken, given our current set of values, and then just grant forgiveness for our failings. This is all a crucial part of developing maturity, which in itself is one of the major qualities people are looking for when asking if someone is trustworthy. Be kind to yourself and show some mercy.

The Trustworthiness Quotient™

In order to be considered a Trustworthy Adviser, two things need to happen. The client needs to be prepared to trust you, and you need to be able to demonstrate that you are worthy of that trust, in other words, trustworthy. This goes beyond honesty and integrity. It requires professional competence to deliver the expected outcome.

A definition of trustworthiness is:

'keeping one's word and being worthy of another's confidence. Being sound in principles, full of integrity, reliable, capable and dependable.'

In their excellent book *The Trusted Adviser*, Maister, Green & Galford described the trust equation, in which they stated what they felt were the four key ingredients of trust. We are indebted to them for this concept but would like to offer an expanded but different approach to trustworthiness:

The Trustworthiness Quotient™ (TTQ)

Simply stated, TTQ says that Trustworthiness comprises several elements:

- Dependability: reliable and loyal
- Integrity: congruence of thoughts & actions
- Credibility: excellent reputation
- Empathy: supportive understanding of others

Dependent upon the level of:

- Self-interest: the degree of selfishness
- In-Consistency: unpredictable and differing responses

$$T = \frac{D + I + C + E}{SI + IC}$$

T = Trustworthiness
D = Dependability
I = Integrity
C = Credibility   SI = Self-Interest
E = Empathy   IC = In-Consistency

Understanding and growing in each element

Dependability

In order to be considered trustworthy, I have to prove myself positively and negatively. I must demonstrate that others can rely on me to do and say what I have led them to believe I will do and say. This breeds confidence through consistent evidence. It is simply proof positive.

I must also show consistently that neither my words nor actions undermine their trust. It is pointless to impress clients with thoroughness and commitment at the early stages of a relationship and then appear indiscreet some months later. All the hard work will have been undone. Not doing those things that undermine our reputations could be described as 'proof negative'.

In every area it is significant to win assurance; small issues are crucial building blocks for trust, long before the greater ones come into the frame. This has to be achieved without continual supervision and the need for someone checking on my methodology and progress.

Ways to Increase Dependability

☑ Try to deliver beyond expectation.

☑ Always keep the commitments you make.

☑ Be faithful in everything.

☑ Don't expect to know all the answers.

☑ Cover all bases, even if that may be the client's role.

☑ Ensure your client is spared surprises.

☑ Discuss even minor details with your client.

☑ Have mutually agreed goals and agendas.

☑ Tell the truth with real care for the other person.

☑ Be passionate in your endeavour.

Dependability means being faithful and keeping promises even when it is costly or inconvenient. Especially when it hurts! It means being utterly reliable, not dependent on whether our feelings or circumstances have changed. The more often we are able to demonstrate that we can be relied upon, the more the dependability factor increases. This is vital in helping trust grow.

> You may find it helpful to select three of the ten items above for immediate application. Circle those that ring your personal bells.

Integrity

In order to be considered trustworthy you must be full of integrity. This includes always doing what you say, but there is more to it. Integrity involves speaking the truth for the greater good of the other party, and never intentionally misleading. It is honestly matching words and feelings with thoughts and actions. There can be no compromise in business dealings through seeking personal financial advantage. Integrity means that speech and behaviour will conform to a high ethical code, and truthfulness will be exercised with wisdom and discretion.

We have all seen the truth used destructively. Integrity is truthfulness with compassion. It is about delivering the right information to the right person at the right time, and in the right manner. Integrity desires the best for others. It has no desire to deceive, take advantage, or manipulate. Integrity denotes having a value system of the highest order.

Ways to Increase Integrity

- ☑ Always speak the truth.
- ☑ Don't be tempted by white lies.
- ☑ Never compromise your value system.
- ☑ Put other people first.
- ☑ Don't tolerate outbursts of personal anger.
- ☑ Avoid being contentious.
- ☑ Persuade but don't manipulate.
- ☑ If you don't know, say so!
- ☑ Don't continually be an opportunist.
- ☑ Always be fair in your dealings.
- ☑ Be teachable in your role.
- ☑ Exercise discretion over what you say and to whom you say it.

From the above twelve items, you might find it helpful to choose two or three to give attention to during the next few days.

Credibility

In order to be considered trustworthy, it is necessary to demonstrate credibility. This speaks about your qualification to do the task in hand. It also refers to your technical ability to hold the title Trusted Adviser.

Credibility is also about your professional ability to achieve what you promised. This may well start with testimonials from those with experience of your work and applies equally to both attitude and performance.

Credibility demands accuracy and honesty. We all experience the sheer boredom created by those who tend to exaggerate or make false claims. Every time a person is observed to be over-stating their achievements and skills the audience reaction is far from the one intended. Everyone takes note never to trust that person's self-assessment and to mistrust their accounts of events, especially when quantities, money, or abilities, are being discussed. The false boast usually deprives the speaker of that which they crave: acceptance and the esteem of others. These essential qualities of a trusted adviser require a careful building of one's credibility.

Credibility qualifies you to offer a considered solution, in a manner that instils confidence in the receiver. In other words, it buys you a hearing. If the truth needing to be expressed is unpleasant, a wise choice of timing combined with a gracious manner usually enables those who trust you to accept your critiques and candid bad news. No adviser has a monopoly on good tidings or being able to encourage every action and idea of their client. (In fact, if every notion was encouraged and every action affirmed, the client would soon become suspicious!)

Ways to Increase Credibility

- ☑ Value your honourable reputation highly.
- ☑ Be thoughtful and cordial.
- ☑ Adopt a positive attitude.
- ☑ Do not criticise or condemn, but constructively critique.
- ☑ Avoid outbursts of anger.
- ☑ Remember humility is power.
- ☑ Give your ego the day off.

Empathy

In order to be considered trustworthy, you must be able to demonstrate empathy. Empathy is the power of imaginatively entering another person's experience, of walking in their shoes, seeing with their eyes, thinking their thoughts, feeling their emotions. It is a gift but it can be acquired by practicing sensibility. Empathy also involves conveying to the other person your understanding of their position, letting them know you are travelling with them on their journey.

To acquire or grow in empathy we have to exercise a genuine interest in others. A client must be a person, not a prospect. It demands being good at valuing individuals, welcoming their contributions and ideas in projects and discussions. The one who has learned to empathise, knows how to make others feel secure, respected, important and appreciated. (Even when you profoundly disagree with them!)

Empathy requires both sensitivity and a commitment of time. A willingness to operate on other people's schedules rather than be focused on our own needs. Empathy produces loyalty which says; 'I will be for you even when others may be against you. I will defend you even when it costs me something or puts me at some kind of risk'.

Empathy marks the difference between military leaders who give orders and those who inspire subordinates to follow. Field Marshal Montgomery – 'Monty' to his troops – was clearly in charge of thousands of strangers, mostly drawn from a totally different social sphere and background. The reason his rank, accent, and social status did not provoke cynicism, mistrust, or hostility, was that he empathised with his men. He made it plain that every action was planned with a view to minimal casualties. He greeted his army as comrades, not inferiors. His pre-battle speeches inspired and produced a deep sense of solidarity among them because he was a man with a developed and acute sense of empathy. Politicians and other military leaders for the same reason could trust Montgomery. He was a trustworthy adviser.

> **Ways to Increase Empathy**
>
> ☑ Develop a genuine interest in others.
> ☑ Try kindness rather than condemnation.
> ☑ Be sensitive to others' feelings.
> ☑ Understand that caring can be costly.
> ☑ Give time generously.
> ☑ Look for the best in everyone.
> ☑ Avoid judging others.
> ☑ Don't think too highly of yourself.
> ☑ Call attention to mistakes indirectly.
> ☑ Use encouragement, make the fault easy to correct.
> ☑ Be an excellent listener.

Try selecting three from the above eleven to apply this week.

In-Consistency

In order to be considered trustworthy, it is important to demonstrate low levels of in-consistency. In-consistency is having unpredictable responses. Consistency requires that we live by principles; in-consistency arises as we live by the way we feel. Consistency means that whatever the task or situation, we analyse the facts as required and give a measured and considered response. It means not acting on a whim or impulse.

Being consistent means being there for people in bad times as well as good, not just a fair weather adviser. It is being an anchor in a storm, or having the qualities of a rock: solid and dependable. An in-consistent person who just reacts according to their moods, or to assuage pressure, never maximises their gifts and skills. Their relationships are destined to remain shallow and their history is usually strewn with the wrecks of disillusioned ex-friends and distanced colleagues. They will never assume significant leadership and are only trusted superficially to be expert in their field.

Consistency is a virtue and its result is that others feel safe with us. We engender security. It demands an even keel. The in-consistent individual who can be pleasant and calm one day, full of anger the next, apathetic before lunch and enthusiastic afterwards is building a reputation and a response. We gauge their moods, aim to 'catch them on a good day', avoid them if the signs are negative. Newcomers to the organisation are quickly advised of their proclivities. No one trusts them beyond the moment. Sadly, this failure is what isolates many gifted people and often ruins their personal lives while requiring that professionally they keep moving on every few years.

Ways to Decrease In-consistency

☑ Be predictable about the positives

☑ Consider all the facts before responding

☑ Remember and be guided by your value system

☑ Don't give in to impulsive feelings

☑ Always hear both sides

☑ Attack the problem not the person

☑ Be secure in yourself

☑ Ask questions rather than give orders

Which of these eight suggestions do you feel immediately challenged to improve?

Self-interest

In order to be considered trustworthy, it is necessary to demonstrate a low level of self-interest, or put another way, a high level of selflessness. That means not always being motivated by getting your own needs met. Rather, being motivated by meeting the needs of the client. On a simple level, a business associate who always chooses restaurants serving his favourite foods and orders the best wines when someone else is paying, will never induce others to trust him.

Greed is often a powerful driver in self-interest. This is best dealt with by always having a desire for the client's greater good rather than being concerned about what you stand to gain. Sacrifice wins people's confidence, so long as we don't draw attention to it.

The person full of self-interest radiates the message 'I am my most important person'. They have a need to always know the answer and be in the limelight. A large ego makes it difficult to truly see beyond oneself. Getting our needs met is best achieved through meeting the needs of others.

We need determination to tackle this issue and will probably become increasingly aware of our own selfish motives once we start to do so. However, it is a marvellous paradox that we achieve what we really want in life by being prepared to sacrifice our immediate self-interest. Every inventor must experience disappointment on the route to the success they long for. Edison's famous dictum about each failure being another step towards success is more than just an anecdote on the value of the light bulb. He got no pleasure out of failure! It cost him something each time! But that cost was integrally part of the desire to succeed. Similarly, we have to pay a price for everything worth holding on to once we get it. Short-term self-interest is part of that package.

Ways to Decrease Self-Interest

☑ Be fully aware of your client's goals
☑ Don't continually seek your own way
☑ Try not to dominate and control
☑ Feel secure and confident in your own ability
☑ Acknowledge the abilities of others
☑ Encourage without the need for recognition
☑ Don't continually seek credit for work done
☑ Be generous with ideas and time
☑ Look for ways to exalt your client, not yourself
☑ Avoid being patronising and paternalistic
☑ Never knowingly exploit others
☑ Be prepared to make sacrifices

You may have ideas for creatively applying some of these twelve issues. It would help to jot down your thoughts at this stage and pause to consider how these ideas might impact any of the other issues you have already determined to resolve. A few, well chosen, personal adjustments can make significant changes to your Trustworthiness Quotient. I wish you success!

Your own Quotient

Allocating 10 marks per element, take the time now to work out your own trustworthiness quotient similar to this example below;

$$T = \frac{D + I + C + E}{SI + IC} \qquad T = \frac{8 + 4 + 7 + 3}{7 + 4} = 2$$

Conclusion

Becoming a Trustworthy Adviser is a double process. It requires building a new type of relationship with your clients and building your character and reputation in the process. Both endeavours will prove rewarding.

Success in this endeavour can be measured:

- **Emotionally**; through our liking of who we are and what we do
- **Economically**; by wise use of time and increased income
- **Spiritually**; by a profound sense of personal satisfaction and more meaningful relationships.

The journey is well worth making

SECTION 2

BEHAVIOURAL STYLE

We now come to the second building block in the process of Becoming A Trustworthy Adviser. In this section we are going to examine the importance of human temperament, its behavioural styles and how they can be modified, or adapted, to maximise our business trustworthiness.

The FOUR behavioural styles are known as:

- **Dominant** (D)
- **Influential** (I)
- **Steady** (S)
- **Compliant** (C)

- How do these styles view their own trustworthiness?
- How is each perceived by the others?
- What is our proclivity to be trusting?
- The 4 elements of trust
- The Behavioural Style Grid
- Advantageous modification of temperament behaviours

4
UNDERSTANDING TEMPERAMENT

An ancient observation

About 2,500 years ago the Greek philosopher Hippocrates identified the four behavioural styles known as 'Temperaments'. Besides giving mankind the oath named after him that still governs all medical ethics, he observed that people demonstrate different behaviours depending upon the climate and terrain in which they grow up. This idea still exists in modern thinking, when, for example, we speak about someone having 'a Latin temperament', or 'being Germanic in style', or having 'an Irish temper'.

Hippocrates attributed the different temperament types to four different bodily fluids, as this was consistent with the thinking and world-view of his time. He called these types choleric, sanguine, phlegmatic and melancholic. Although we no longer adhere to the four body fluids theory, that initial work by Hippocrates formed the foundation of the Four Temperament type behaviour model we use today. Each of these terms is still in common use when describing what we now refer to as 'personality' or 'mood'. For example, a casual, easy-going, unexcitable person could as easily be referred to as 'phlegmatic' as he might be called 'laid back'.

At times, we all display behaviours of which we can be proud, ones we would regard as strengths. These might be determination, charm, empathy or attention to detail. Unfortunately, we all know that these strengths can be accompanied by behavioural weaknesses that serve us badly such as aggression, impulsiveness, worry and negativity. The challenge is to accentuate our strengths and modify those weaknesses, thus propelling oneself towards personal growth and 'maturity'.

There is little doubt that one of the biggest single influences on our behaviours is our Temperament. I would define temperament as *'the combined variety of inborn traits, the raw material that constitutes our unique nature. It governs our mood as well as the manner and intensity of our reactions and responses – thinking, feeling and behaving'* . We are born with a unique temperament and will die without it being significantly changed. The good news, however, is that we can modify our behaviours within our temperament, thereby becoming 'victors' over it, rather than victims of it.

Modern developments

Early in the 20th century, the psychologist Carl Jung developed a type theory where he described four basic 'functions': thinking, feeling, sensation, and intuition. He also described four different 'attitudes': extroverted, introverted, perceiving, and judging. His research suggested that everyone exhibits one of four different functions and four different attitudes by and through which they approach the external world.

Dr William Moulton Marston received his doctorate from Harvard University in 1921, and went on to publish 'The Emotions of Normal People' in 1928. In this book, he further described the patterns of behaviour seen in the Four Temperament model, first described by Hippocrates. Most of the D.I.S.C. temperament models in use today are based on Marston's work.

Achieving **'Behavioural Transformation'** is not just about applying some new tips or techniques. It starts with an awareness of the inner self. Depending on our temperament, we each have predictable patterns of behaviour, which I will refer to as 'behavioural style'. Our behavioural style determines how we react or respond to given situations. It also moulds the way in which we communicate, ultimately determining both the way in which we are perceived, and our ability to develop relationships with those having the same or different behavioural styles.

My objective is not to change you as a person, but to encourage modification of some of your behaviours. Our behaviours are a mixture of all four Temperament types, but we have a core set of behaviours, positive and negative, which are usually prevalent.

The four behavioural styles

Most people are acquainted with the two basic personality types, extravert and introvert. To begin with, we therefore have the following basic picture which can be seen in figure 1.

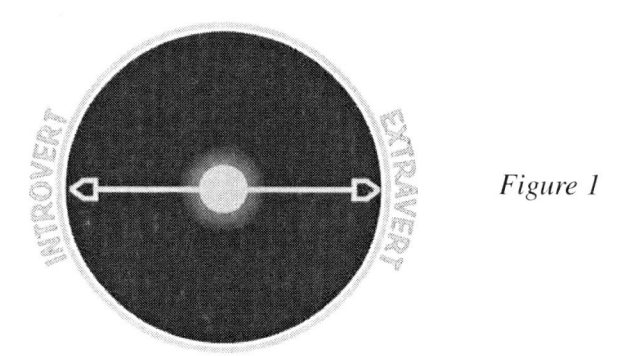

Figure 1

What this fails to take into account is the style of behaviour within which people prefer to operate. For example, an outgoing 'extraverted' person may be highly motivated and comfortable with others, or they might be more task orientated, socially competent but essentially independent. The same can be true of the reserved 'introverted' person.

These two aspects are referred to as 'Task' and 'People'.

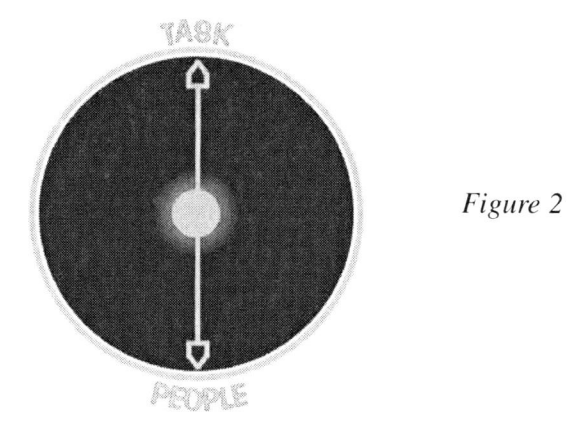

Figure 2

Now, if we lay the preferred style (fig. 2) over the personality type (fig. 1) we start to build a picture that expresses our variety.

Understanding Temperament

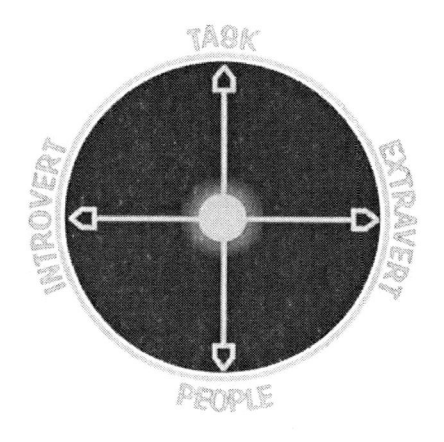

Figure 3

Each quadrant (fig 3) represents a 'Behavioural Style'. Each style has its own strengths and weaknesses; we all have good days and bad days! Remember, these four behavioural styles are morally neutral; they are not character assessments, nor do they represent good or bad individuals. These are comfort zones within which we generally, but not exclusively, prefer to conduct our relationships. They also represent those gifts and tendencies that we find motivating and frequently offer us a sense of personal reward and satisfaction.

The four behavioural styles, which correspond to the four temperaments identified by Hippocrates are:

STYLE	TEMPERAMENT
Dominant	**Choleric**
Influential	**Sanguine**
Steady	**Phlegmatic**
Compliant	**Melancholic**

The Style Grid now looks as follows:

Figure 4

Let's look at each in turn but first of all remind ourselves of the purpose.

The aim is to become a Trustworthy Adviser. Understanding ourselves, how we are wired, why we react as we do, what pushes our personal buttons, explains why some people find us easy company and others regard us as hard work. It also helps to explain the reason we instantly click with some people, often at first meetings, yet experience ongoing struggles with others whose manner and motivation are alien to our own.

Knowing the behavioural style of clients and colleagues, plus understanding our own, provides us with invaluable tools for building better working relationships. The goal, therefore, is to know when, and how, to adapt our behaviour, in order to facilitate better communication, easier dialogue, make others feel comfortable with us, and achieve positive relationships that engender trust, intimacy and partnership.

The Dominant Temperament

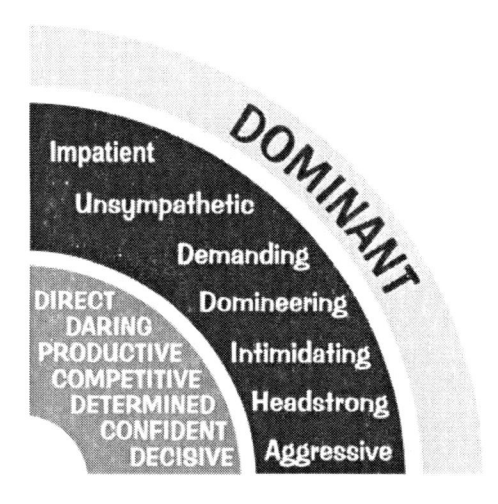

You may be someone who likes to be in charge. Someone has to be! Better an individual who enjoys that role and makes others secure within their confidence. An unwilling leader exudes uncertainty and never, ever, inspires others.

People who possess the Dominant Temperament come across as active, assertive, independent and ambitious. When you meet them, they usually demonstrate a considerable amount of self-confidence. They enjoy being in charge, and readily take the initiative with other individuals and in groups. This is a natural leader, a born pioneer, one for whom risks are more enjoyable than stressful, a high achiever.

They are normally strong-willed individuals, prepared to challenge and confront other people about their ideas and attitudes. They love challenges and readily take on new assignments. Decision making usually comes easily to them. Their drive for achievement appears insatiable. They like to run their own lives, and are wary of anyone who has power over them. They need to be in control. Their appetite for new challenges can make them appear restless to those of a different outlook.

At work, the dominant person performs best in a fast moving, dynamic and demanding environment. Being very task orientated and needing to achieve, their main focus is on measurable, bottom-line results. They are good at setting objectives, quickly work towards achieving their goals without delay, and don't allow themselves to be easily distracted.

Others tend to accept the dominant person's natural authority and leadership. Due to their innate restlessness, they continually seek new horizons, and may lose interest or patience in a project once the novelty has passed and the challenge has become routine. They prefer others to complete the job in hand while they look for pastures new. These people are self-starters, resourceful, able to adapt to most situations without difficulty. As those who get bored easily, their work should not involve repetitive detail or maintenance.

In relationships, Dominant individuals come across as somewhat cool, independent and competitive, possibly appearing aloof. They are direct, say what they think, and may be regarded as blunt and aggressive. They are perceived as proven achievers who do not readily give encouragement or support. In their effort to attain their goals, they can sometimes come across as demanding, having a tendency to push too hard whilst being rather critical of others. They are not particularly concerned about what others think of them, and will continually press towards the goal regardless of where they stand in the popularity stakes.

In a commercial environment this type of individual provides cutting edge leadership, is highly competitive, and values that characteristic in others. They excel in a crisis because it is a stimulating and exacting challenge to be wrestled with, overcome and dominated. Their focus is on results, not processes, on the achievements of a team, not its synergy.

As you might expect, and have probably deduced already by comparing this analysis with yourself and those you know, people with this temperament type tend to lack patience. They get bored quickly and can be prone to angry outbursts when under extreme pressure. At worst, this might result in ranting, and pointlessly challenging the commitment of others. This is an unfortunate by-product of their tendency to ignore other people's views and feelings. While this venting helps them to reduce their stress levels, other temperament types may feel intimidated by such behaviour.

This person is motivated to accomplish and win, whatever the environment. Freedom from control, in both their work and personal life, is important because it enables them to take the risks associated with seeking new challenges. They continually search for variety; they love to conquer a problem; they derive energy from facing difficulties; they set high personal targets; and they use all these as means of measuring their success.

The Influential Temperament

Those possessing the Influential Temperament are usually gregarious, outgoing, and energetic. They like to live in a fast paced environment. This is the classic 'people' person; naturally preferring interaction with people to involvement with tasks. Their behaviour is characterised by a high level of enthusiasm for life. They are generally optimistic and spontaneous, although at times impulsive. They tend to use these attributes, coupled with genuine warmth and charm, to persuade others to their way of thinking. They like activities that provide excitement and inspiration. Detailed analysis is not their style, so there may be a tendency to view facts superficially, which can result in jumping to conclusions. They are good starters of projects, but tend to lack follow-through. Feelings – rather than reflective thought – dominate their decision processes.

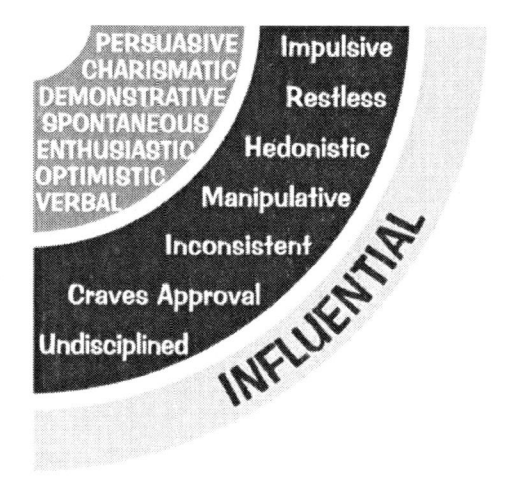

In the job situation, Influential people like a fast moving, exciting environment, where they can use their natural skills of persuasiveness to the full. They effectively harness people and ideas, spreading their enthusiasm infectiously. Being of a creative and imaginative disposition, this temperament type inspires others and enables newcomers to gel quickly and feel at home. They are accepting, generous, and inclusive. Where poise and smoothness are essential factors, they usually perform particularly well.

One of their key needs is approval. Consequently, they will continually search for people who respond well to their outgoing ways.

Influential style people associate with those they admire and whose recognition they desire. However, because they get bored easily and like to move on to new, exciting projects, they tend to start well but not always complete the task. They will benefit greatly from working in an environment that provides some form of structure without removing the variety. Help in planning and follow-through enable an organisation to get the best from those with the Influential temperament.

Relationships are very important to the Influencer and are characterised by warmth and friendliness. These are persuasive people always trying to win colleagues, clients and friends round to their point of view. People view them as socially outgoing; however, because of their high degree of persuasiveness, they may at times be perceived as manipulative, or even given to using people. They are concerned about the feelings of others, sharing their own feelings readily. Some might say they wear their hearts on their sleeves. They are concerned about status and prestige, and like to associate with those who can help them achieve these goals.

The Influencers' natural weaknesses are lack of discipline, impulsiveness, and the tendency to get bored easily. When taken to extremes, their behaviours can be perceived as superficial, erratic, and overly emotional. There can be an over dependence on verbal ability because it is such a natural strength and combines with their charismatic personality. This can lead to an overselling of their vision, their projected expectations, and even their colleagues' abilities, as they tend not to adequately assess people's weaknesses. Due to their need for popularity and recognition, they tend not to cope well with criticism, occasionally feeling personally rejected if their ideas or actions are questioned or subjected to scrutiny.

These people are motivated by popularity, public recognition, and the necessary financial rewards that enable them to live well, be hospitable, and make others feel special. They desire freedom from controls in a fairly liberal environment, and work best for a democratic boss able to offer support in the form of planning and structure.

The Steady Temperament

People who possess the Steady Temperament are noted for being dependable, persistent and kind. They tend to dislike confrontation because their natural role is that of a peacemaker. They are life's diplomats: full of patience and genuine empathy. Initiating confrontation goes against their desire to always make others feel good, while receiving it can seem to them like an injustice. They therefore always try to minimise personal conflict.

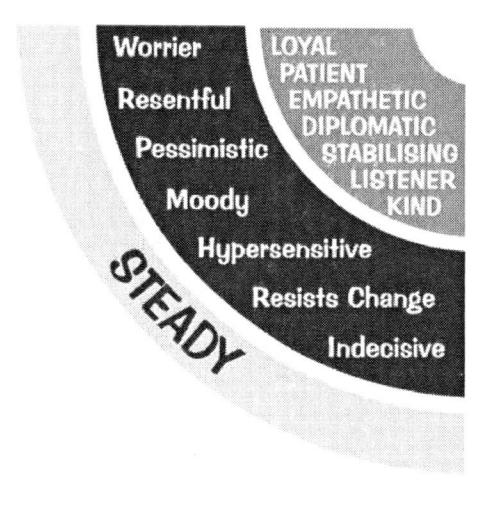

STEADY

Worrier, Resentful, Pessimistic, Moody, Hypersensitive, Resists Change, Indecisive

LOYAL, PATIENT, EMPATHETIC, DIPLOMATIC, STABILISING, LISTENER, KIND

Not being naturally competitive, these people will tend to let others take the initiative. This is a work trait as well as a social one. They enjoy people. Steady individuals are instinctively compassionate and concerned for the needs of others. Their responsiveness to others, along with a friendly, understanding, non-threatening approach, makes them easy to be with. Long-standing, personal relationships are of paramount importance to them. Hence they focus on building trust and getting acquainted. They do not rush into friendships, but are particularly good listeners; prepared to take time with others, helping them to relax and be at ease. Indeed, their approach to relationship building could also be described as 'Steady', but it is thorough and has depth.

These individuals tend to be perfectionists, with a very sensitive emotional nature. They find pushy and aggressive behaviour to be threatening and irritating. They tend to resist it passively by avoiding those who exhibit this social style, preferring to maintain stability in a fairly constant environment. They generally wear well with others.

At work, people with the Steady temperament prefer a predictable, familiar environment. 'Status quo' represents security – definitely not something to be challenged! Not being natural leaders, they welcome direction from other temperament types and are generally co-operative and willing to serve. These are the hard working team players, committed to their leader and the cause. Having started a task, they are able to see it through to completion with great patience. They are known as good finishers. When they do put their ideas forward, their manner is gentle, usually humble, non-threatening, and free from aggression or competitiveness. They tend to be good team players that develop a consistent work pattern.

Because change can be perceived as threatening, or uncomfortable, by the Steady Temperament individual, they need to be carefully prepared for it by being given time to work out in their own minds how such changes will affect their jobs and everyday life. They thrive on sincere appreciation, like to know they are doing well and respond positively to personal attention from superiors.

Steady people readily accommodate all different styles of people. This is partly because they need to be liked and appreciated, which at times can make them too eager to please. Because they are sensitive to the needs and feelings of others and try not to hurt anyone, they may pretend to go along with those with whom they disagree, despite their decision to withhold their ultimate consent. This can lead to a lot of personal frustration, tending to be smothered with a belief that things will improve. If not, they reason, escape is the final solution.

Their focus on trying to maintain the status quo tends to result in a lack of interest in planning and goal setting. Help may be needed with structuring their schedules when change arises and specific descriptions of what is expected of them can become necessary.

Lack of assertiveness, especially with more forceful types, may lead to resentments and stubbornness. They are easily hurt, and may carry grudges. Standing up for their ideas needs to be trained into their behavioural responses, as it is alien to their nature.

Steady people need security, stability, time to adjust, and little pressure. Easygoing and slower paced, they demonstrate calm, measured behaviour. Their dislike for conflict requires that they have all the necessary documentation and facts, along with time to work things through.

The Compliant Temperament

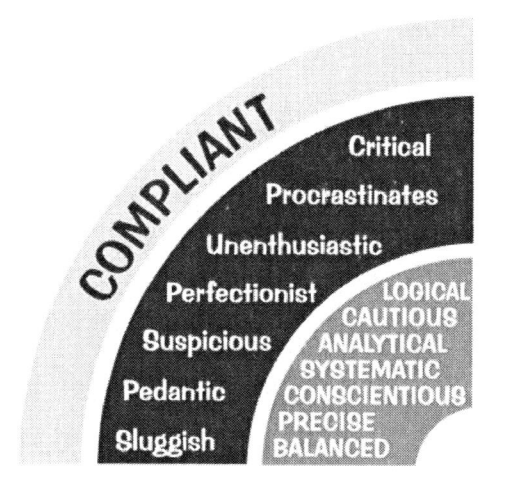

Those with a Compliant Temperament are comfortable with facts, rather than feelings. They prefer precise, well-researched ideas, to emotionally charged inspirations. Their tendency is to adopt a problem solving approach employing pertinent questions, analysis, definitions, and agreed procedures. They like to get it right first time and will go to great lengths to gather all the facts, giving lengthy consideration to each possibility before making decisions. They demand proof and love to provide it. Evidence must always be precise, relevant, and presented in a restrained and objective manner.

Thoughtful and non-aggressive, they usually wait for others to approach them rather than offering their opinion. They tend to proceed in a logical, sometimes clinical fashion, and dislike displays of uncontrolled emotion and irrational actions by others, fearing this may hinder or prevent the achievement of an agreed goal. They like to be in control of themselves, their emotions, and their environment. They usually appear calm and unruffled no matter what is going on around them. Their outlook and responses tend to be fairly predictable.

At work, people with the compliant temperament generally take an orderly and systematic approach to both their role and their job. They are detailed, thorough and accurate, setting and maintaining high standards of personal and corporate performance. They like things to be rational and well organised. Unless a task is clear and defined, they prefer not to get involved. However, they will work with persistence and conscientiousness until a task is completed to their satisfaction. 'Suck it and see' is never their maxim!

Their methodical efforts will be most effective in an environment where rules and procedures are well established. Faced with confusion and ambiguity, they can become tense, even immobilised. They value logic and deductive reasoning over intuition and gut feeling. What they don't have and cannot quantify, they don't trust. Their steady and quiet manner, make them ideally suited to an advisory role. Because they need to be right, they need to be given time to find the right answer.

In relationships, they tend to be hesitant and formal. They find it hard to develop instant rapport and trust, preferring to get to know people gradually, in a controlled way. Although they tend not to initiate new relationships, others often seek them out because they are known to be non-threatening and quiet. Compliant individuals are good listeners, only offering their opinions when sure of their ground. They do not usually seek personal recognition, but prefer to use their problem-solving abilities to establish and build relationships. They dislike interpersonal confrontation and conflict, and although they appear unemotional, can be tough, and at times arbitrary, under pressure. They may get too involved with analysis and still be seeking more data when it is actually time for actions or decisions.

Often lacking the ability to be casual in interpersonal situations, they are sometimes perceived as cool, aloof, or even stuffy. A tendency to be critical, and over-meticulous easily distances them from others. Fun does not come easy to them, and their need to loosen up and enjoy themselves can hinder their effectiveness. They are logical thinkers, more concerned with the quality of work rather than with the volume of output. They prefer a quiet, well-organised workplace, where correctness is valued and socialising is kept to a minimum.

--------------oooOooo-------------

The above descriptions embody the traits of each temperament. Obviously individual differences and degrees of characteristics will vary between people. These define what those with each temperament have in common, not how they may differ. The more extreme the type, the more pronounced the traits.

- So, you might be a doer who can be quite argumentative (known as the 'D' style).
- Or you may be someone who likes to have fun, a real people person who can be a bit undisciplined (known as the 'I' style).
- Alternatively you may be a very kind individual who enjoys serving others although not always sure of yourself (known as the 'S' style).
- Finally you may enjoy gathering data, doing a quality job, although sometimes critical of others (known as the 'C' style).

Understanding Temperament

What matters is for us to know ourselves, and others. We all tend to enjoy finding out about our personalities and characteristics. Evaluating our strengths and weaknesses is the next step, which requires a willingness to admit our failings and acknowledge that our strengths are often over-played. Applying some effort to personal growth and self-improvement will demand some application but it is the logical next step after appreciating who we are and what we are really like.

In order to be effective as Trustworthy Advisers, we also need to appreciate what others are like, how they perceive people like us, and how to modify our behaviour in order to serve them more effectively. Before going on to do this, it might be helpful to pause and evaluate.

- Which temperament is mine?
- Do I possess any characteristics of other temperaments?
- What kind of people do I find it easiest to get on with?
- With whom do I experience the greatest conflict?
- Which temperament types am I least willing to trust?

5

TEMPERAMENT AND TRUSTWORTHINESS

This chapter will examine and explain the following:

- Reasons why each Temperament style regard themselves as trustworthy
- Reasons why others might instinctively doubt this
- Each Temperament Type's approach to trusting others
- The four elements of trust

Temperament and Temperaments

Part of the wonder of human personality is that our behaviours are a blend of all four temperament types. We have predominantly one 'core' style, often a strong second, and sometimes a third. Our temperament is the combination of all four styles in relationship and degree to one another. People will ask 'which style make the best leaders?' or 'what is the best blend for a sales person?' I firmly resist giving an opinion because I can see and value the strengths and the weaknesses of all four types. I have seen good 'D' type leaders who have learned patience as well as good 'S' type leaders, who have learned to be more assertive. The important thing I have learned is, it is not which style you are that shapes your future, it is how 'mature' you are within it that will govern your progress and ultimately your success in life.

Learning to mistrust

Trust and trustworthiness are very personal traits. We are all born trusting – remember the baby who trusts complete strangers, especially if they are women and make the appropriate gentle sounds of appreciation and care? Even as we grow up, childhood is characterised by an innocence often expressing itself in trust. To become mistrusting and suspicious is therefore a learned behaviour.

This change can occur for various reasons. As our memories begin to hold records of the failings and broken promises of others, they also store the feelings of hurt and disappointment. Our expectations might have been unreasonable and never encouraged in the first place. Promises may have been uncritically believed because that was the natural response of childlike naivety. Whatever the reason and no matter how much the fault may have been with us as well as the other party, the emotional effect of being let down made its mark. Gradually we all tend to build defence systems against having our trust breached.

An architect once told me that his partnership never did business for anyone whose surname ended in the letter 'I'. His explanation was simple and even he found it amusing; 'We've had three clients over the years who kept changing the specification, built up the costs, ignored our warnings about the charges that would be incurred, and then finally paid us nothing and declared themselves bankrupt. It sounds silly, but we just decided to make it a policy to refuse work from anyone with that kind of name'. He knew it was irrationally absurd! Broken trust produces behaviours of which we can be fully aware yet deeply entrenched in, just as much as it can result in attitudes and habits of which we are entirely ignorant.

> **'Mistrust and suspicion are acquired, or learned behaviours.'**

The influence of temperament

Our temperament also has an influence on whether we find it difficult to trust, as well as how trustworthy we may appear to be. Each temperament type will regard itself as trustworthy for different reasons, based upon its strengths.

Unfortunately that has no influence whatsoever on those who are very different from us or find our behavioural style difficult to comprehend! We cannot assume that we are considered trustworthy just because of our personal integrity. Trust is emotional as well as rational. It requires that fears be allayed and doubts satisfied. What I know about myself, and my strengths, is no recommendation to the person who finds me an utter mystery even after several months of meetings and discussions!

Sometimes a person may trust us implicitly for superficial and unjustifiable reasons. How many times has an elderly person who has been conned out of their savings or robbed of their valuables, explained why they placed their trust in a complete stranger by saying; 'Well, she had such a nice face, you see'?

Our social comfort zone is often defined by our temperament. We tend to avoid those who are vastly different from us. Equally, we feel at ease with our kind of people. In other words, our trust might have nothing to do with a person's trustworthiness. Nor may it have any connection with their lack of trustworthiness. The next step, therefore, is to examine the different temperament types for how they influence our self-awareness and contribute to the trust, or mistrust, of those with whom we come into contact.

Trust and the Dominant Temperament

Those with a Dominant temperament regard themselves as trustworthy because they know that they are very principled in their approach to others. They can

> **'People are bound to trust me because I have such strong principles.'**

usually be relied upon to fulfil their promises, and they expect others to see this quality in them. In fact, because they are often results driven, they can persevere in keeping their word despite the fact that it hurts them. They usually have the ability and strength of personality to force through obstacles and difficulties, bending circumstances to submit to their efforts and driving through the agreed agenda. Of course they keep their word!

Others, however, may be wary of trusting this temperament, because dominant people are not naturally warm. Trust involves feelings as well as facts – hence the 'nice face' victims. Dominant temperament individuals tend to find it difficult to be vulnerable. They are therefore not easy to get close to. Their natural force of personality can lead others to feel that the Dominant person is not to be trusted; they may be taking advantage, or just taking over! 'Oh, I just didn't like him, he was too pushy, too self-confident.

Everything I raised as a difficulty had either been already thought through or it was no trouble at all. 'No worries', he kept saying. I just thought he ought perhaps to have some worries of his own.' How often does a tradesman or professional fail to land a job because his client would prefer him to have a few uncertainties and share some of their fears?

When it comes to trusting others, the Dominant temperament has a natural fear that a competitive agenda lies behind the other parties' request for trust. They suspect that someone wants to 'get one over on them', as we would say. Their inclination is to be suspicious of others, in particular their motives. As a result, they tend to find trusting others something of a strain.

Trust and the Influential Temperament

Individuals with an Influential style temperament see themselves as trustworthy, because they love people! It is natural for them to freely make promises to others, due to their warm and generous nature.

> 'Anyone can see that I'm a people person. They trust me instinctively because of that.'

They always have every intention of keeping their word. They want others to feel good, especially about them. However, they can easily become sidetracked by the very enthusiasm that led to their first commitment. Something else just seizes their attention and demands their energies.

Consequently they can fail to deliver on promises they have made, which eventually leads to others not trusting them. They can, on occasions, be indiscreet in their quest for popularity. This might result in their taking on projects that are beyond their abilities or resources. It may lead them to undertake commitments without any thought as to the consequences of failure. It frequently leads to disclosing confidences they should keep to themselves. Remember, this temperament is impulsive.

The Influential style can be overly trusting of other people. Especially those they like and who are of a similar temperament. They can also be naive about the ability of others. In some cases a totally unrealistic attitude towards the ability of another person or group, can result in persuading a third party to place their trust in the wrong people. This is caused by an enthusiasm for friendship that exceeds sober judgement. The result will be a loss of trust in them, which they may well protest as being totally unjustified.

Trust and the Steady Temperament

People possessing the Steady temperament believe themselves to be trustworthy because they are conscientious.

Relationships matter to them. They would never want to be

> 'The reason people place their trust in me is that they can see I genuinely care about them.'

responsible for letting someone down. However, in their quest to please everyone, they may not always be as honest with others as they should be, especially where they perceive the truth to be blunt, or unpalatable. This can result in failing to win the trust of others, because they are perceived as withholding the full story.

They are by nature sceptical and want to develop a deep and meaningful relationship before they are prepared to trust completely. The corollary of this is that they expect others to share their boundaries; time has to be taken to win them over, sudden changes in relationships are seen as threatening and to be avoided.

Remember, this is a sensitive disposition, easily hurt and finding it hard to forgive because the impact is considerable when they are offended. If trust is broken with these people, it is a long road back before they are willing to trust once more. They are also disinclined to confront or complain openly. Small matters that need to be smoothed out in a trusting relationship may never see the light of day if these people are rushed into things ahead of their own pace.

Trust and the Compliant Temperament

People with a Compliant temperament think of themselves as trustworthy, because they pride themselves on doing things 'correctly'. Duty is a strong motivator for such an individual. They are very discreet and will not readily betray a confidence. This is something upon which they place a high value. They can, however, be perceived as aloof, and may be reluctant to get involved in relationships. Their tendency

> 'People like me do things properly, efficiently, thoroughly. That's why others put their trust in us.'

towards control can make it very difficult to admit their mistakes, thus obstructing the development and growth of trust.

People with this temperament tend to see everything that could go wrong, first of all. They need time and space to express these fears, needing much reassurance and adequate data before they are prepared to trust. It takes a long time for this temperament to be prepared to share their inner selves, often because that is a place they rarely go to, preferring the world of quantifiable facts and reasoned opinions.

However, because of their orderly approach to everything, they are more prepared to be vulnerable to those who share their values. For them, trust is less an emotional equation than it is an analysis of data and information. Personal chemistry is not what they look for. Proof and persuasive logic holds the key, because that is the realm in which they feel secure.

Trust is both an event and a process

Trust as an event happens at a specific time. Think of a new boss or member of staff. We tend to reserve our trust until they have demonstrated trustworthiness. During this initial period there may be uncertainty, you might vacillate from one opinion to another, you could even find your assessment of them varies according to whom you speak with, or with whom you see them getting along. However, if the relationship is going to develop, there comes a time when you have to make a decision. A point where you say; 'Yes, I am going to trust that person' or; 'No, I will not trust them'. That decision is an event.

Trust is also a process. A single event of trust is not sufficient to sustain a long-term trust based relationship. Trust has to go through the process of growing and maturing over time. As the relationship deepens, there will be more opportunities for trustworthiness to be demonstrated. It therefore has opportunity to deepen and grow.

As a Trustworthy Adviser, it is important to build a personal as well as a professional relationship with clients, in so far as one can. The event of their choosing to trust you will require as much supportive evidence as you can offer, especially during the early days. The process aspect needs your attention; you cannot rely on their decision to be permanent. For this reason the personal element of the relationship is crucial. We are often convinced that our decisions about people are correct when we find their interest in us extends beyond the immediate task in hand, yet somehow respects our boundaries and never becomes intrusive. This is where we need great sensitivity and insight concerning our own temperament and the behavioural style it represents, as well as an understanding of how we impact and influence others. Moreover, we need to develop the ability to assess the temperament and style of our clients and modify our own behaviour accordingly.

In conclusion, all Temperaments see themselves as trustworthy. However, they do not necessarily see those with other Temperaments as trustworthy, nor always feel inclined to trust those with similar Temperaments. For some Temperaments trust comes easier than it does for others, but it may be superficial.

The following table is a broad summary of the perceptions we tend to hold regarding others and ourselves.

	See themselves as	Seen by others as	Can they trust?
Dominant	• Principled • Reliable • Confident	• Lacking warmth • Aloof, difficult to get close to • Liable to walk over you	• Find it hard • Suspicious of the motives of others
Influential	• Happily making promises they fully intend to keep • Credible	• Easily sidetracked • Failing to deliver on promises • Liable to be indiscreet in quest for popularity	• Can over-trust the motives of others
Steady	• Conscientious, therefore trustworthy • Hate letting others down • Extremely loyal	• Inclined to reserve their feelings and not be fully open and honest	• Sceptical by nature • Will trust when the relationship is well developed
Compliant	• One who 'does things right' - therefore who is trustworthy • Strong sense of duty in all things	• Discreet - will not betray confidences • Aloof and reluctant to develop trusting relationships	• Over-cautious so find it hard • Require constant reassurance and lots of information first • Need time before they will share themselves

One thing the table should make clear above all else, is that people approach the issue of trust and relationships from very different perspectives. Even if their aims are the same, the methods of making the connections will be very different.

To conclude, it would be worth considering the four elements that make up trust between individuals and how they are significant to the four temperaments.

The elements of trust

Subjective
This would be summarised as; 'I feel confident that I can trust him'. It may refer to your daughter's new boyfriend, a plumber, your investment adviser, a doctor. They have passed a test without any formality or set standard. It is purely intuitive. You may have flagrantly ignored all sorts of warning signs or silenced the voices of perceptive criticism. Alternatively, you may be unaware of any reason for concern whatsoever. The feeling could have strong foundations based upon previous experiences, which you have yet to recall and process. What you rely upon is the feeling, not its source. Equally, this might just be a matter of personal chemistry; they support your football team, listen to your kind of music, like your choice of décor, laugh at your jokes and respond with similar anecdotes. It might go much deeper and register at the level you would refer to as discernment.

> **Trust is an emotional transaction.**

This sort of assessment is common to the Influential type temperament. Those of a Steady disposition may employ it as well but with far less weight being placed on external indicators and more time given to making the judgement.

Objective
'I've checked all their figures, taken several references from associates I respect and done my own projections, which come out pretty close to their own.' Guess who might be speaking? This is Ms. Compliant assuring her board that the proposed project management team are reliable. Forget the chemistry, she's done the checks!

The objective element of trust requires hard work, research, analysis, deep thought, and comparison. It also demands that we run the scenarios of

> **Trust is an intellectual exercise.**

'What if it goes wrong?' more carefully than 'What are the benefits if it works out?' That is not to deny the intuitive aspect of personality in the Dominant and Compliant Temperament types. However, they invariably choose to lean on knowledge far more. They are driven less by their feelings than by the facts.

Active

Assuming we have employed both the subjective and objective elements, according to the degree they influence us as individuals, we come to the point of decision. This is crunch time. It may be to share a confidence, possibly a confession, perhaps to disclose a fear, or explain our behaviour in terms of past experiences, of which no one else is aware. Whatever we are about to say has been preceded by varying degrees of thought and feeling. Now is the time for us to act on our assessment of the party in whom we choose to place our trust.

The action may be far less personal and more related to business activity. Choosing a new member of the team, employing a designer, engaging a construction contractor, or allocating a tranche of investments to a stockbroker, it all involves the same processes and attaches the same anxieties as personal disclosure would do.

> **Trust may be a noun, but we still have to do it.**

What you have to do as a Trustworthy Adviser is allow your clients to make their assessments of your trustworthiness based on their Temperament type, without your personal style getting in the way and communicating an unhelpful impression.

Reflective

Every person who trusts in you will need to reflect. If not, they are extremely naive! The normal pattern of behaviour is that people exercise their choice to trust but do not suspend their critical faculties. They watch. What they look for is a positive outcome in which your competencies are demonstrated and their personal interests are seen to be of supreme importance to you.

They will want to see that your billing represents good value for money. Your timekeeping should reflect commitment. Preparation for meeting has to prove that their confidence in you was not misplaced. Behaviour with their other associates needs to convince everyone that you are a good find, not a mistake.

I once introduced to senior management an external associate with whom I had mutually profitable arrangements. I had briefed him about who would be at the luncheon, what interests they represented within the conglomerate, why they were prepared to meet with him, and what the minimum was that we would be looking for if his proposals were to be considered. It was a meeting with a strong potential for a win-win result. All it required was a little negotiation. The meeting took place in one of our company's private dining rooms. By the time we had finished the first course he had swallowed two double gin and tonics, and two glasses of wine. I was worried. Half way through the main course my fears were justified. He forgot my advice, pushed for a one-sided deal, and completely lost the plot. He also lost credibility and respect. I never introduced him to anyone else, even though we maintained a valuable working relationship for a few more years. My reflection was concluded before the coffee was served!

> **Trust is organic. People watch it grow and check out its fruit.**

- Every satisfactory and positive outcome confirms the decision to trust. This applies to all temperament types.
- Confidence is built incrementally and leads to our being regarded as trustworthy.
- Because each Temperament type finds their own way to the place of trusting, a sensitive approach facilitates an easier arrival.

6

ADAPTING OUR BEHAVIOUR

This chapter examines and explains:

- The Behavioural Style Grid
- Behaviours that prevent success
- Modifying behaviour in order to win

You will probably be fairly sure about which of the four Temperaments best describes you. We refer to this as our 'Core Style'. From among the other three, you will quite likely have identified some characteristics that also feature in your behavioural style. These prove to be complementary, providing us with breadth and balance.

The aim now is to examine how we can adapt our behaviour, given our Temperament types. We cannot change who we are, but through understanding and application we are able to accentuate our strengths and manage our weaknesses. For example, there is no justification for someone with a Dominant Temperament to be domineering.

This chapter focuses on those aspects of our Temperament that enable us to be successful and those aspects sometimes responsible for preventing that. The aim is to prepare the way for making whatever necessary changes are required in order to achieve our objective: becoming Trustworthy Advisers.

Wherever I have explained these principles and people have found them to be personally applicable, their testimony has been that the benefit of working through the changes has been to add value to their personal lives as much as their careers. In other words: whatever the challenge, the reward outlasts the effort.

Adapting Our Behaviour

The Behavioural Style Grid™ below separates those traits we find acceptable in ourselves, and others, from those we find less desirable. I refer to those in the inner ring as being 'Good Day Traits' and the outer ones as 'Bad Day Traits'. These are not moral judgements!

TASK

COMPLIANT / **DOMINANT**

INTROVERT / **EXTRAVERT**

Outer ring (Bad Day Traits), Compliant/Task quadrant: Critical, Procrastinates, Unenthusiastic, Perfectionist, Suspicious, Pedantic, Sluggish

Outer ring, Dominant/Task quadrant: Impatient, Unsympathetic, Demanding, Domineering, Intimidating, Headstrong, Aggressive

Outer ring, Steady/People quadrant: Worrier, Resentful, Pessimistic, Moody, Hypersensitive, Resists Change, Indecisive

Outer ring, Influential/People quadrant: Impulsive, Restless, Hedonistic, Manipulative, Inconsistent, Craves Approval, Undisciplined

Inner ring (Good Day Traits), Compliant: LOGICAL, CAUTIOUS, ANALYTICAL, SYSTEMATIC, CONSCIENTIOUS, PRECISE, BALANCED

Inner ring, Dominant: DIRECT, DARING, PRODUCTIVE, COMPETITIVE, DETERMINED, CONFIDENT, DECISIVE

Inner ring, Steady: LOYAL, PATIENT, EMPATHETIC, DIPLOMATIC, STABILISING, LISTENER, KIND

Inner ring, Influential: PERSUASIVE, CHARISMATIC, DEMONSTRATIVE, SPONTANEOUS, ENTHUSIASTIC, OPTIMISTIC, VERBAL

Centre: **MATURITY**

STEADY / **INFLUENTIAL**

PEOPLE

In most cases you will identify some of yourself in both the inner and outer rings.

75

Taking our Temperaments to work

You may well have had the experience of working with someone who seems to always be suspicious of your motives. They ask; 'Explain the real reason you said that?' or; 'What actually lay behind that action?' It seems that any selfless act or constructive statement you make is deemed to be serving some hidden agenda. Even when they say nothing like that for weeks on end you still feel that the thoughts are there, unexpressed, but simmering. This diagram points to those attributes that can often create a lasting impression. It should help us to understand why those with temperaments that have very different characteristics from our own, often see our milder behaviour in more extreme terms. And vice versa, of course!

> ✱ **Although we cannot control the way in which all our words and actions are interpreted, we do have control over whether or not we allow our weaknesses to develop and take on a life of their own.**

John Cleese is probably one of Britain's leading comic actors. The nature of his style of sit-com (situation comedy) is a classical drama device. Students of Shakespeare will know that all his tragic characters are people with one major fault whose circumstances, usually contrived by the scheming of others, cause it to be exposed to the point of extreme vulnerability. Their weakness, at that point, becomes their predominant characteristic and inevitably leads to their ruin and destruction, along with a number of others. Shakespeare's body counts can be quite high!

Cleese creates, and brilliantly plays out, tragi-comic characters with one enormous flaw. In the film Clockwise, his character is a man with a hidden past; he was always incapable of managing his time. This fault comes back to haunt him when, due to his over-massaged ego, he gets on a wrong train. His trip was to attend a conference of school head-teachers, to whom he was scheduled to give an address about his success in revolutionising the standards of his school by meticulous, even paranoid, control of what everyone did with their time. As the tension of his impending lateness grows, Cleese exhibits all the worst of his character's faults. We could say that, as his day progressed, he moved inexorably from the centre of the Behavioural Grid to its outer extremities, and even beyond! Maybe we can all identify with those sorts of days, which is what makes this kind of humour so successful. Someone else suffers far worse than we do for being more stupid than we are, even at our worst moments.

A day of two halves

Let's rework that old cliché used about sports matches and apply it to the working day of each Temperament type. The assumption is that all of our individuals have had very little sleep, perhaps after returning from an overseas trip, they had a row with their partner just before leaving home that morning, their journey was delayed and someone broke the off-side mirror of their car and failed to stop. They are frustrated, tired, disappointed by others, and self-critical.

At lunchtime a respected colleague takes them out and shows genuine interest in their welfare. The trustworthiness of this person enables them to share confidences about the morning's problems and they are helped to see how this affected their performance. The afternoon reflects the behaviours they prefer to see in themselves.

Derek Dominant

At a meeting to discuss a new project, colleagues raise doubts about projected costs, completion dates for each stage, a lack of adequate marketing statistics and the need for a more robust legal examination of the consequences of failure.

Mr. Dominant demands to know why the marketing figures are late. He is completely insensitive to the cause of this delay: the bereavement of one of his staff due to losing a family member. He insists that the project will go ahead, on time, on budget, as projected.

One of the team attempts to calm him down and protect the already damaged feelings of the marketing researcher. Derek tells him to sort out his legal advisers first, before intruding into other areas.

The accountant is intimidated by interruptions to his quiet and systematic presentation of why costs are spiralling. The project co-ordinator attempts to turn the discussion to a review of target dates for each phase and is met with the assertion that this will happen on time, within budget, without mishap. All objections are judged as negative and 'Not our style'.

A quick pep talk, littered with threats and denunciations of poor commitment, defeatism, and weakness brings the meeting to a silent conclusion.

After lunch, the team is hurriedly reassembled for a review of several older projects nearing completion. Normally Mr Dominant exhibits very little interest at this stage. Today, he ensures that each participant has opportunity to speak, asks for their opinions on any foreseeable difficulties, and thanks each in turn for their contributions. He is very direct, yet sensitive.

Derek has no problems in making two significant decisions but he takes a little time to explain his thoughts. He makes sure that he gets his way in these areas, but he listens, considers, and reasons. Everyone feels secure about his decisions.

His determination to end a project early is forcefully presented. He tells them it is vital if the outcome of the morning's discussion indicates the need for extra attention to the newer project. Everyone agrees, noting that perhaps they were heard after all.

He announces when he intends to take a holiday, something he never negotiates or discusses, and then proceeds to talk about their need to take a rest as well. They feel a little appreciated. His marketing researcher, to whom he gives double the compassionate leave set out in the staff handbook, is surprised by his display of concern this afternoon, but not surprised to learn that Human Resources were not consulted about this departure from policy.

The meeting concludes with a brief exhortation to be the best of the best and a request for suggestions about how this can become a reality. He then briefly apologises for the manner with which he conducted the morning meeting and asks that there be no hard feelings. Everyone smiles, nods appreciatively and is glad to be part of a team that gets things done, and done fast.

This is not a case of Jekyll and Hide. (A literary character created by Robert Louise Stevenson, whose personality was dramatically changed from a caring physician to an evil monster by drinking a potion he created, but to whose effects he becomes addicted.) Nor is it a description of the popular but distorted view of schizophrenia. This is a description of possibility. It details what could reasonably be expected to happen when individuals realise that they are speaking and behaving according to the weaknesses of their Temperament type and consequently makes the choice to adapt their behaviour.

Imogen Influential

Ms Influential depends on her charm, her wit, her quick thinking, creativity, and cheerfulness. She usually gets her own way just by talking; it saves lots of pointless documentation. Tired, irritable, and not feeling too kindly disposed towards herself or others, she enters the meeting without the emotional preparation she normally relies upon.

The figures sound bad but she talks them into insignificance, offering fantastical alternatives. Projected sales results are not yet analysed and assurances of them coming through soon are not convincing anyone but Imogen just loves to display trust, even when it seems unfounded. She keeps smiling at her researcher to offer some joy in her sadness. It fails to touch the spot.

She admits not to having read an earlier report, explaining that it was somewhere on her desk between yesterday's stuff and the wood buried far beneath. 'I'll look at it, sometime,' she says dismissively, forgetting that only last week she gave an inspirational talk on the benefits of a clear desk policy and how people felt valued when you paid attention to their work. The team were split between those who smiled and those who frowned.

A suggestion was instantly seized upon as the way forward despite her legal adviser expressing severe reservations and a little flirtation and flattery seemed to silence him temporarily. Later he looked dissatisfied and unhappy. The meeting ended early with some witty reminders that the word 'Problem' was 'Bad speak' for 'Brilliant opportunity for success'. The theme was old, the jokes were new, she seemed to need their affirmation more than usual and they gave it willingly yet wishing they hadn't.

Ms Influential hates a project once it is under way. The afternoon meeting has to carefully chart a course to maintenance and conclusion. She is expected after the morning's behaviour to yawn frequently, doodle energetically, and gaze out the window.

She sums up each position thoroughly, factually, obviously well prepared. She apologises for not issuing notes, saying it seems easier if she just speaks, requests a minute taker and holds their attention with ease. The team are encouraged, thanked, affirmed and inspired.

One project offers itself for early completion, according to Imogen. Seizing that opportunity, she explains, will release time for the troubled one, which they considered that morning. The argument is cogently presented; no one demurs. In fact, everyone is invited to raise objections, all of which are considered.

She skilfully returns their thoughts to the earlier issue, apologises for not showing the appreciation for effort and thought they all deserved. Ms

Influential has thought it over and believes that the team's skills are more than a match for the issues raised. She gives them hope, courage, and self-belief, without making anyone feel inadequate for having expressed reservations.

She advises her researcher to take a few days compassionate leave, assuring her that the workload will be covered and gets a commitment from all the team to that end. They leave, happy that their team is led by such a creative and inspirational woman.

Imogen reined in her weaknesses, accentuated her strengths, and chose to behave maturely within her Temperament.

Sofia Steady

Sofia is worrying about the broken car mirror and the journey home. Turning attention to the agenda, she becomes severely anxious. This has all the elements of a disaster! The accounting model looks bad but she asks for a worse case scenario and proceeds to tell everyone what a commercial meltdown that would create.

The legal implications require a decision about seeking external advice. Sofia dithers and seems caught between incurring greater costs and trusting their own staff. A passive silence takes hold and strangles creative suggestions.

Project delays are explained but Mrs Steady is quietly angry. She resents the fact that this had been foreseen and she had given clear warnings. Why did no one ever appreciate a frank discussion of negative issues? Why did they always compare her style to that of the bubbly Imogen who talked her way out of problems that were avoidable in the first place?

Sofia can see that her researcher needs time off. A temporary replacement might be needed in order to get the figures out. She does not want a new face on the team. It works well, usually. Disruption is always negative.

The meeting concludes with warnings. It is right to be concerned, even anxious. Hasty decisions would be counter-productive. They must think long and hard, matters are complex and things could go either way.

That afternoon, the team gathers for what they fear will be a depressing two hours of gloom and prevarication.

Sofia forces a smile and apologises for being so downbeat that morning. She explains about feeling tired, the traffic, the wing mirror and even the row with Stan. Everyone smiles, nods in sympathy, identifies thoroughly.

She listens attentively and patiently, making notes and exploring possibilities. The projected finances are the result of hours of work and she shows appreciation for all the effort and presentational skills employed.

There will not be any panic or rush to react and this feels safe to the team, not claustrophobic.

The researcher is advised to go home early and take the full entitlement of compassionate leave. Later a card is circulated for the team to sign and some flowers are sent. Her reputation for supportiveness is legendary.

A tension between their legal adviser and project co-ordinator is smoothly handled. Both egos are stroked and emotions are calmed. Neither feels they lost face but value a better example. Sofia refuses to see any of her people upset.

She enables the team to agree to conclude a project early and use their efforts to resolve the morning's headache. She announces that they need to make a decision on that one today and takes them confidently to where they wanted to go. The meeting ends with everyone silently agreeing that their team leader builds them together at every opportunity.

This is not the result of a lobotomy! Sofia has played to her strengths and turned her day and her team around. Wisdom leads us to choose the mature responses.

Carl Compliant

Carl is wary of making mistakes. His bad morning projects onto the team as he sighs wearily after announcing that he has reviewed their findings very thoroughly. They fear him, he fears the outcome; they all fear the future.

Mr Compliant is suspicious of the legal considerations. They may be a justification for inaction or for exalting the role of the legal adviser. He focuses on their validity, challenging each point and quickly finds an area where his knowledge exceeds his adviser. He exploits the advantage to no purpose; it brings them no nearer to a solution.

The lack of marketing data receives a stinging criticism for a paucity of forward planning. He is interrupted on behalf of the researcher and his coldness to her situation is gently reproved. Carl feels trapped. He defends his attitude, argues that it was nothing to be taken personally, rhetorically asking why he is being misinterpreted.

The accounts projections require a decision, not analysis. It seems that intuition is needed and Carl enumerates every possibility he can come up with. He concludes by asking for more information, greater detail, up to the minute data and caution about reaching conclusions from incomplete statistics.

The afternoon meeting is stimulating from the start. Everyone is encouraged to think about each project and successful conclusions. Carl's razor sharp mind is leading the way but space exists for all to participate. He helps them analyse their progress, and sift the facts. Nothing is vague, the order of thought is clear and flawless.

Mr Compliant is able to listen to good news without pouring cold water on it, or predicting wild successes. He is cautious but thorough. His case for an early completion of one project is well presented and easily accepted. He smoothly links it to the need for paying greater attention to the new project discussed that morning.

Carl uses this as an opportunity to apologise for his insensitivity and dogmatism, disclose that he had a very difficult morning (no details given), and to offer the appropriate compassionate leave, which he has looked into since lunch. The team departs feeling good to have such a clear thinking leader.

Carl Compliant did all this without medication! He took stock of his weak points and resolved to build around his strong ones.

This 'Day in the life of a Temperament Type' is just a cameo. It shows the best and the worst of each one. The crucial moment was not when the team realised that things could be better. The moment of private decision to act differently in order to achieve the best results was the one that defined the day, and the relationships. This decision is a daily one and should form part of a process of self-development. We never arrive at complete maturity with regard to our behaviours. However, each decision to adapt and employ our strengths while modifying our weaknesses make every subsequent decision that much easier. It also builds its own testimony of satisfactory results.

- Becoming A Trustworthy Adviser involves adapting your behaviour so as to maximise your effectiveness in winning others.
- Trustworthy Advisers have acquired the ability to discern the behavioural style of others and guide them accordingly.
- We can all make the choice to act maturely. Each decision builds habits of success and memories of achievement. They also build our testimony of trustworthiness to which others refer.

7

COMMUNICATION AND TEMPERAMENT

'Successful communication should be measured by the reaction and response it receives, not the intent and desire with which it was sent.'

Extensive research by psychologists and educationalists has revealed some uncomfortable facts about communication. We are foolish to ignore them, treat them as unscientific, or only relevant to those we judge to be less verbally skilled than ourselves. This research has been conducted according to the strictest of scientific disciplines in a wide range of settings. Here are the results:

- **words** account for only 7% of communication
- **tone of voice** accounts for 38%
- **body language** accounts for 55%

Each one of us looks instinctively for different things that persuade us to trust, believe and co-operate, or distrust, disbelieve and resist. These 'Instincts' of ours, often operating beneath the level of rational appraisal, are largely to do with the outlook of our personal temperament and how that programmes our interaction with others. Words, tone of voice, and body language, are all means by which our temperament finds expression.

With this in mind, the challenge to every aspiring Trustworthy Adviser is to maximise their communicability with each different temperament type. This chapter is therefore dedicated to equip you in three crucial areas:

- recognising the temperament of others
- improving your communication
- adapting your communication to suit all.

What we have established thus far is that there are four temperaments. Each of these has a distinctive behavioural style, characterised as:

Dominant	(D)	**Influential**	(I)
Steady	(S)	**Compliant**	(C)

Better connections

Think of a person with whom you would like to have a better connection. How would you describe his or her behaviour the last time you met? In order to understand behavioural style better, your first task is to study the words in each of the quadrants of the Behavioural Style Grid™ below. Look first at the positive words in the inner circle and choose which quadrant best describes this person. Once you have chosen which of the four is your best estimate, have a look at the words in the outer circle of the same quadrant to confirm your selection. This is not an exact science but is the first step in identifying your connection's 'core behavioural style'.

Recognising the Temperament of others

Remember we said each person is a blend of all four styles. The purpose of this exercise is to enable you to at least make an assessment of the core style of the person you are trying to connect with. On the TPI website, we have a 'Connections Tool' which will not only allow you to accurately determine the style but give you clear instruction on how to effect a smooth communication and better connection with people you choose to assess. The value in doing this, is that as you begin to analyse behaviour, two things occur. Firstly, you identify groups of behaviours that accompany one another. Secondly, you develop an aptitude for making quicker, but accurate, assessments. The advantage of this is to adapt your own behaviours, not just to be able to predict those of others! Take a few minutes to plot some clients and colleagues you know reasonably well.

Now give a little thought to any communication problems or misunderstandings that might have arisen with these individuals. The objective is not to apportion blame, nor is it to justify oneself. The aim is to understand, improve and adapt, so as to be more effective.

Improving your communication

The key to good communication is summed up in the line of an old song: 'It ain't what you say, it's the way that you say it; that's what gets results'.

The following tables provide guidance for handling our communication with different temperament types. By comparing the advice given with the characteristics outlined in the previous section you will see the practical benefits quite clearly. A Trustworthy Adviser must be seen to be reliable, technically competent, and to have the best interests of the client in mind. By making conscious efforts to improve communication with those of different temperaments from our own, we are actually going that second mile with those concerned.

> **We often talk of a 'personality clash' – a 'temperament misunderstanding' would be more helpful as it leaves room for a solution.**

It takes discipline as well as self-denial to break with life-long, harmless habits of communication in order to serve others more effectively. The effort entailed may go unnoticed but the results do not. Simply taking the trouble to ask oneself 'What kind of person am I dealing with here, and how best can I get through?' is an action that has a profound affect on your relationship.

- It puts your client in the leading role, even if you do most of the talking.
- It sets their agenda as the priority, even though the meeting may be taking place at your request.
- It ensures that your motives come into line with the objectives of demonstrating trustworthiness and value.

To begin, let's look at ways to improve communication with 'D' Temperaments – extroverts whose motivation is results.

Do ...	Don't ...
• always demonstrate loyalty from the outset	• leave any doubt that you are for them during any discussion
• invite them to contribute to the outcome of any discussion	• dominate and try to control all the potential communication
• keep to the agreed agenda, aim for professional rapport	• focus initially on personal relationship building
• be specific, getting quickly to the point, avoid being long-winded	• be vague, illusory, or waste time
• ask relevant open questions, preferably using the pronoun 'What?'	• ask rhetorical or pointlessly theoretical questions
• prepare thoroughly and order your communication	• extemporise, forget points, or mislay material
• present a structured and logical flow of thoughts and material	• obfuscate, or create ambiguities
• provide options and choices for them to make decisions	• present fait accompli decisions or announce the conclusion
• offer plausible solutions to actual problems	• simply focus on problems and negative scenarios
• attempt to predict the likelihood of success for each option	• give promises and assurances that cannot be entirely guaranteed
• be sure that your disagreements only take issue with the facts	• enter into disputation with the 'D' over personal issues
• focus on action based results	• leave anything to chance, hoping 'it will be alright on the night'

All these guidelines express sensitivity to the nature of those with 'D' type temperaments. Nothing is to be avoided as an issue in itself. This is not about indulging their weaknesses or ignoring deficiencies; it is about communication and how to make it work better. You may well have someone in mind that is clearly of this temperament. Think back over recent encounters in the light of the advice given above:

- Can you identify any difficulties that you would now handle better by means of a different approach?
- Are you less inclined to blame yourself for communication failures now that the tools of success are in your hands?
- Do you feel less inclined to blame the other party for what seemed like deliberate awkwardness but was actually quite unintentional and an issue of temperament?

Communication and Temperament

Now let's examine ways of improving communication with the 'I' Temperaments – extroverts who looks for recognition.

Do ...	Don't ...
• be positive and cheerful, choosing pleasant surroundings and environment	• project negativity by only focusing on what is wrong.
• allow time for socialising, fun, and personal rapport building	• be impersonal, aloof, or curt
• take sufficient time to be stimulating and keep things moving quickly	• make everything too formal and businesslike
• focus on people and their aspirations	• weigh them down with facts, figures, and too much detail
• demonstrate support for their visions and their schemes	• inhibit or attempt to control or dampen their aspirations
• ask and answer specific questions, preferably usine the pronoun 'Who?'	• ask excessive questions of a detailed or technical nature
• ask for their opinion, and show that you value it by listening	• ignore them by focussing only on the task
• suggest focus and vehicles to implement their ideas	• allow time to be wasted on perpetual 'fantasy'
• provide testimonials from those they respect and admire	• allow them to feel isolated
• focus on short-term projects with clear incentives	• engage in discussions that lack identifiable action plans
• give them personal recognition for achievements	• belittle them or their ideas in front of others
• offer sincere compliments and plenty of encouragement	• be paternalistic or sycophantic during your discussions

Before moving on, are there some specific points you want to remember and apply when working with someone you can identify as having this Temperament?

As an aid to memory, jot them down now and give some thought as to how best you can affirm this person without appearing to patronise them.

_____

_____

_____

Trust Me – Becoming a Trustworthy Adviser

Let's go on to consider improvements we can make when communicating with the 'S' Temperament – introverts who are concerned with reassurance.

Do ...	Don't ...
• build personal rapport, show a sincere interest in them as a person	• rigidly adhere to only the business at hand
• demonstrate empathy for them and their situation	• be self-centred and seen to be uncaring, focussed only on the issue
• ask personal questions first, before work related 'open' questions	• interrupt their speaking, or complete their sentences
• elicit their thoughts and feelings with patient listening and responsiveness	• force quick responses or be too direct and intimidating
• discuss the implications for everyone involved	• just take a selfish stance, only interested in what it means to you
• give sufficient time for their reflections when decisions are required	• force quick decisions but explain issues in detail
• provide personal assurances and guarantees, whenever possible	• make any promises where your ability to fulfil is in doubt
• ask 'How' questions to ensure they feel involved in the solution	• impose your thoughts and solutions without agreement
• present your case logically, without emotion, and devoid of any threat	• assert your status or appear demanding
• conduct meetings informally but professionally	• act threateningly, raise your voice, get too close physically, or stare at them
• give time to adjust when things impact them directly	• mistake their willingness and complicity for agreement
• affirm their value and show appreciation for their contributions	• allow them to feel unimportant or under-valued

Think of a client or colleague who fits this temperament type. In order to deepen their trust and respect, what three adjustments could you usefully make to your normal style when next you meet with them?

_____

_____

_____

Communication and Temperament

Finally, let's explore improving our communication with the 'C' type Temperament. An introvert primarily interested in reality.

Do ...	Don't ...
• aim to build professional rapport, focus on the task in hand	• be over personal, casual, informal or personal
• focus on security, safety and the elimination of any potential fear	• introduce any fear-producing concepts that will hinder progress
• respect and not invade their physical space	• invade their space and use a lot of touching
• prepare thoroughly what you have to say beforehand whenever possible	• appear to be disorganised, rushed, untidy or unprepared
• employ a legal or accounting style; establish pros and cons for all issues	• force an uninformed, quick decision based on 'Gut feelings'
• ask and answer specific questions, preferably with the pronoun 'Why?'	• ignore their questions or refuse to respond
• draw up action plans with targets, measurable aims and specific dates	• overestimate or exaggerate possible achievements, or surprise results
• take time to convince, be persistent and go over points where necessary	• become frustrated by detail, or exhibit haste and abruptness
• allow them time for themselves to think through possible outcomes	• 'bully' your way in, expecting an immediate answer
• use facts and respected testimonials in support of any disagreement	• cite opinions or feelings as evidence for your standpoint
• supply the information they need and allow time for their decision process116	• force closure or conclusions, or use incentives to obtain your goals
• stick to the rules and follow the acknowledged procedures	• attempt to 'buck' the system and try to persuade them to do it 'my way'

If you were responding to an immediate crisis and therefore had no opportunity to prepare data or give much time for reflection, how might you quickly get someone of this temperament on side and make use of their skills?

_____

_____

_____

Adapting your behaviour to suit all

Behavioural preferences are like styles of clothing; some people look untidy in business suits, while others give the impression that they iron creases into their underwear! Some behavioural mannerisms and methods of approach may come naturally to us but they can alienate or cause discomfort to others. If our aim is to win their trust, these obstacles need to be overcome.

In ancient Greek theatre, an actor held a mask over his face to denote his character. He could therefore fulfil several roles in one play. The mask was the 'Persona'. Adaptive Communication is not about developing personas. It is about being truthful with facts, while being sensitive with people's feelings. It is about winning people's confidence because we are worthy of their trust. It is about making the most advantageous use of our faculties and skills in order to further the aspirations of our clients, and ourselves.

The following table is a summary of how to employ the guidance given in the previous section. It is never an alternative to honesty, integrity, and maturity. However, it will enhance all these qualities and enable you to communicate more effectively with others as you grow in your ability to recognise Temperaments and make valuable adjustments in your communication style.

Communication and Temperament

	D	I	S	C
BODY LANGUAGE	Steady eye contact	Friendly eye contact	Intermittent eye contact	Direct eye contact
	Controlled gestures	Lots of gestures	Small gestures	Few gestures
	Proactive	Relaxed and fun	Reactive	Firm and unbending
	Firm handshake	Can use a lot of touch	Gentle handshake	Avoid contact
TONE OF VOICE	Forceful	Enthusiastic	Warm and steady	Little inflection
	Loud and confident	Dramatic	Lower volume	Quite cool
	Challenging intonation	Energetic	Kind not forceful	Pensive
	Direct	Lots of inflection	Measured	Quiet and slow
KEY WORDS	I expect	I feel	I consider	I think
	Challenging assignment	This is exciting	Step-by-step	Here are the facts
	Excellent results	Fun and sociable	My guarantee	Proven track record
	Beat the competition	Visionary	Let me hear you	Analyse the data
	New and unique	Make you a hero	No risk attached	Let's think about that
PACE	Fast	Fast	Considered	Deliberate
	Decisive	Spontaneous	Easy-going	Systematic

Although a bit contrived, I like to use the diagram overleaf to remind me of the different temperament traits, the way I am and how I should assess and adapt to improve communication.

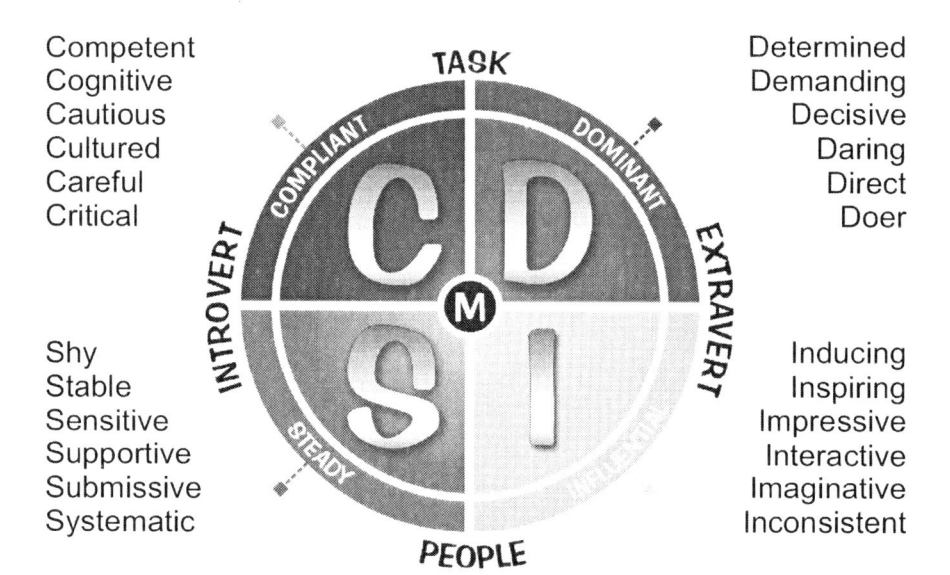

Competent	TASK	Determined
Cognitive		Demanding
Cautious		Decisive
Cultured	COMPLIANT / DOMINANT	Daring
Careful	C / D	Direct
Critical		Doer
	INTROVERT / EXTRAVERT	
	M	
Shy	S / I	Inducing
Stable		Inspiring
Sensitive	STEADY / INFLUENCING	Impressive
Supportive		Interactive
Submissive		Imaginative
Systematic		Inconsistent
	PEOPLE	

A Trustworthy Adviser …

… is someone who is seen as reliable, faithful, dependable, professionally competent and worthy of being included in the early stages of planning development because his or her counsel is valued. Making adjustments to the way we communicate enables us to win trust in the early stages of a business relationship and to establish a rapport with those we would normally consider distant, and perhaps difficult, to get along with.

> **'Successful communication should be measured by the reaction and response it receives, not the intent and desire with which it was sent.'**
> - Be careful with your words.
> - Be extra careful with your tone of voice.
> - Be especially careful with your body language.

SECTION 3

EMOTIONAL MATURITY

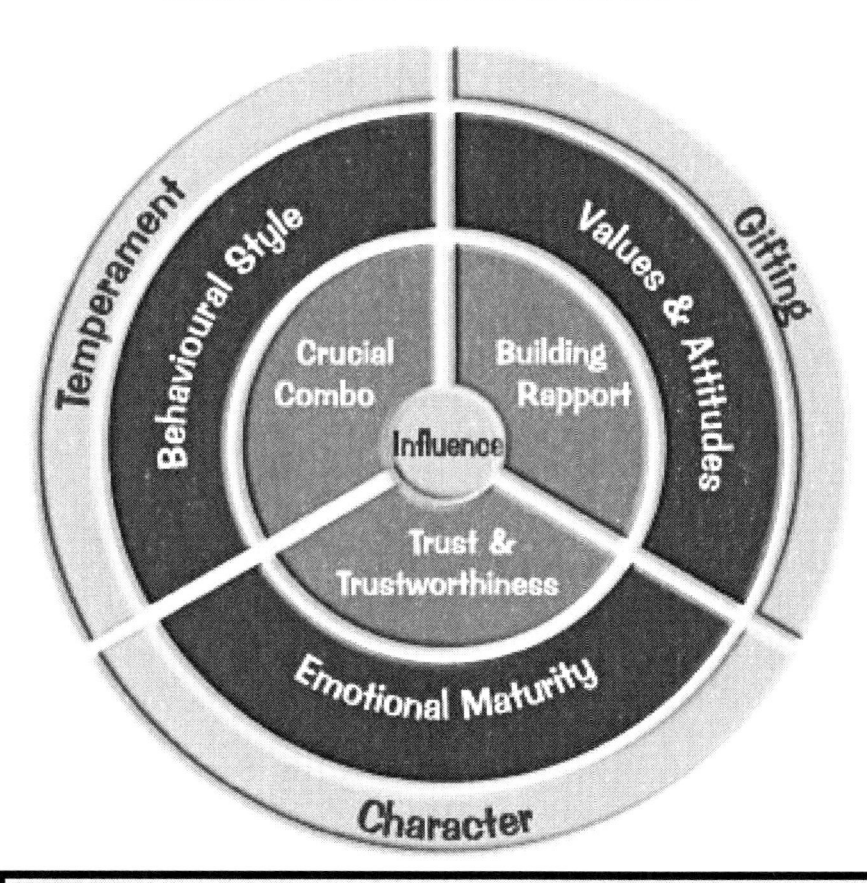

- Can We Really Change?
- Defining Maturity
- The 16 Character Traits
- Overcoming Barriers to Emotional Maturity
- Developing Winning Habits
- Achieving Personal Growth

This part of our journey deals with personal development. We are going to examine the most common barriers to achieving personal growth and identify specific ways they can be overcome. This material has the potential to change your life. It can affect how you feel about yourself and therefore how you feel and behave towards others. It has the capacity to enable the reader to make substantial and measurable changes without feeling as though they are experiencing a total personality overhaul. The steps provided are incremental, yet significant.

Since 1992, I have used this particular material in a number of workshops and seminars, addressing many delegates from vastly different cultures, in several nations. People are essentially the same the world over. Our needs, fears, strengths, skills, weaknesses, and personalities do not differ, even though they find infinitely variable expression through national and ethnic culture systems. My professional experience, measured by objective testimony, is that this material equips people to address deeply personal behaviours and make actual, lasting changes. Without hyperbole, I can state that this material has the potential to change your life.

Transforming individuals by enabling them to achieve Emotional Maturity is a vital key to improving business performance. It also brings a great deal of personal wholeness and happiness in the process.

Anyone wishing to become a Trustworthy Adviser will be aware that their clients are assessing two things about them, simultaneously. They are looking for evidence of professional competence and at the same time examining the signs of character maturity. In the world of recruitment and human resources, it is recognised that hard skills competencies are not the factors separating those employees with outstanding performances from their colleagues. Many recruits and incumbents have equally impressive skill lists and well developed career paths. Skills and experience are important, but the vital factors are those frequently referred to as the competencies of emotional intelligence. My aim in this stage of our journey is to enable you to achieve a degree of emotional maturity, so that by reputation and personal standing you are regarded as capable of fulfilling the role of a Trustworthy Adviser.

The specific attributes addressed in this section are 16 character traits that can be identified, measured, and developed. The material offers an opportunity to progress towards Emotional Maturity within each of these traits, providing practical and achievable goals.

Many attempts at self-improvement are as doomed as New Year's resolutions. They usually begin with a mixture of guilt and ambition. The goal is quite well defined, the steps necessary to get there are generally vague, or even nonexistent, and there is usually no allowance for failure or setback. They therefore result in yet more guilt and feelings of failure. Pessimists write off the entire project as pointless, deciding to accommodate their bad habits, or lack of good ones. Optimists develop the notion that perhaps next year will prove more successful. We need to be more thorough, and more radical!

The thoroughness will be provided by examining each of the 16 character traits, developing ways of achieving Emotional Maturity in all of them, and setting one's own goals, which are reasonable as well as challenging. This will take the form of making a contract with oneself. However, there need be no penalty clauses!

The radical element of this process lies in dealing with root issues. The term 'Radical' has been corrupted by the idea that it always has to mean 'Alternative' or 'Extreme'. In botany, the word refers to root systems, and in language studies, to the underlying concept that a word contains. It means: 'That which is fundamental' or 'foundational'.

In order to facilitate lasting success, rather than short-term results followed by disappointment and frustration, we are going to examine the major obstacles to personal growth and set out ways in which these can be identified, confronted, and overcome. We will be dealing with those deep-rooted aspects of our behaviour that can so often cause us to react in a way we would regard as 'out of character', yet can, over time, easily develop into habitual responses and attitudes. This is the radical part: not only looking at root issues, but offering insights and guidance on addressing any obstacles we may identify.

My intention is that both as potential Trustworthy Advisers, and fellow human beings, you will receive hope and help from this material.

8

CAN WE REALLY CHANGE?

The following story is adapted from a report in The Times newspaper, dated 6th December, 2001. It describes an actual event. I want to invite you to imagine yourself to be in the position of the main character and honestly consider what your own reactions might have been under the circumstances.

David Robertson is a master distiller of Scotch whiskey, from Fife in Scotland. At the back of his drinks cabinet he kept an unmarked bottle of scotch, reserved for a special celebration. The bottle in question contained a Macallan single malt and was worth two thousand pounds.

It was Mr Robertson's birthday. His wife had made him a trifle to accompany his birthday meal, trifle being his favourite dessert. The trifle on this occasion, however, was so delicious that Mr Robertson ate it all. On inquiring of his wife what made it so special on this occasion, she advised him she had used whiskey because they had run out of sherry. That was its only variation and accounted for the improvement he so enjoyed.

'Which whiskey?' Mr Robertson asked.

'The one in the unmarked bottle at the back of the cabinet,' Mrs Robertson replied.

David Robertson went to the cabinet, took out the bottle of Macallan and poured himself a stiff drink. It was time for a celebration. The celebration of an expensive mistake!

As a fellow Scot, I can appreciate the value of that single malt. Drinking it is about heritage and history, as well as a fine drink, unequalled throughout the world. A bottle like that contains the wisdom and skill passed down through generations of distillers. To drink it is to taste the Highlands and imbibe our culture and traditions. It isn't the sort of whiskey that anyone of discernment would be found diluting – dare I say, polluting – with dry ginger or lemonade.

Can We Really Change?

Now here was a man with a wealth of expertise and understanding of the distillers' arts, who realises that he has just eaten a trifle flavoured with this exquisite single malt! He is confronted by the fact that his wife has used the most expensive drink in the home, probably in the town, possibly even in the country, to flavour a trifle. Imagine that you are David Robertson.

- Would you raise your voice just a little?
- Is it likely that Mrs Robertson might suffer some sarcastic reprimand for her thoughtfulness?
- Would you go out and buy a padlock for the drinks cabinet?
- Might you insist that no one should be told about this affair, in case you become the butt of every distiller's jokes throughout the entire nation?
- Would you declare that your birthday had been ruined?
- Are you tempted to buy your wife a case of sherry for her next birthday?
- Does a call to your solicitor cross your mind?
- Are you the kind of person, man or woman, who would think of toasting her mistake?
- Would you tell the story so freely that a national newspaper not only reports it, but also interviews a friend who freely offers his comments on the episode?

Putting myself into David Robertson's shoes, I would have to say that reacting according to the last two possibilities listed above would amount to highly mature behaviour, for someone of my temperament! How about you? How many times has failing to see the funny side of something caused you to exhibit behaviour you later regretted?

What this chapter addresses:

- Defining maturity
- The Behavioural Style Grid™
- Is change possible?
- The 16 Character Traits

Putting the pieces together

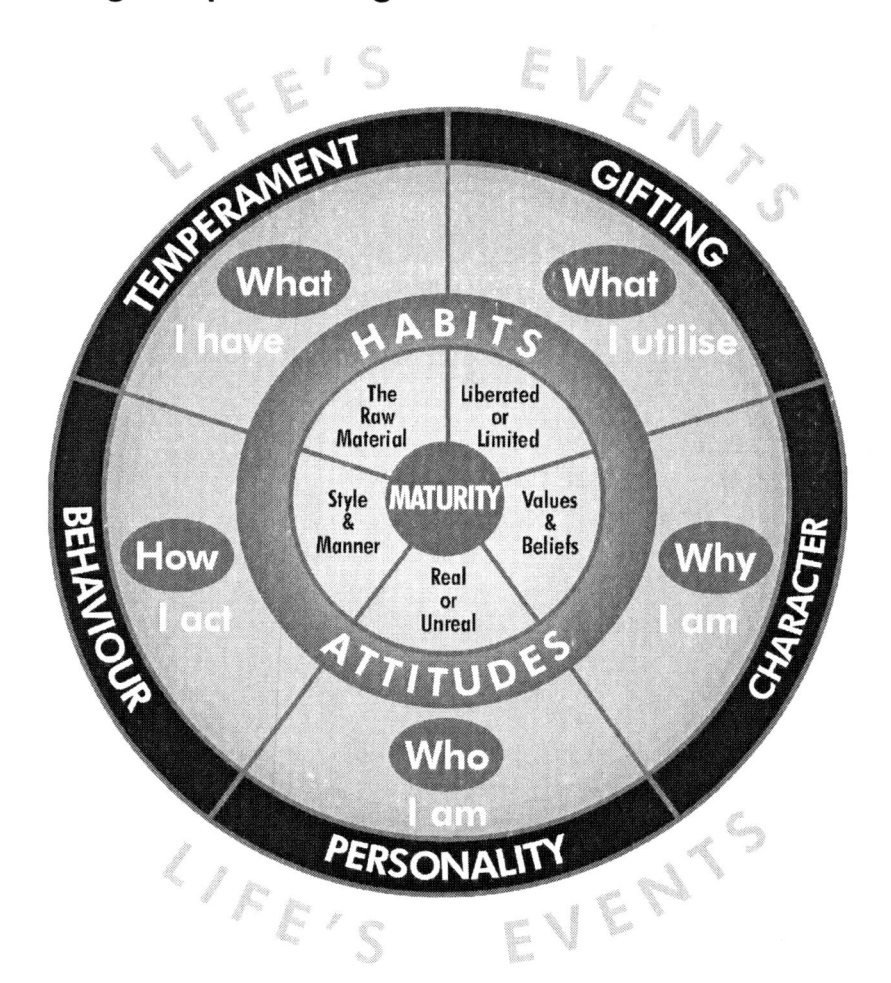

Temperament and behaviour

TEMPERAMENT – (WHAT I have) we have discussed at length in the previous chapters.

BEHAVIOUR – (HOW I act) – (see grid on page 101) is influenced greatly by our temperament and could be described as our style and manner. On a good day, our behaviours will be those in the inner circle, the outer ones could describe our bad days, or stressed behaviour.

Character, gifting and personality

CHARACTER – (WHY I am) this is what we build onto our temperament. It is driven and maintained by our beliefs system and our values. It is judged by our behaviour, good or bad, and is a measure of quality, rather than activity. To develop maturity is to grow in character.

GIFTING – (WHAT I utilise) sometimes expressed as aptitude, it is the natural ability given to every single person e.g. ability to write, ability to influence. Once identified and understood it can be a liberating experience from which individuals go on to realise their full potential. It can also be self-limiting if a person fails to press through and use it to the full.

PERSONALITY – (WHO I am) this is the product we demonstrate to the outside world. It can be real or unreal. Personality is the 'whole person' and the means by which we relate, react, and respond. It outwardly manifests those inward traits that make us unique.

Attitudes and habits

ATTITUDES are HABITS of thinking that produce certain patterns of inward feelings which find expression through our behaviours. They act as filters for our belief system. The two are very closely linked and are choices we make and decisions we take. They are situated within the act of our will and are solely within our control.

Mature, mellowed, or just plain older?

When violent male criminals reach the age of forty, something often happens. They tend to give up hurting people and sometimes give up crime altogether. Some of them engage in studies they previously thought pointless, or even beyond them. They discover their intellects, their powers of analytical reasoning and observation. Occasionally they write books. Although some of this takes place inside prison cells, the cause of this reflectiveness and self-discovery is not simply due to regret or incarceration. Sometimes it happens in freedom without any apparent demands for introspection or a change of attitude. It may lead to regrets, even apologies, but not necessarily. They just refer to it as 'A mellowing process' or 'Calming down'.

Some footballers and rugby players experience the same thing after parenthood causes them to focus on the protection and care of a vulnerable dependant. It means less yellow cards, or trips to the sin bin, but not really a lot else besides. Genuine emotion has affected their attitudes, but one rarely hears anyone intimate that their previous behaviour was at times wrong and to be regretted. They just say 'I've mellowed a lot lately, but I think it makes me a better player'. Transfer fees are still important and their value still needs to be affirmed!

What has happened in both cases is usually emotional, very genuine, but might be short-lived. It may have involved decisions, it may not. Expediency might easily cause their behaviour to revert to its previous levels of aggression, whether in a career of crime, professional sport, or even management. 'Mellowing' can have a lot to do with lower levels of testosterone, especially in career criminals reaching forty years of age. Whatever chemical or neurological causes there are for this change of behaviour, it would only be appropriate to call it 'Maturity' where there has been a conscious decision to change and become a better person. That would build in new habits. Not wanting to get imprisoned again hardly signifies a better attitude towards other peoples' property or person!

Some changes in behaviour are simply about getting older. Energy levels drop and testosterone fuelled aggression can be replaced by a more calculating and manipulative form of competitiveness. No overall change – just a different instrument playing the same old tune. Maturity is not about age. The human will does not grow stronger because of the passage of time; it gains strength by a process of exercise in just the same way as our muscles do.

'Maturity involves both a journey and a destination. The destination is a place of completeness, where strengths are accentuated and weaknesses are appropriately managed. The journey is one of constant learning and growth, enabling the full development of emotional and moral behaviour.'

This statement is not meant to imply a state of perpetual dissatisfaction with oneself. We can reach a place of maturity in a particular area of our character and still continue to grow in that trait. For example, you may well be a patient person when it comes to waiting, fixing equipment, or dealing with detail, but very conscious of your need to extend this to dealing with all types of people, especially when you feel tired or under stress. You have reached maturity but are still travelling towards completeness.

Emotional Maturity is also about freedom. Freedom in all three aspects of the dimension of time: past, present and future. Freedom from the negative impact of experiences (the past), freedom to respond to life's events rather than react to them impulsively (the present), and freedom to make right choices about the next step (the future).

Behavioural Style Grid™

TASK

COMPLIANT
- Critical
- Procrastinates
- Unenthusiastic
- Perfectionist
- Suspicious
- Pedantic
- Sluggish

LOGICAL
CAUTIOUS
ANALYTICAL
SYSTEMATIC
CONSCIENTIOUS
PRECISE
BALANCED

DOMINANT
- Impatient
- Unsympathetic
- Demanding
- Domineering
- Intimidating
- Headstrong
- Aggressive

DIRECT
DARING
PRODUCTIVE
COMPETITIVE
DETERMINED
CONFIDENT
DECISIVE

MATURITY

INTROVERT

EXTRAVERT

LOYAL
PATIENT
EMPATHETIC
DIPLOMATIC
STABILISING
LISTENER
KIND

STEADY
- Worrier
- Resentful
- Pessimistic
- Moody
- Hypersensitive
- Resists Change
- Indecisive

PERSUASIVE
CHARISMATIC
DEMONSTRATIVE
SPONTANEOUS
ENTHUSIASTIC
OPTIMISTIC
VERBAL

INFLUENTIAL
- Impulsive
- Restless
- Hedonistic
- Manipulative
- Inconsistent
- Craves Approval
- Undisciplined

PEOPLE

You remember the four temperament types and their respective strengths and weaknesses? At the centre of this grid is Maturity. Our destination. On our good days, when stress levels are low, when colleagues are co-operative, trains run on time, we've had sufficient sleep the night before and not had a row with someone close to us, we tend to operate mostly in the centre circle. When life is stressful, we graduate towards the outer circle and call it 'A bad day'.

Under normal circumstances, we tend to find ourselves displaying a mixture of behaviours from the inner and outer circles. Under stress we may not necessarily exhibit the weaknesses of the outer circle representing our predominant temperament type. We all have a mixture of temperaments and therefore one with the Dominant Temperament style may under stress become resentful and inactive. If the cause of the stress is not getting his or her own way, this response is quite likely, especially if they have a High D coupled with a Low S.

Our aim is to become mature within the temperament with which we were born and from which we will never be separated. We will return to this later in the chapter as we examine the 16 character traits.

Can we really change?

We have a saying in the English language that is derived from the Old Testament book of Jeremiah: *'A leopard never changes its spots'*. If that statement is final and absolute, it is a very sad reflection on the entire human race. However, there are basically two reasons why people do not change and therefore two reasons why they may.

The issues have to do with intention and knowledge. Firstly, do we want to change? Secondly, do we know how to change? The first question is the challenge. We each have to make a personal decision to change for the better – to become someone whose behaviour is spent within the inner circle of the Behavioural Style Grid, for most of the time.

- An individual who acknowledges his or her weaknesses and resolves to set about modifying, and managing, them.

- Someone whose strengths are accentuated and not compromised or undone by corresponding weaknesses.

- A person who grows internally in order to achieve his or her external objectives.

Having made that decision, the process has already begun! A leopard *can* change its spots. The secret is to change from the inside out. What one has to bear in mind is that it took a long time to get to the point where one's behaviour became what it is. It is therefore unrealistic to expect overnight transformation. We each need to recognise that, in the matter of maturity, we are 'A work in progress'.

The 16 Character Traits

These aspects of our character are grouped into four headings to denote the way in which they are manifested. One trait does not necessarily lead to the next. For example, a person able to exercise courage under duress may be extremely impatient whatever the circumstances. Equally, the absence of maturity in one trait need not imply immaturity in the next, or in many others.

Group 1: OUTWARD EXPRESSIONS

Each of these, reflect ways in which we relate to others. They are what we actively demonstrate in our relationships.

Group 2: INWARD EXPRESSIONS

This group of characteristics impact our motives and denote the internal state from which our behaviours derive.

Group 3: DYNAMIC ATTRIBUTES

These four define the ways, or manner, in which we act. They touch the outside world with our inner world.

Group 4: PASSIVE ATTRIBUTES

This group are often to be found in our actions or speech, but exist without the need to be socially expressed. We might describe them as characteristics we 'hold' or maintain.

The rest of this chapter establishes a definition for each of the 16 traits. It also provides some indicators, or diagnostics, for mature and immature behaviours within each characteristic. It will show the general level of each characteristic to be found within the four Behavioural Styles, based upon our temperament.

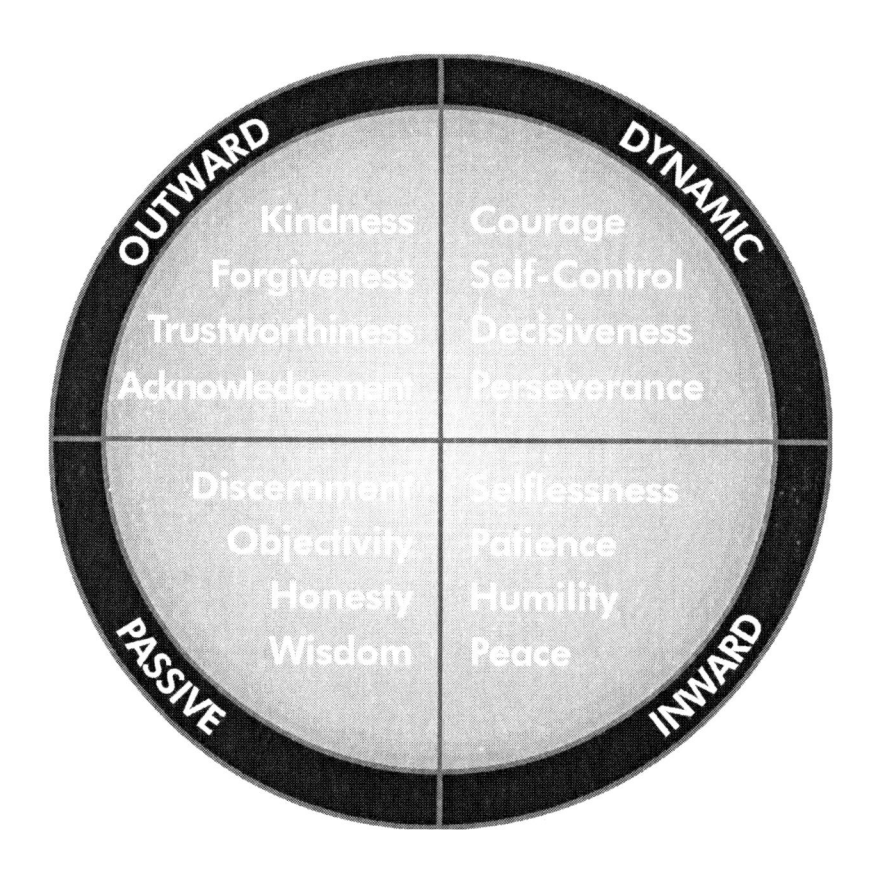

[Circle diagram with four quadrants:
- Outward/Dynamic (top right): Courage, Self-Control, Decisiveness, Perseverance
- Outward/Passive (top left): Kindness, Forgiveness, Trustworthiness, Acknowledgement
- Passive/Inward (bottom left): Discernment, Objectivity, Honesty, Wisdom
- Inward/Dynamic (bottom right): Selflessness, Patience, Humility, Peace]

Chapter 9 will examine the predominant barriers to Emotional Maturity and in chapter 10 we follow up with an action plan for personal development within each trait. This is where you can make a contract with yourself.

Now let's proceed to examine these characteristics that others look for in their Trustworthy Advisers under the four headings shown above.

We will start opposite with Group 1: Outward Expressions

Can We Really Change?

GROUP 1: OUTWARD EXPRESSIONS
Each of these reflects ways in which we relate to others. They are what we actively demonstrate in our relationships.

Kindness

Definition: To demonstrate consideration, respect and graciousness. To have the desire to be actively helpful and generous, treating people with compassion.

Good Day

- Actively helpful and generous
- Treats other with sensitivity and compassion
- Rarely quarrelsome
- Adopts the role of peacemaker
- Seeks to protect and support those who appear less fortunate
- Meets needs without looking for acclaim
- A willing volunteer

Bad Day

- Lacks concern for others
- Self-centred and lacking compassion
- Can be mean and miserly
- Prone to rudeness and sarcasm
- Not a volunteer
- Can take advantage, even 'use' others
- Intolerant

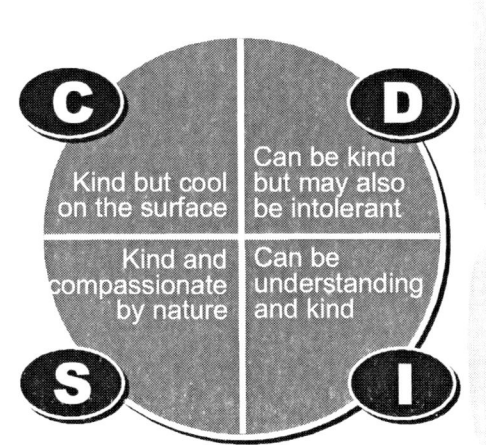

C — Kind but cool on the surface
D — Can be kind but may also be intolerant
S — Kind and compassionate by nature
I — Can be understanding and kind

⚠ Caution!

Kindness, when over-extended may make you appear saccharine sweet and stifling. It can make others feel awkward in knowing how to respond, wondering about the person's genuineness.

'Kindness is very indigestible. It disagrees with proud stomachs.'
William Thackeray

'Kindness consists of loving people more than they deserve.'
Joseph Joubert

105

Forgiveness

Definition: To keep no record of wrongs and be prepared to forgive; choosing to remember no more. To show mercy, not seeking to get even.

Good Day

- Not allowing resentment to build up
- Able to 'pardon' a hurtful word or action
- Has a deep sense of being forgiven
- Not recording wrongs, hurts or humiliations
- Willing to act graciously towards those who apologise
- A developed sense of magnanimity
- Does not seek revenge

Bad Day

- Unwilling to let go of an offence or hurt
- Prone to anger
- Resentment has grown deep roots
- Tendency towards self-pity; blaming others
- Lacking empathy
- Not easy to get along with
- Looks to get back, even vengeful

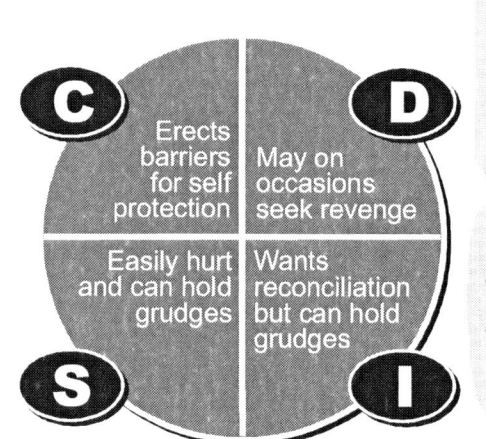

	C: Erects barriers for self protection	D: May on occasions seek revenge
	S: Easily hurt and can hold grudges	I: Wants reconciliation but can hold grudges

⚠ Caution!

Forgiveness, when over-extended, can be superficial, never dealing with the root cause unconditionally. Time may be required for the emotions to settle before forgiveness can be released.

'Do not seek revenge or bear a grudge against one of your people, but love your neighbour as yourself.'

Leviticus 19:18, The Bible

Trustworthiness

Definition: To keep one's word and be worthy of others' confidence. Being reliable, full of integrity, and someone others can depend upon.

Good Day

- Speaks the truth and will not intentionally mislead others
- Regarded as reliable and principled in word and action
- Keeps promises
- Clear value system
- Commitments are taken seriously
- Discreet - able to keep confidences
- Level-headed and sensible

Bad Day

- Difficulty in admitting mistakes
- Forgetful
- Unreliable timekeeper
- Prone to make empty promises
- Low priority in keeping commitments
- May 'leak' sensitive information
- Perceived as one who cuts corners

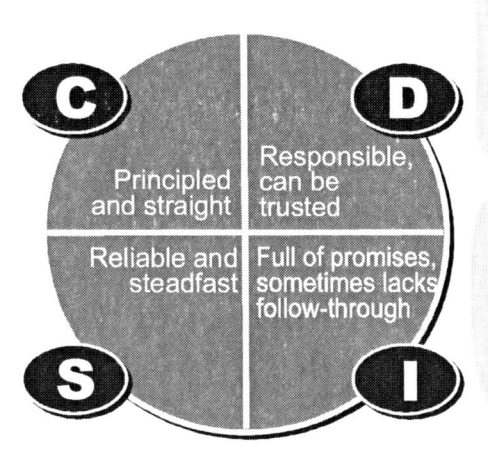

⚠ Caution!

Trustworthiness, when over-extended and over-emphasised, may lead to pride. There can be a revelling in being perceived as being trustworthy.

C — Principled and straight
D — Responsible, can be trusted
S — Reliable and steadfast
I — Full of promises, sometimes lacks follow-through

'Ultimately, trust and respect are hallmarks of a high-performing team.'

Tsun-Yan

Acknowledgement

Definition: To show genuine pleasure at the success of others. Expressing appreciation for others, their individuality or accomplishments.

Good Day

- Able genuinely to recognise the accomplishments of others
- Gives praise to others
- Expresses gratitude
- Conscientious in giving credit to sources used in speech and writing
- Willing to admit their need for the talents and contributions of others
- Easily able to recruit volunteers

Bad Day

- Can appear ungrateful at times
- Neglectful of people's needs
- Ungracious
- Takes people for granted
- Finds it uncomfortable to give or receive praise
- Marginalises or ignores the achievements of others
- Considers subordinates unimportant

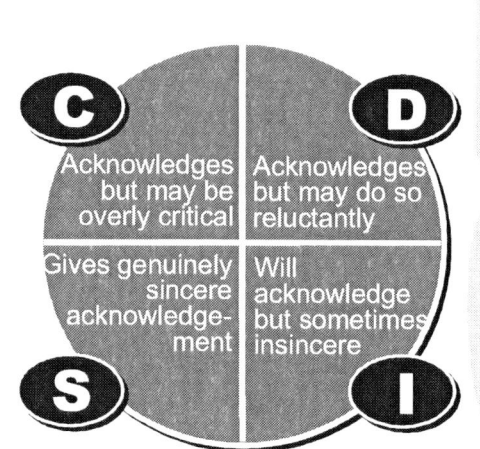

⚠ Caution!

Acknowledgement, when over-extended, can become flattery, that lacks substance. It may be seen as insincere praise rooted in selfishness. It may also appear to others as false humility or fawning.

C — Acknowledges but may be overly critical
D — Acknowledges but may do so reluctantly
S — Gives genuinely sincere acknowledgement
I — Will acknowledge but sometimes insincere

'I believe public recognition is almost as important as financial reward. Public praise is very seldom given in the industrial world. Very seldom is enthusiasm shown, or thanks given.

John Harvey Jones

Can We Really Change?

GROUP 2: INWARD EXPRESSIONS
This group of characteristics impacts our motives and denotes the internal state from which our behavious derive.

Peace

Definition: To be composed, untroubled, content and at ease with oneself. Being free from worry and anxiety; able to plan for the future whilst living one day at a

Good Day	Bad Day
• Collected and composed	• Prone to worry
• Untroubled, free from anxiety	• Anxious about the future
• Relaced and unperturbed	• Tense
• At rest with oneself	• Not at rest with oneself
• Confident	• Restless
• Free from stress and agitation	• Unpredictable in response
• An ordered lifestyle	• Easily ruffled
• Secure in family and relationships	• Prone to lose one's temper

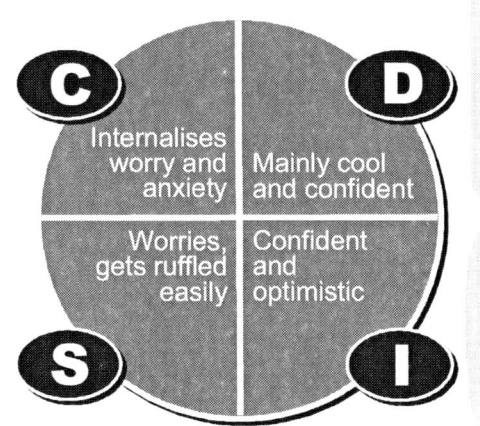

C Internalises worry and anxiety
D Mainly cool and confident
S Worries, gets ruffled easily
I Confident and optimistic

⚠ Caution!

Peace, when over-extended may make an individual look so laid back that they appear unfocused, lazy or unmotivated. It may be the result of having created their own little safe world, screening out uncomfortable realities.

'Peace comes not by establishing a calm outward setting so much as by inwardly surrendering, whatever the setting.'

Hubert van Zeller

Humility

Definition: To hold a modest view of one's own worth and importance compared with others. The quality of being humble, not given to pride or pretentiousness.

Good Day

- Not self-important
- Able to value oneself in an objective rather than an egocentric way
- Natural unpretentious lifestyle
- Able to recognise the value of others in an objective way
- Willing to learn and receive instruction
- Able to offer service from a place of personal strength and security
- Able to learn from criticism

Bad Day

- Little sense of personal worth
- Self-important
- Fears loss of status
- Tendency to boast and act arrogantly
- Exaggeration of abilities
- Often takes the credit
- Overbearing and intimidating
- Compensating behaviours to boost ego

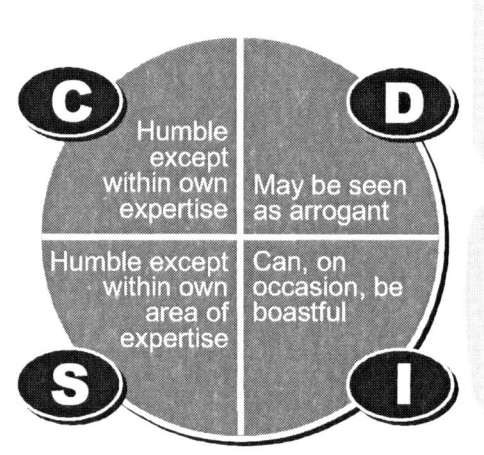

⚠ Caution!

Humility, when over-extended may communicate a lack of self-confidence and could appear self-deprecating. There is a danger that it may communicate weakness rather than meekness.

	C	D
	Humble except within own expertise	May be seen as arrogant
	Humble except within own area of expertise	Can, on occasion, be boastful
	S	I

'Nothing is more scandalous than a man who is proud of his humility.'
Marcus Aurelius

Patience

Definition: The ability to endure with composure and without complaint. Displaying a willingness to pass up immediate pleasure in favour of long-term

Good Day

- Able to endure difficult circumstances
- Shows self-control under provocation
- Bears the faults and limitations of others
- Accepts and values people
- Prepared to come alongside others
- Prepared to forgo short-term gains for long-term rewards
- Tolerant and long-suffering of people's idiosyncrasies

Bad Day

- Intolerant and easily exasperated
- Unable to endure or wait
- Easily irritated by people
- Unwilling to wait for things to happen
- Makes decisions too quickly
- Easily provoked to anger
- Impulsive, rash and hasty

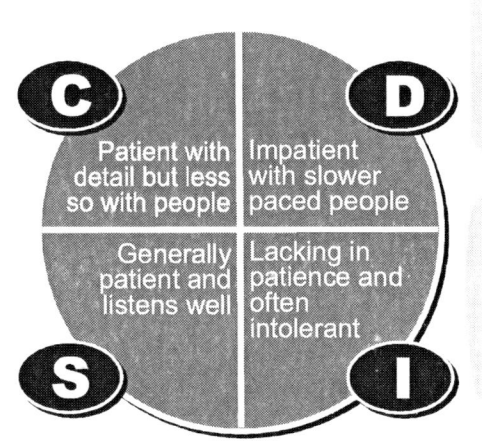

C — Patient with detail but less so with people
D — Impatient with slower paced people
S — Generally patient and listens well
I — Lacking in patience and often intolerant

⚠ Caution!

Patience, when over-extended may lead to passivity and apathy. This can result in others continually taking the lead whilst you go with the flow. You may lose direction and not move forward in your endeavour.

'Our patience will achieve more than our force.'
Edmund Burke

'At the least bear patiently, if thou canst not joyfully.'
Thomas à Kempis

111

Selflessness

Definition: To not always demand one's own way and being able to subjugate one's own interests and concerns in deference to the need of others.

Good Day

- Secure and confident in oneself
- No desire to exploit or manipulate
- Ability to keep working without looking for recognition
- Unselfish and generous
- Able to recognise the talents and abilities of others
- Willing to support and encourage others without needing recognition
- Keen to serve others

Bad Day

- Only interested in own goals
- Looking to get one's own way
- Lacking concern for others
- Tending to dominate and control
- Bossy
- Reluctant to acknowledge the achievements of others
- Behaving as if possessing authority or knowing what is best

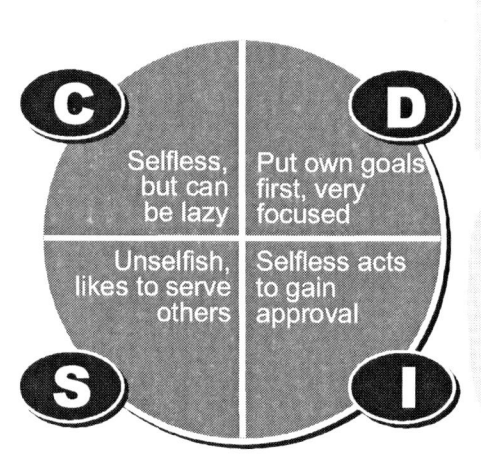

C: Selfless, but can be lazy
D: Put own goals first, very focused
S: Unselfish, likes to serve others
I: Selfless acts to gain approval

⚠ Caution!

Selflessness, when over-extended can make a person appear as a 'doormat', to be taken advantage of by others. Trying to improve one's self-respect and sense of worth by continually pleasing others may have a selfish motive.

'Desire nothing for yourself, which you do not desire for others.'

Spinosa

Can We Really Change?

> **GROUP 3: DYNAMIC ATTRIBUTES**
> These four define the ways, or manner, in which we act. They touch the outside world with our inner world.

Courage

Definition: To have the resolve to change that which should be changed. To show a willingness to confront challenges and take risks, while not giving in to timidity or lack of resolution.

Good Day

- Confident and optimistic
- Willing to confront rather than avoid challenges
- Able to swiftly recover from failure
- Characterised by bravery during opposition, danger or difficulty
- Able to overcome fear
- Boldly going where others fear to tread
- Inner strength maintained even when changes are impossible

Bad Day

- Easily intimidated
- Unable or unwilling to confront
- Avoids new or difficult challenges
- Lacking in determination
- Lacking in self-confidence
- Avoids risk taking
- Tendency towards timidity and fear

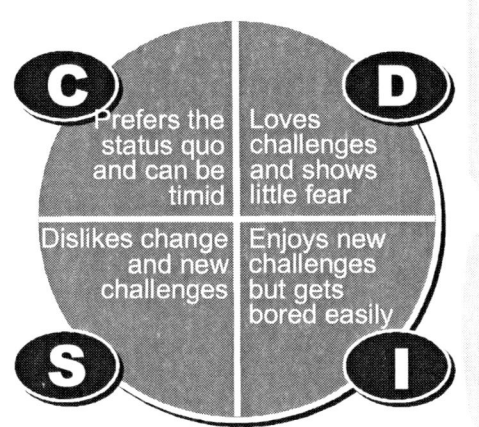

C — Prefers the status quo and can be timid
D — Loves challenges and shows little fear
S — Dislikes change and new challenges
I — Enjoys new challenges but gets bored easily

⚠ Caution!

Courage, when over-extended can appear to communicate recklessness towards life and others. Such a person will not be easily trusted or quickly followed. Courage needs to be tempered by discernment and objectivity.

'The credit belongs to the man who is actually in the arena ... if he fails, at least he fails while daring greatly, so that his place shall never be with those timid souls who know neither victory nor defeat.'

Theodore Roosevelt

Self-control

Definition: The ability to exercise self-restraint; holding oneself in check by applying control over thoughts, speech, actions and emotions

Good Day

- Demonstrate mastery over temper and difficult circumstances
- Emotions will be harnessed when appropriate
- Not given to 'knee-jerk' reactions
- Equitable in dealing with others
- Able to settle disputes with wisdom and grace
- Focused yet sensitive
- Able to check negative responses

Bad Day

- Given to emotional outbursts
- Aggressive in approach
- Decision-making tends to be impulsive
- Prejudging before ascertaining the facts
- A poor listener
- Liable to over-indulge and give in to bad habits
- Lacking willpower

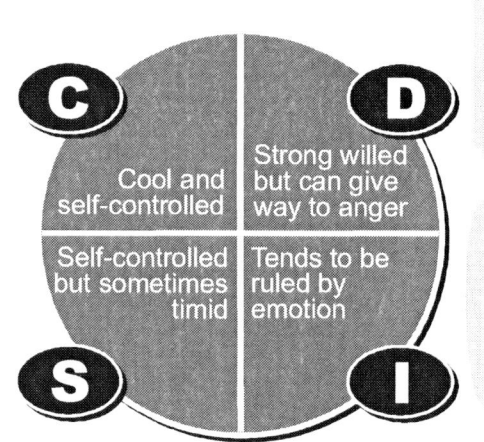

⚠ Caution!

Self-control, when over-extended may make you appear cool, aloof and disinterested when emotions and feelings are kept buried. You may appear machine-like to others, following set procedures and routines.

C Cool and self-controlled
D Strong willed but can give way to anger
S Self-controlled but sometimes timid
I Tends to be ruled by emotion

'No man is free who is not master of himself.'

Epictetus

Can We Really Change?

Decisiveness

Definition: To be able to make decisions quickly and effectively. Being resolute and conclusive and keen to remove doubt as quickly as possible.

Good Day

- Able to decide or determine conclusively
- Determined, firm and fair
- Keen to remove all doubt as quickly as possible
- Positive leadership; a sense of purpose and progress
- Incisive and able to discriminate between large and small issues
- Personally secure and unthreatened
- Clear priorities

Bad Day

- Avoids making decisions
- Indulges in exploring endless possibilities
- Prefers the broad brush to clear focus
- Rarely resolute, often inconclusive
- Lacks control and fails to see what is important
- Not producing much progress, often procrastinating
- Unwilling to give a positive lead

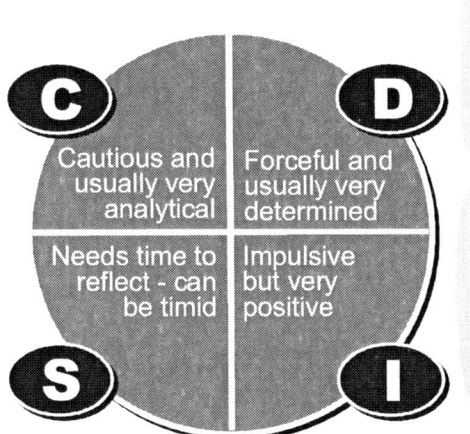

C — Cautious and usually very analytical
D — Forceful and usually very determined
S — Needs time to reflect – can be timid
I — Impulsive but very positive

⚠ Caution!

Decisiveness, when over-extended can appear brutal and harsh to those who feel they have a place in the decision-making process. Decisions taken too quickly can have unforseen circumstances.

'Make unimportant decisions fast so that perfection doesn't stand in the way of progress. On the other hand, if the decision is important, a poor decision could be disastrous. Start by deciding when the decision should be made.'

Martin Scott

115

Perseverance

Definition: To be able to produce constant persistence to achieve something against the odds. To face discomfort and defeat without complaint or giving up.

Good Day

- Generally wins through despite the odds
- Determined - unwilling to give up
- Holds fast to goals and vision in times of discomfort or trial
- An inspiration to others
- Able to patiently endure adversity
- Self-motivated
- Disciplined

Bad Day

- Easily gives up on a task or project
- Lacking in resolve
- Will look to 'cut corners' and find an easy way out
- A tendency towards laziness
- Unreliable under pressure
- Easily daunted by difficult challenges
- Not tenacious

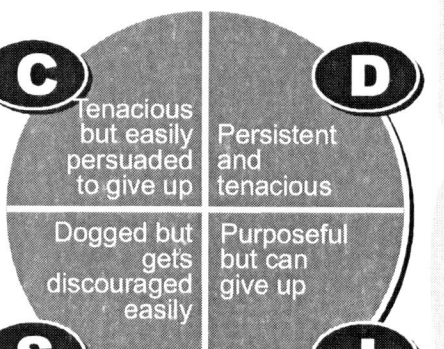

⚠ Caution!

Perseverance, when over-extended can become an unattractive stubbornness. These people are characterised by being poor listeners, not applying the counsel of others and may be seen as arrogant regarding their own judgements.

C	D
Tenacious but easily persuaded to give up	Persistent and tenacious
Dogged but gets discouraged easily	Purposeful but can give up
S	I

'The tendency to persevere, to persist in spite of hindrances, discouragements and impossibilities - it is this in all things that distinguishes the strong soul from the weak.'

Thomas Carlisle

Can We Really Change?

GROUP 4: PASSIVE ATTRIBUTES
This group are often found in our actions or speech, but exist without the need to be socially expressed. We might describe them as characteristics we 'hold' or maintain.

Wisdom

Definition: To be thoughtful and judicious in the application of knowledge, experience and learning. Using insight and understanding of people, issues and situations

Good Day

- Able to distinguish 'the wood from the trees'
- Making good choices from many options
- Comprehending outcomes through insights into others
- Renowned for prudent, tactful speech
- Knowing when to compromise and when to stand firm
- A respected counsellor and mentor

Bad Day

- Becoming confused by detail and trivia
- Making decisions too quickly
- Failing to learn from mistakes
- A reputation for being rash, naïve and gullible
- Poor listening, distracted and disinterested
- Blurring the lines between opposites

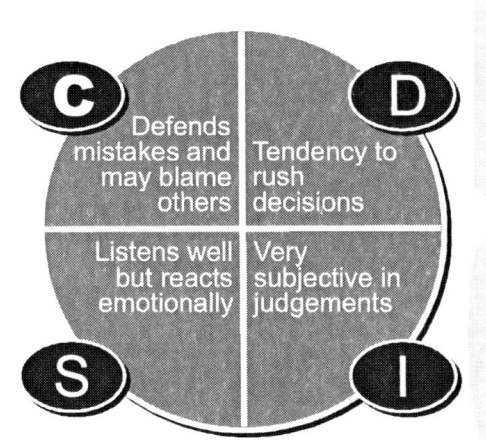

C — Defends mistakes and may blame others
D — Tendency to rush decisions
S — Listens well but reacts emotionally
I — Very subjective in judgements

⚠ Caution!

Wisdom, when over-extended may come across as preaching and pontificating. It's okay to be the wise old owl but avoid being the pompous 'know-it-all'.

'Knowledge is power but applied knowledge - wisdom - is even more powerful.'

Ken Buist

Honesty

Definition: To be truthful, virtuous, just and fair towards others, frank and candid in one's views of oneself. Being neither deceitful nor devious in one's dealings with others.

Good Day

- A person of honour and integrity
- A reputation for uprightness in disposition and conduct
- Not manipulating people or circumstances for personal favour
- Not resorting to half-truths
- Candid in self-assessment - strengths and weaknesses
- Respected by others, if grudgingly or secretly

Bad Day

- Lacking integrity
- Trying to cover up shortcomings
- Unfair in dealings with people
- Perceived as being untrustworthy
- Insincere
- Perceived as being deceitful

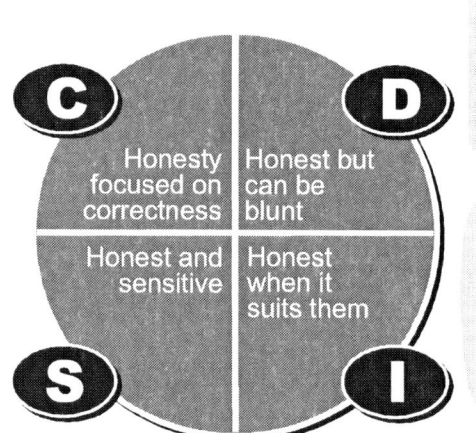

⚠ Caution!

Honesty, when over-extended can appear indiscreet and naïve. It is vital that it is combined with the ability to judge how much should be said, and to judge the right timing and context. How you deliver honesty is as important as the honesty itself.

C: Honesty focused on correctness
D: Honest but can be blunt
S: Honest and sensitive
I: Honest when it suits them

'Honesty is the first chapter in the book of wisdom.'

Thomas Jefferson

Can We Really Change?

Objectivity

Definition: To respond rationally rather than reacting. To understand one's feelings and be able to put them to one side and focus on behaviour.

Good Day

- Primarily concerned with the facts of a situation
- Able to take a detached perspective without partiality
- A genuine desire to be equitable and fair in assessment
- Withstanding emotional pressure from others in decision making
- Ability to recognise the value of differing views
- Willing to be corrected if judgements are shown to be inaccurate

Bad Day

- Proneness to follow feelings rather than facts
- Tendency to be selective about facts
- Judgements coloured by prejudices
- Easily persuaded to change position
- Impulsive decision making
- Reacting to circumstances emotionally
- Selective about information gathering

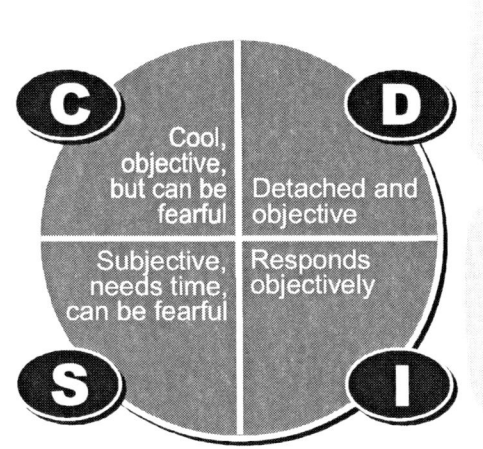

⚠ Caution!

Objectivity, when over-extended, slows down the decision-making process. It is a continual search for relevant data, and ignores human intuition and creativity. It can lead to procrastination.

C — Cool, objective, but can be fearful
D — Detached and objective
S — Subjective, needs time, can be fearful
I — Responds objectively

'We see things not as they are but as we are.'

Immanuel Kant

Discernment

Definition: The ability to distinguish one thing from another using insight to get to the heart of the matter. An acuteness of mind with the ability to penetrate

Good Day

- A developed sense of perception about people
- Able to recognise lies
- Capable of uncovering the underlying issues and cause of problems
- Enjoying the insights of others
- Good at scrutinising the 'small print' and underlying motivations
- Continually seeking insights into one's own personality
- Astute, shrewd and wise

Bad Day

- Either gullible or cynical
- Naïve and prone to being deceived
- Tending to be unaware if the inner motivations and intentions of others
- Analysis of people and situations can be superficial
- Liable to make impulsive and inaccurate judgements
- May lack sensitivity towards others

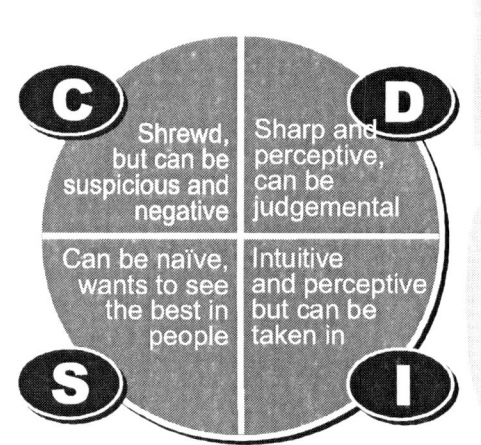

⚠ Caution!

Discernment, when over-extended could be perceived as judgementalism and convey an air of superiority towards others. Continually wanting to bring the need for change to the attention of other people can be irritating.

C — Shrewd, but can be suspicious and negative

D — Sharp and perceptive, can be judgemental

S — Can be naïve, wants to see the best in people

I — Intuitive and perceptive but can be taken in

'The sensibility of man to trifles, and his insensibility to great things, indicates a strange inversion.'
Pascal

Emotional Maturity is not an examination with an impossible pass mark. Neither is it a condition we somehow contract, or even catch! We do not attain maturity by achieving some arbitrary standard or through a mystical experience. Maturity involves daily decisions, life-changing choices, and constant application. Like peddling a bike up a hill, stopping will inevitably result in falling off. This is why we sometimes see strong, capable, disciplined people make a series of bad decisions, and their lives subsequently become chaotic, even tragic.

Lighting scented candles, listening to ambient music in a darkened room, or concentrating on my inner child, or animal psyche, will not help. Short-cut routes to inner peace and enlightenment are very appealing but can no more bring me to maturity in all, or even any, of my behaviours, than the use of psychedelic drugs. However, we can set a course and apply ourselves to making measurable progress from the 'Immature' symptoms to the 'Mature' ones.

The commercial world is full of capable and highly motivated individuals. What gives a professional the edge in either expanding or contracting markets is the opinion their clients hold of them. That is what determines a 'Favoured Supplier' status. It is also what underpins all recommendations to other prospective clients. Ultimately, it is what enables us to become Trustworthy Advisers and achieve the status that puts us ahead of the field.

Emotional Maturity is crucial in attaining this position.

9

SHEDDING THE SNAKESKIN

Every creature with skin has to keep producing new cells. It has been estimated that 90% of household dust is actually dry skin! The snake, however, is unique in moulting in one complete exercise. By rubbing itself against a hard surface, the snake loosens the old skin around its eyes and mouth, pushes through the now redundant tissue hanging from its face, and crawls out of its old skin entirely. What emerges is a shiny, new-looking creature, still bearing the characteristic markings, but now far more attractive, supple, and flexible a predator.

Unlike the snake, behavioural transformation cannot be expedited within two hours! Yet the difference has many similarities:

- → greater ability to adapt to our social surroundings
- → more personable, therefore more professionally effective
- → increased freedom to express our skills and contributions.

My research and experience have repeatedly highlighted five major barriers to Emotional Maturity. Each one needs to be shed if we are to develop ourselves fully, both as professionals and sociable individuals. These five barriers are:

| Anger | Fear | Unforgiveness | Pride | Greed |

Our tendency is to adopt each of these into our emotional makeup and regard their presence as normal. We make excuses and adjustments for them and develop our strengths in order to compensate. Maturity, however, is accentuating our strengths, moderating our weaknesses, and removing those barriers impeding our personal growth in each of the sixteen character traits.

Growth agents

This is the good news! There are two attitudes that facilitate the removal of all five barriers and accelerate our growth in each character trait as we apply them diligently. They are **honesty** and **willingness**.

Honesty
Having reviewed the 16 character traits, you will probably have observed three things about yourself.

- In some characteristics you are relatively strong.
- In others you would admit to being weak.
- In the remainder you would describe your performance as variable.

Quite simply, this is honesty, which is where the process of maturity begins. We each need an accurate view of our lives. A true perspective of our behaviours, attitudes, and motives is vital, along with an understanding of our choices. Why we make them, are they good and positive, or bad and destructive? Our insights need not be absolutely clear. What matters is agreeing with oneself to apply honest self-appraisals.

Willingness
The theologian Jonathan Edwards described the human will as the power by which the mind chooses things. Without that ability, he argued, our decisions would simply be a series of random impulses. He went on to conclude that our choices are informed by what we believe to be in our best interest.

Being fully convinced of the need to change a behaviour, or attitude, means that I believe it is in my best interest to do so. The personal cost is a price worth paying. This could mean adapting my style of communication, or denying selfish tendencies, by putting the needs of others first. Willingness is the second essential agent for personal growth.

Honesty and willingness are personal decisions. They represent deep inner convictions derived from sober reflection and serious thought. However, they very quickly become experiential. The moment I choose to exercise these faculties they have a direct and significant impact on my life.

> 'Sow a thought, reap an act,
> Sow an act, reap a habit.
> Sow a habit, reap a character,
> Sow a character, reap a destiny.'

This little stanza is packed with dynamic truth. Our specific destiny is *Becoming a Trustworthy Adviser*. Along the way, it is likely to involve some personal transformation, so don't allow feelings of inadequacy or victimisation to rob you. As you embark on this journey, focus on what can be accomplished. You are a unique individual capable of finding and enjoying freedom within your mature behaviours.

Anger

Dealing with anger

Anger is a natural human reaction. It is morally neutral. At times it is a wholly appropriate response and a thoroughly legitimate feeling.

Two men, two reactions

> Nelson Mandela walked free from Robin Island after months of intense negotiations with FW De Clerk. Both men had far more reasons to mistrust one another than to believe the other could be relied upon. Yet, as they embarked on a process of developing mutual respect and trust, the man with the greater reasons for anger, resentment and bitterness emerged as a genuine statesman, respected and admired by all world leaders. What Mandela achieved within himself during his imprisonment empowered him to bring healing, reconciliation and hope to the entire nation. He had dealt with anger in the most positive and constructive manner.

Injustice demands a response; part of which is to be angry. Anger can become a phenomenal energy source, either wreaking destruction and further misery, or fuelling our efforts to oppose wrongdoing and achieve a meaningful conclusion.

By contrast, the atrocities of September 11th show how one man's anger can turn into bitterness, and then fury. Osama bin Laden believed Saudi soil was defiled by the presence of Americans during the Gulf war. His actions were intended to avenge this perceived offence.

The lesson from these two men is that anger must be managed and when it is, the result can bring overwhelming good.

Hostile anger

This normally takes the form of aggression. However, venting anger in this way develops a habit that eventually forms our character and defines our reputation.

Hostile anger at work takes the forms of sarcasm, severe criticism, rudeness and vengeful behaviour. If you occasionally slip into these, take time to consider ways in which you can better manage your reactions. If these are behaviours you frequently exhibit, there is a real need to examine what lies behind them. Trustworthy Advisers are known for their maturity when handling pressure, difficult people, and even injustices.

Passive anger

Equally destructive, this manifests through:

- moodiness
- tense body language
- withdrawal
- atmospheric silences
- withholding affection.

It is silent and non-violent. Those who hold this emotion avoid confronting those responsible, choosing instead to brood in self-pity, building resentments around their pain which is often genuine but needs expression and release.

The substitute for confrontation is often gossip. Suppose a report gets rejected for lacking creative proposals. The criticism might be unreasonable or simply communicated in a curt manner. Whatever the rights or wrongs, we initially feel disappointed, perhaps demotivated, and possibly angry, with good cause. The challenge is what to do about it.

If we waste energy complaining to those not responsible, or time in following prolonged periods of sulking inactivity, we have clearly indulged in passive aggression. It renders us ineffectual. I watched a highly capable but undisciplined subordinate eat an entire packet of chocolate biscuits in sullen silence immediately after addressing his failure to meet specific objectives within agreed target dates. He was angry with himself for failing and with me for pointing this out. His parents, apparently, had always discouraged emotional expression; he was trained to express his anger passively.

Unexpressed anger festers, ultimately turning into bitterness and resentment. It is relationally destructive, professionally damaging, and ruins effective teamwork.

Intolerance is another indicator, usually expressing itself in censoriousness and strongly disapproving remarks. Prejudices are often a way in which passive anger finds a route to the surface.

Not all, but many cases of depression are attributable to repressed anger. In extreme cases, this can have devastating consequences. Fortunately, once the cause is uncovered, there is help available.

Common causes in the work-place

Frustrated Plans
We rarely get our own way in negotiations. The principle for success is to enter negotiations determined to achieve a win-win result. Nobody should lose face or feel humiliated, everyone must come away with something, and all parties concede some of their opening position. However, if our reaction to being told we cannot possibly have all we ask for is to display our frustration or withdraw from the discussions, we have allowed anger to cloud our judgement and block our progress. We have effectively created a lose-lose situation. Becoming angry when we fail to get our own way is simply an expression of profound selfishness. It is extremely immature behaviour.

Unmet Expectations
A lot of the anger we experience is rooted in the pain and disappointment we feel when our expectations fail to be met. A new colleague failing to fulfil your expectations may require a calm and reasonable appraisal of his or her performance and behaviours. Failure to deal with the issues will eventually lead to an unhelpful outburst. The longer the disappointment lingers, the

greater the frustration, and the deeper the well of resentment that results.

First, our unmet expectations must be acknowledged, reappraised, and adjusted. The corrections and confrontations can then be handled appropriately.

Being our own slave-driver

Corporate deadlines, performance benchmarks, market share projections, and profit forecasts are enough to worry about! However, if personal targets are too demanding the result will be a profound sense of failure. This can easily lead to a loss of proportion which projects itself onto the smallest failing in others. Honest appraisal of our feelings will be required to overcome this self-condemning attitude.

Jealousy

Being missed off a circulation list, or not consulted, creates understandable annoyance. Left unresolved, this is likely to leave one suspicious of others. Their conversations become potentially threatening and everything begins to be tinged with mistrust. Feeling excluded or overlooked produces jealousy, which in turn may lead to residual anger.

Four steps to dealing with anger

- **1. Pause**

    If anger is influencing our behaviour, or attitudes, we need to take time out.
    - Is this feeling justified?
    - Has it another source: unmet expectations, jealousy, frustration?
    - Am I feeling bad about myself?

    We may need to talk it through with a close friend, or our partner. Preferably someone not involved directly, or with prejudicial views formed by our earlier complaints.

    Write down exactly what caused the anger, and the range of feelings accompanying it. Remember to destroy this document once a satisfactory conclusion has been reached. It is also advisable to keep it at home.

- **2. Reflect**
    - Who are you angry with?
    - When did this start?
    - What specific issues gave rise to these feelings?
    - How often and how easily does this occur?
    - Why do you believe this has happened?
    - Are your feelings entirely appropriate, or perhaps excessive?
    - What result would resolve the feelings?

    Angry people see the offence and feel the hurt. The object of reflection is to gain perspective. We need to take our own behaviour into account while putting ourselves into the shoes of the responsible party. That is not to excuse the inexcusable, nor to blame ourselves if we are genuinely blameless. It is, however, to reflect maturely because what we want is not revenge but closure.

- **3. Control**

    To control anger we must first control our thinking. Internal pain projects our attention onto the cause. This is a powerful and basic survival instinct. Anger is a protective measure that heightens awareness of our environment, sharpens our senses and discernment to spot potential threats, and empowers us with aggression for self-defence. We therefore need to take control of our thought patterns without denying the legitimacy of our feelings. Remember, anger is morally neutral. The issue is how we express it.

    Feelings of anger do not subside simply by choosing to control one's thoughts. To expect that would be unreasonable. As we control the extent and expression of our anger it becomes ours to manage and process. We then start to acquire a habit of self-control and anger management.

- **4. Grow**

    Having gained control of our thinking, we can constructively deal with the issues. Confrontation can now take place without becoming a series of hostile accusations. It can be tactful, discreet, persuasive and undemanding. None of these require us to compromise but they do enable us to set out to win the person, not the argument. Our goal should be complete forgiveness and reconciliation.

Confrontation may not be possible if the issue involves an organisation, for example. I can however, seek to make them accountable. In setting out to win the other party, or promote best practices within organisations, we are growing. Our focus has moved from our pain to the good of others. We are seeking correction, not revenge. We are aiming to be supportive, not destructive. The anger has become positive, useful, and a means of personal growth. We have overcome a common barrier to maturity and employed it to attain greater maturity.

Fear

Overcoming fears

Fear, like anger, has its place. Our concern is to deal with those fears that prevent us from attaining Emotional Maturity by distinguishing their source, their impact on our behaviours, and our response.

- ➤ Distinguish the source
- ➤ Recognise its impact
- ➤ Identify our response

A protective device

Fear is another instinct for survival. To expect to be entirely free of fear is unrealistic and inadvisable.

We rightly fear danger and avoid unnecessary risks. Caution when walking on an unguarded cliff-top is healthy. It ensures I go home afterwards. Yet fear preventing me from climbing a ladder to clear leaves from my gutters is clearly undesirable. Fears that create panic demand that I sculpture my life to avoid the possibility of danger.

Learned fear

This is acquired – not instinctive. It appears to be protective but is actually very restrictive, even harmful. Learned fear derives from bad experiences, anxieties imposed on us by others, and superstitions.

Bad experiences are to be avoided. We therefore develop defence systems to prevent their repetition. Unfortunately these are sometimes so deeply woven into our makeup that we are completely unaware of their presence.

A colleague observed that whenever he raised his hand above eye level, the man to his right instinctively ducked. Scratching his head evoked fear in his accountant! Later he asked if the man was aware of this reaction.

'Oh, yes. I do it all the time. Except at home.'

'So you aren't afraid that your wife will hit you. How about other women?' he inquired.

The accountant thought carefully. 'Do you know, It's only men' he replied. It seemed to be a revelation.

The discussion revealed that his father had slapped him around the head from an early age. Realising his reaction was a learned fear, he began to discipline himself to hold his head up whenever his heart said: 'Duck!'

After a few months of patchy but gradual success, he braved himself to share this development with his father in a non-accusatory manner. His father had seen a gentler, more gracious model of discipline at work with his grandchildren and asked for forgiveness. Both men grew closer as a result. They also grew as individuals. We never need to stop maturing. The accountant has said that he and his father are now friends, rather than just family, and he no longer ducks when others scratch their heads!

Many employees stifle their imagination and fear taking initiative. The reason is often that their parents valued compliance above everything else. This left their creativity in cold storage. Encouragements to think 'outside the box' sound to them like an exhortation to embrace reprimand! Fears like this must be recognised, and personally confronted before their shackles can be released.

Superstitions have a unique power to produce irrational, even laughable, behaviour. It seems odd that a sportsperson who trains so diligently, should rely on something so capricious and unreliable as luck. Some tennis professionals wear the same shirt throughout an entire competition, frantically washing it themselves between matches.

Many Singaporeans believe that fortune is carried by a southerly wind. A waterfront office block has been imaginatively constructed in the shape of a south-facing arrow, in order to offer the wind of fortune to businesses in both sides of the building. Rents are at a premium!

'Touch wood' is part of the English language. The idea is that if I say this, and do it, I can avoid creating a curse that automatically results in the opposite of what I just said. For example, 'Providing the global economy remains stable, we can maintain our market share. Touch wood.' It looks so silly in print, doesn't it? Who would think that such a gesture could ensure the stability of global business markets? The power of superstition is the fear of not having control over events.

Fear leads to superstition, and superstitions keep us in fear of consequences. If you are a mildly (or even seriously) superstitious person, ask yourself:

> ➢ What is the source of this?
> ➢ How does it impact my thoughts and feelings?
> ➢ What are my responses if I omit to follow the prescribed routine?

The fear filter

Once we start to see most things as potentially harmful, we develop a filter of fear through which everything must pass. It becomes an automatic response, demanding answers before any course of action

> **Surveys have indicated that up to 98% of the things people fear never actually happen!**

can be entertained. You may know people who interrogate every suggestion like this:

- How will this affect me?
- What harm might it do?
- Could this result in embarrassment?
- What is the worst-case scenario?
- Why shouldn't the worst possible outcome be the most likely?
- How costly might this become in personal terms?
- Where is the threat?
- Just because it appears safe, why trust it?

A lack of positive objectivity leaves someone focused on negative possibilities. Their memory will always record bad results. It may even fail to register any good results. By only remembering failures and bad outcomes, their fears are apparently proved accurate by the available evidence. Fears become reinforced and self-fulfilling.

Controlling fears

The fear filter takes control by developing attitudes that often lead to social timidity, hesitancy, and sometimes withdrawal. Suspicions are formed that stifle personal development and prevent open relationships from offering the positive input of others.

These descriptors may sound extreme but we are skilled at masking our inner thoughts and adapting shrewdly to our environment. On first impression, an aggressive, highly picky individual could appear to be strong, but anti-social. Such behaviour is often due to fear – of being victimised, embarrassed, marginalised or ignored.

Negative goals often express controlling fears. 'When this happens, which it probably will …' In order to avoid the charge of negativity, people often adopt a worldly-wise cynicism to mask their underlying attitudes. What actually takes place is the 'wet blanketing' of new ideas and innovative schemes. Controlling fears easily debilitate and consume the creative energy of individuals and their colleagues.

Controlling fears are tyrants. They demand constant attention, create relational barriers, and ultimately frustrate a person into becoming a contracted version of their true self. The solution is to control the fears.

Taking control of our fears

The rescue workers entering the Twin Trade Towers on September 11th were ordinary men and women, properly trained to do their jobs. These courageous individuals did not leave their emotions at home each day. They knew fear, as well as the joy of saving lives. They were realists who knew the facts and understood the risks.

How then were they able to calmly risk their lives in order to save others? Their courage derived from the same source available to us all of us. They took control.

'Sow a thought, reap an act.'

Choose your thoughts

We can each exercise our will to choose what we think about. Our anxieties may remain, but we can still make that choice. We can choose to think about the job in hand, its necessity, the rewards for success, the lives of others that are involved or might be benefited.

We must also choose what not to think about. As a fear expresses itself with 'Oh no, what if ...?' we have to seize and reject it, denying that thought the opportunity to dominate our inner life. It is by the renewing of our mind, through the discipline of our thought world, that our behaviours can be transformed. It begins with choosing our thoughts and restricting them to those that are positive and constructive, directed towards achievement and success. This is not a brittle optimism. It is about setting a course for our lives.

Distinguishing the source
If you are prone to particular fears, ask yourself, 'Where did this originate?' Fearful thoughts and feelings are not random. By seeing that a fear has been learned, we are enabled to live without it! Fears are normally a product of life's experiences and childhood influences, not traumas. Knowing their origin explains how they were formed, and defines what to reject, correct, or adjust in order to take control.

Verbalise
The accountant saw the significance of his reactions when asked an appropriate question. Verbalising our fears is often the next step in defeating them. Talking facilitates calm analysis and can often reveal techniques for dealing with them. It also makes us feel more secure to experience understanding from another person.

Free your imagination
Most fears live in the imaginary realm and how we employ it is entirely our responsibility. Many people feed their imagination with a diet that exacerbates the very fears inhibiting their emotional maturity. Like the film advertised under the banner: 'You'll never sleep without the light on again!'

Focussing on every bad experience suffered by complete strangers can take its toll. It feeds the imagination with material that is the ideal diet for fearing the motives and likely behaviours of others. There are some things it is just pointless to know about.

Your imagination is the birthplace of your creativity. It has the potential to enrich your life, solve working problems, diversify professional opportunities for success, express your unique personality and develop your relationships. By engaging in positive goal setting, and fixing your thoughts on those things which are good, strong, dignified, and valuable, fears become starved of their nutrition. They will be replaced by growing optimism and courage.

Questions to make fears accountable

> - Is this concern reasonable?
> - Is it realistic?
> - Is it reducible?

Some concerns are exaggerated but require our attention. Others are extreme and actually foolish. Some are valid but wise actions will lessen their effects.

Unforgiveness

Resolving unforgiveness

> The television journalist had gained an interview with a parent in North Belfast whose son had been accidentally killed only two hours before. It was a time of grief and extreme pain. The only question asked was:
> 'Do you feel bitter about this?'
> Not a word of condolence was offered. 'Bitter' was put into her mouth and she quite naturally repeated it. Sadly we will never know how she dealt with that tragedy or whether she has been helped. Unfortunately many people are left holding on to their hurts.

Those who take their hurts home and then take them to bed, usually find themselves resentful of their jobs, colleagues and employers. Ultimately they become their own victims.

Recognising unforgiveness

> - bearing grudges
> - enjoying bad news about those who have caused hurt or offence
> - recounting wrongs suffered and the faults of those responsible
> - being wary of others

Bitter feelings are a natural part of any grieving process. Bitterness that remains, however, is a different matter. It severely hinders emotional development.

Another symptom of unforgiveness is inappropriate or excessive reactions. These often reveal past hurts that need to be faced, forgiven, and buried. Finding closure is crucial if we are to avoid living in the darkest recesses of past experiences.

Resentments and bitterness cause stress, which ultimately needs to find a release valve. Usually it is directed at an innocent event, or person, capable of being made a vicarious target of retribution. Psychologists refer to this as 'Transference'.

> Forgiving someone does not make them right,
>
> Nor is it an act of weakness or surrender.
>
> We forgive people because they were wrong.
>
> Forgiveness brings emotional freedom.

Why unforgiveness must be resolved

- It taints our view of life.
- It breeds suspicions.
- Enjoyment of life becomes distorted.
- Personal development is inhibited.
- Relationships become fragile.
- Physical illness can result.

It becomes difficult to enjoy the moment when one's focus is on the past. Attention is split between now and the moment of pain, the future holds no meaning because it moves me away from the object of my resentful feelings.

Unforgiveness drives us towards a self-centred perspective that militates against kindness, empathy, good manners and the service of others.

Bitterness demands affirmation. Relationships get judged on the basis of whether the other person agrees with one's feelings. Conversations drift inexorably to the same old subject.

Medical studies have concluded that in some cases arthritis and other painful complaints affecting muscles and joints can be caused by the bitterness of unforgiveness.

> The mature person aims to live in the present.
>
> Unforgiveness keeps us in the past.
>
> Maturity focuses on a vision of the future.
>
> Unforgiveness has nowhere new to take us.

Four steps towards forgiveness

- **1. Recognise the hurt**

    Vagueness is unhelpful. So is making excuses for someone.

    The prevalent emotion is probably anger, which needs to be expressed. This facilitates proper identification of pain, rather than the obscured version clouded by subsequent resentments. Recognise the hurt for what it is.

- **2. Take an objective view**

    Did we hold unreasonable expectations of the other party? Do we share responsibility for what occurred?

    Blaming others unfairly will never be resolved by forgiving them unnecessarily. That is plain unreality. Objectivity is vital but may require the advice of a supportive but detached individual.

- **3. Understand the other point of view**

    There may have been no malicious intent. It could have been a genuine accident, mistake, or misunderstanding. That possibility has to be taken seriously. Look at the facts from their perspective. Forgiveness may still be necessary but it will be far less demanding.

    Understanding another's viewpoint reveals those elements that can, and should, be excused.

- **4. Make it an act of the will**

    Having examined the hurt, its cause, and the other party's viewpoint, a clear choice now remains. This is a matter for personal responsibility: to forgive or to withhold forgiveness.

> Forgiveness is the unconditional pardoning of one who has done wrong.
>
> It is the relinquishment of all rights and expectations of compensation.
>
> Forgiveness means actively replacing resentment with acceptance.

Pride

Taming our pride

A healthy attitude
Beaming with joy, a flag-draped Olympic medallist waves jubilantly from the podium. We enjoy the athlete's success, happily affirming speed, strength or skill.

Pride in one's ability need not become arrogance. Pride in one's achievements does not necessarily lead to boasting. Pride in our culture or nation need not become chauvinistic. All these forms of pride are reasonable and socially acceptable. No one should be offended by them or expect them to inevitably lead to excess.

The same is true of pride in our children and partners, which can be supportive, affirming, releasing, and empowering. It breeds encouragement and thoughtfulness. I would naturally place more trust in a person who took care about how they presented themselves than someone who was dirty, and unkempt. Pride in one's appearance need not be narcissistic.

Pride can be a healthy attitude, properly motivating us to achieve our full potential. We usually call it self-esteem, or confidence, and find it attractive in others and valuable in ourselves. It is psychologically recognised as an invaluable emotional competency.

Ugly in excess
Unfortunately, pride can become our primary motivation, turning to excess and thus corrupting our character. It has shifted from self-esteem – a healthy emotional attitude – to self-centredness, which inhibits our growth to full emotional maturity.

Attitudes towards people, tasks, and situations become an exercise in superiority, rather than interest or empathy. They are all there for the sole purpose of feeding the ego.

Achievements are targeted solely at personal aggrandisement. If there is no praise, there is no purpose. Noble schemes are shunned and altruism is neglected, unless there is a guarantee, or strong probability, of significant recognition.

Abilities are paraded in front of others for their admiration and adulation. Success stories are repeated ad nausea; acclaim is expected from every audience. Those who fail to comply will be ignored, possibly shunned.

Associations only find significance by reflecting glory to the one at the centre. A child is valued for his sporting success, or her academic achievements. A partner is important for her beauty, or his charm, a colleague is valued because they contribute to the success of their esteem driven manager.

Damaging effects

When a person's motives are dominated by pride, they become isolated. The process is inevitable. The significance of others becomes progressively diminished, effectively alienating the self-centred individual. Excessive self-esteem undermines good teamwork because one or more members wants to be the star.

One seriously damaging effect in the workplace is when genuine competitors are foolishly held in contempt. Having a leading market share for several years can too easily lead to assumptions of superiority, rather than maintaining that lead through professionalism and creativity. What can easily follow is derision. As this becomes part of the culture it cascades from competitors and their products, to clients and customers.

When Nick Leeson attempted to manipulate the markets of the far East, his massive gamble resulted in the collapse of Baring's, Britain's oldest merchant bank. Leeson was not a 'rogue trader' by nature, even though his practices had been wrong. Nor was he motivated by personal gain. His motivation was pride. Leeson wanted to be the man who could bend huge equity markets to obey his will. His failure put him into a Singaporean prison and turned Baring's into a by-word for weak managerial control.

Peter Davies, Sainsbury's chairman, recently led the company into a new office changing its ethos to reflect a support centre, rather than a domineering head office. Davies gave everyone the same office furniture, including himself, and created an ambience of humility and partnership, taking the company forward into the new century, away from its old style, hierarchical pomposity. His diagnosis about losing market share, and the remedy to restore it, included bringing humility into the organisation's culture. If successful, he can rightly be proud of his achievement!

Recognising proud traits

Pride has the power to ruin lives, destroy relationships, and de-rail our ambitions. It needs to be tamed. This following list is short but you may recognise yourself:

- frustration about time and energy spent on tasks going unnoticed
- reflecting on personal witticisms, and points well made
- basking in the affirmation and praise of one's peers
- repeating stories that make you look tough, determined, smart, wise
- a compulsion to make people aware of your achievements
- exaggerating your role in successes.

Ruling your esteem

When General Schwartzkopf organised the formal surrender in the Gulf War, he specifically instructed his officers not to dishonour or humiliate Iraqi military leaders. The conquering hero did not gloat over his victory. Allied forces obeyed his words and the president listened to his insights. But Schwartzkopf never let it go to his head. Self-esteem and personal confidence can also be humble, serving, collaborative and supportive. Even towards ones' enemies!

Four ways to exercise control of our self-esteem

Acknowledgement

- ☑ Admit faults and failings.
- ☑ Don't justify proud actions or boasting.
- ☑ Recognise tendencies to indulge some of the list above.

There is no 'Humility Pill' we can swallow: it starts with acknowledgement.

Accountability

- ☑ Ask your partner or a close friend to help keep you in check.

- ☑ Be prepared to ask: 'Did I overdo it?' or 'Was I too pushy?'
- ☑ Confess occasional lapses or arrogant attitudes.

You will be amazed how liberating it can be to make yourself vulnerable in this way. Remember, the other person will have already noticed your behaviour. Accountability helps us maintain diligence.

Affirm

- ☑ Give praise wherever possible.
- ☑ Congratulate others, acknowledging their significance.
- ☑ Show appreciation for the efforts of others.
- ☑ Honour those whose ideas you implement.
- ☑ Acknowledge your sources and quotes.

These practices will help you develop moral transparency, while provoking collaboration and contribution from others. Be generous, but genuine, in your affirmations.

Act

- ☑ Give as much, or more, than you take.
- ☑ Introduce others to those who may be useful to them.
- ☑ Watch out for the disabled, the quiet, the less socially adept.
- ☑ Help others find recognition and significance.
- ☑ Demonstrate concern and compassion.

Humility is not a condition; it's a way of behaving. Above all, remember that your own unique significance can only be enhanced by taking control of your self-esteem.

A word of insight

In applying these principles, you may become more aware of your failings, not less. This is not a sign of deterioration and a worsening condition! Actually it signifies the opposite. It means you have sensitised yourself to be alert for excesses. Mature people have strong self-esteem and deep reserves of confidence. These come from a developed security in their own identity, not through successful competition in every encounter. Those who are motivated by more than their own self-interest achieve the most and are always the best remembered.

Greed

Avoiding greed

'Excess is not enough!!' is how one journalist described New York during the 1980s. That ironic phrase makes the value system it represents look pathetically absurd. Emelda Marcos' three thousand pairs of shoes seemed to typify it most.

Yet some of the world's richest people are renowned for their generosity, work ethic and self-control. The head of AOL is known for his industriousness, Wal-Mart's CEO lives modestly, while Bill Gates pledged $1bn to charitable causes, irrespective of anti-trust litigation threatening to dramatically reduce his personal wealth. Clearly, status, wealth and power are not synonymous with greed and indulgence.

Greed is the excessive gratification or indulgence of legitimate appetites or pleasures. It takes hold when they become our priority. Food, alcohol, sex, money and possessions are its territory.

Greed ruins lives, destroys relationships, and steals our dignity. The more indulged, the greater it grows. It is a cruel master; never satisfied, always demanding.

Understanding the causes

Greed often expresses our need for comfort. 'Shopping therapy' and 'Comfort eating' describe substituting pointless indulgence for an un-met emotional need. A substitute represents second best, at best. It is often nothing more than the easiest available option.

Feelings of insignificance and personal rejection are often causes of greed. A sense of futility and emptiness can cause sexual greed that is never truly satisfying. Such feelings also lead to excessive drinking or jealousy; the former making us ill, the latter making us bitter. Sometimes these causes are so deep they require counselling, even therapy, but for most of us the answers lie within our grasp. Life is to be enjoyed, not dominated by uncontrollable forces.

Unseen paybacks

Some results of greed are all too obvious: mounting debts, jealousy, eating and drinking to excess. Others are subtler. Individuals driven by greed can be curiously unaware of their behaviour until it hits them with devastating results.

Looking Foolish
Profligate spending – 'Shopping therapy' – can mean that all one's credit cards get refused at a crowded cash till. Vilifying finance companies and fulminating against banks will simply shift the queue from sympathy to hostility. The shopper feels utterly humiliated. Self-esteem has actually been damaged.

Easily Exploited
Government officials who succumb to relatively small bribes can shipwreck their careers. Enron executives have been accused of lavishly entertaining those whose attention to detail might have been blunted by such excesses. Greedy weaknesses are easily exploitable, making us vulnerable to manipulation we later regret.

Bad Reputations
These always follow bad behaviour. Many politicians in Western democracies have in the past decade lost their good names, their careers, been publicly disgraced, even imprisoned, because of greed which led to corruption. A former French Prime Minister's taste for hand-tooled shoes became a subject of national interest. False applications for company shares, two former cabinet ministers imprisoned, even brown envelopes stuffed with cash, have all become part of the political landscape in Britain.

Those who get caught are the last to see the obvious; their reputations were tarnished long before they were exposed to the glare of publicity and the scrutiny of the media. A ruined reputation is difficult, sometimes impossible, to recover.

Setting the boundaries
To avoid these life-ruining experiences and ensure control of life's pleasures requires that we audit our behaviour, create personal boundaries, and regulate our appetites. Regularly taking stock of what really matters in life helps to put materialism into perspective. Being grateful for all we have is a practice that prevents us from always wanting more.

Health is another area in which greed can have deleterious effects. Giving regular time to looking after our bodies and evaluate the impact of our lifestyle will help keep us free from excessive indulgence.

Developing qualitative relationships with faithfulness and loyalty at the centre enables us to avoid the risk of sexual greed. This crucial area of our lives should be characterised by the fulfilment and satisfaction derived from a loving sexual experience. This enjoyment increases as we discover the value of meeting the needs and desires of our partner. Faithfulness creates boundaries that increase pleasure.

Teachers of wisdom have throughout human civilisation warned against the destructive power of greed. Their words have never been more appropriate than in the 21st Century.

10

ACHIEVING PERSONAL GROWTH

- Practical guidance on personal development
- Specific actions designed to facilitate substantive growth
- Initiating changes to acquire positive attributes
- Developing good habits

These are the 16 character traits we need to develop and strengthen if our perceived maturity is to convince others that we should be regarded as having the status of a Trustworthy Adviser.

OUTWARD EXPRESSIONS	INWARD EXPRESSIONS	DYNAMIC ATTRIBUTES	PASSIVE ATTRIBUTES
Kindness	Peace	Courage	Wisdom
Forgiveness	Humility	Self-control	Honesty
Trustworthiness	Patience	Decisiveness	Objectivity
Acknowledgement	Selflessness	Perseverance	Discernment

In order to grow our character we need to remember how long it took for us to get to where we are today. It is as important to be patient with ourselves, as it is to be committed to the process. Nearly all failures at self-improvement occur because individual expectations are too high. We want to be perfect and we want it to happen today!

Even when people approach the issues with reasonable and achievable targets, they usually lose patience over failures and setbacks. A Trustworthy Adviser needs to be one who has learned the art of being merciful. Our aim is maturity, not perfection. Maturity implies process, growth, evolutions, and transformation. We therefore have to forgive ourselves whenever we fail to live up to our expectations and standards. This should help to develop both humility and perseverance. In other words, we apply some of the character traits in order to progress in developing them to maturity.

Forgiving myself for failure, being honest with myself about the causes, exercising patience with myself where I am in need of improvement, and resolving to persevere, are vital exercises in personal growth. I can therefore apply four character traits, one from each section, in order to address a failure or setback. This is how we turn things to advantage. To do this, we have to acquire some good habits, which will govern how we respond to ourselves, to our circumstances, and to our relationships. The simple behaviours that enable the development of good habits are referred to as '**Change Catalysts**' in the material that follows. They facilitate a speeding up of the maturity process as we focus our thoughts and actions on personal growth.

Lasting and effective transformation is ensured by the development of good habits.

Many of the recommendations will be familiar to you. They will be things you already practice. However, as you examine the whole agenda for developing each character trait, you will probably identify several **Change Catalysts** that fall outside your current sphere of behaviour. There will be others you might categorise as: 'These are occasionally true about me'.

> **The two change agents are honesty and willingness**

Look at each page reflectively and analytically. The idea is not to tick or cross what you do or don't do; this is not a score chart! Allow your **honesty** to compare your normal behaviours and attitudes with each **change catalyst**.

Then select maybe two in which you are active, but do not excel, and make a contract with yourself to achieve growth. After that, choose one or two in which you would consider yourself lacking or inconsistent, and again make a personal contract to apply this change catalyst to your behaviours. In doing this you have applied **willingness**. The process has begun!

The reason for not attempting to apply the entire list of **change catalysts** is one of personal kindness. It would be too great a number of actions to remember, and too great a commitment. The result would be frustration and a feeling of failure. Our aim is success!

At the foot of each page is a cautionary statement. This is because over the years of working with people, I have observed the tendency for individuals to 'Get good at their virtues'. In other words, they try to always apply and display their better nature, or more enhanced characteristics. It might be to achieve popularity, or to demonstrate credibility through a particular strength. When these are not appropriate, or are over-applied, it actually gives others a false impression. The chairwoman of an interviewing panel once commented to me about a candidate that he was 'Such a lovely person. And that's why we can't give him the job.' He over-extended his gentleness and humility. What they were looking for was the ability to exercise authority and be assertive.

Just as a tennis player with a service arm twice the size of the other one, would look grotesque, we also need to develop all sixteen character traits equally in order to be balanced. It is this mixture of strengths that characterise the Trustworthy Adviser.

The nature of the **change catalysts** is that while having direct impact on the development of the character trait under which they are listed, they also have a transferable influence on several other character traits. This enables you to focus on just a few of the possible actions per trait, and yet achieve the maximum growth possible within the entire range.

Achieving Personal Growth

KINDNESS – an outward expression of character

Choose any 2 or 3 of the change catalysts you are currently exercising but wish to develop further. Then choose 1 or 2 in which you recognise a need to grow and strengthen.

Change Catalyst

- Suspend bias and judgement of others.
- List some people you would like to know better and plan how.
- Practice smiling at others and cultivating warmth and openness.
- Quit looking down on others.
- Value others for who they are.
- Exercise hospitality and generosity.
- Be aware of the damage caused by careless words.
- Develop the skill of encouragement.
- Consistently express concern for the well-being of others.
- Decide to serve rather than wait to be served.

The change catalysts I aim to practice in order to develop the characteristic of kindness are:

_____
_____

Signed _____ Date _____ Review Date _____

Ask a good friend to monitor your progress and encourage you.

! Caution Over-extended kindness can appear saccharine sweet and stifling. It causes doubts about sincerity, leading to awkward responses. Be kind but purposeful.

FORGIVENESS – an outward expression of character

Choose any 2 or 3 of the change catalysts you are currently exercising but wish to develop further. Then choose 1 or 2 in which you recognise a need to grow and strengthen.

Change Catalyst

- Thoughtfully examine the following questions:
  - What or who is hurting me right now?
  - Against whom do I hold grudges?
  - Do I tend to keep a record of wrongs?
  - Do I talk to others about those who have offended me in the past?
- Name the specific people and actions you want to forgive.
- Own up to your responsibility in the issues to be resolved.
- Identify when, or against whom, you react angrily.
- Choose to forgive yourself and the other parties and verbalise that choice.
- Plan a near date to discuss and resolve any possible misunderstandings.
- Decide to resolve interpersonal difficulties quickly from now on.

The change catalysts I aim to practice in order to develop the characteristic of forgiveness are:

_____

_____

Signed _____ Date _____ Review Date _____

Ask a good friend to monitor your progress and encourage you.

! Caution Over-extended forgiveness will be superficial, failing to deal with the root cause unconditionally. Time may be required to allow emotions to settle before releasing forgiveness is practicable. Always avoid making excuses for yourself and others.

TRUSTWORTHINESS – an outward expression of character

Choose any 2 or 3 of the change catalysts you are currently exercising but wish to develop further. Then choose 1 or 2 in which you recognise a need to grow and strengthen.

Change Catalyst

- Examine times you have broken your word.
    - Evaluate the reasons for this.
    - Consider how you can regain the other parties' confidence.
    - Where possible, make amends.
- Take responsibility for your mistakes and be open about them.
- Correct any misrepresentations you may have made.
- Make a list of your personal values and the beliefs that underpin them.
- Keep your diary and to do lists updated but avoid being over-committed.
- Determine not to gossip or betray confidences.
- Be sure that your word is capable of being fulfilled.
    - Review your time schedules.
    - Ascertain the availability of other resources needed for each undertaking.
    - Do nor rely on the performance of another without obtaining their buy-in.

The change catalysts I aim to practice in order to develop the characteristic of trustworthiness are:

_____
_____

Signed _____ Date _____ Review Date _____

Ask a good friend to monitor your progress and encourage you.

! Caution Over-extended trustworthiness can lead to pride in being perceived by others as having this virtue. It is important to ensure that being trustworthy is the colour of ones actions, not the sole aim.

ACKNOWLEDGEMENT – an outward expression of character

Choose any 2 or 3 of the change catalysts you are currently exercising but wish to develop further. Then choose 1 or 2 in which you recognise a need to grow and strengthen.

Change Catalyst

- Ensure that your feedback is not just negative or highly critical.
- Never take others for granted – let them know you value them.
- Accept that no-one is perfect and look for the good in them.
- Plan how and when to give recognition and express appreciation.
- Be sincere in your praise – specify what was right or good.
- Examine yourself for jealousy and suspicion and deal with it.
- Involve others in as many decision making processes as possible.
- Consciously draw quieter individuals into discussions and show affirmation.
- Avoid innuendo and gossip about those in authority.

The change catalysts I aim to practice in order to develop the characteristic of acknowledgement are:

_____
_____

Signed _____ Date _____ Review Date _____

Ask a good friend to monitor your progress and encourage you.

! Caution If acknowledgement is over-extended it becomes flattery. This will lack substance and appear insincere. It can also seem to be a false humility, or appear ingratiating.

PEACE – an inward expression of character

Choose any 2 or 3 of the change catalysts you are currently exercising but wish to develop further. Then choose 1 or 2 in which you recognise a need to grow and strengthen.

Change Catalyst

- Acknowledge any personal anger and plan how to deal with it.
- Identify your fears and anxieties – ascertain which are valid and rational.
- Aim to live one day at a time, keeping your focus on today's tasks.
- Ensure you get adequate sleep, relaxation and leisure time.
- Balance the needs of your body, emotions, intellect, and spirit.
- Resist negative thinking that centres on the worst case scenarios.
- Build on your self-confidence, gradually adding to what you do well.
- Pace yourself within your levels of energy and creativity.
- Plan for unallocated time.

The change catalysts I aim to practice in order to develop the characteristic of peace are:

_____
_____

Signed _____ Date _____ Review Date _____

Ask a good friend to monitor your progress and encourage you.

! Caution Over-extended peace takes the form of appearing unfocused, lazy, and without motivation. It can become an unrealistic outlook, shielding the individual from uncomfortable facts.

HUMILITY – an inward expression of character

Choose any 2 or 3 of the change catalysts you are currently exercising but wish to develop further. Then choose 1 or 2 in which you recognise a need to grow and strengthen.

Change Catalyst

- Meditate on your own self-worth; your talents, uniqueness, and value.
- Do not compare your gifts to others but recognise everyone's talents.
- Be sure never to boast, even subtly, about your abilities and achievements.
- Refrain from taking all the credit for successes, whenever possible.
- Practice modesty, aware that pride precedes most falls.
- Actively value others and express this attitude.
- Allow others to see your vulnerability.
- Identify any areas of pretentiousness or arrogance.
- Consider reasons why you may need to feel better than others.

The change catalysts I aim to practice in order to develop the characteristic of humility are:

_____
_____

Signed _____ Date _____ Review Date _____

Ask a good friend to monitor your progress and encourage you.

! Caution Humility will communicate a lack of self-confidence when over-extended. It can appear self-deprecating. This would tend to indicate weakness rather than meekness.

PATIENCE – an inward expression of character

Choose any 2 or 3 of the change catalysts you are currently exercising but wish to develop further. Then choose 1 or 2 in which you recognise a need to grow and strengthen.

Change Catalyst

- Resist the temptations to judge others as inadequate.
- Accept that some people have slower responses and thought processes.
- Practice valuing the strengths of others, for example, their caution.
- Examine your tendencies towards impulsive behaviour.
- Control anger and avoid responding to provocation.
- Practice tolerance and understanding towards those who are different.
- Learn the art of Exemplary Listening™.
- Be prepared to persevere and treat testing situations as positive events.
- Display open and accepting body language.

The change catalysts I aim to practice in order to develop the characteristic of patience are:

_____
_____

Signed _____ Date _____ Review Date _____

Ask a good friend to monitor your progress and encourage you.

! Caution Apathy and passivity can result from over-extended patience. The result might be that others always take initiative while you just go with the flow. This will result in under-achievement and loss of direction.

SELFLESSNESS – an inward expression of character

Choose any 2 or 3 of the change catalysts you are currently exercising but wish to develop further. Then choose 1 or 2 in which you recognise a need to grow and strengthen.

Change Catalyst

- Look for ways to put others first.
- Take yourself off the throne.
- Be prepared to meet the needs of others.
- Never be patronising or paternalistic.
- Aim to regularly do favours and good turns for others.
- Examine whether there is anyone you tend to exploit.
- Consider recent examples of a willingness to make sacrifices.
- Recall any selfish behaviour others might have pointed out to you.
- Plan some actions that will reduce self-centredness.
- Do unto others as you would have them do unto you.

The change catalysts I aim to practice in order to develop the characteristic of selflessness are:

_____
_____

Signed _____ Date _____ Review Date _____

Ask a good friend to monitor your progress and encourage you.

! Caution   Over-extended selflessness can make a person easy to be exploited, or appear to act as a doormat. Pleasing others is an end in itself, not a means of finding identity or expressing feelings of inadequacy.

COURAGE – a dynamic attribute of character

Choose any 2 or 3 of the change catalysts you are currently exercising but wish to develop further. Then choose 1 or 2 in which you recognise a need to grow and strengthen.

Change Catalyst

- Identify your main fears.
- Start to confront assertively, not aggressively.
- Devise plans to take some calculated risks and follow them through.
- Consciously develop an outlook of boldness.
- Face difficulties with determination.
- Refuse to allow opposition to put you off pursuing your objectives.
- Keep a list of achieved goals and review it regularly.
- Begin to stand up for what you know to be right.
- Welcome challenges, smile at them.
- Spend time with those you admire for their courageousness.

The change catalysts I aim to practice in order to develop the characteristic of courage are:
_____
_____

Signed _____ Date _____ Review Date _____

Ask a good friend to monitor your progress and encourage you.

! Caution Courage will appear reckless if over-extended. This will cause apprehension and mistrust in others. It needs to be tempered by discernment and objectivity.

SELF-CONTROL – a dynamic attribute of character

Choose any 2 or 3 of the change catalysts you are currently exercising but wish to develop further. Then choose 1 or 2 in which you recognise a need to grow and strengthen.

Change Catalyst

- Consider strategies to help maintain control in emotional circumstances.
- Refrain from giving in to your impulses.
- Avoid situations you know are likely to trigger a loss of self-control.
- Identify negative patterns of thinking and behaving.
- Stop, think, and breathe deeply before responding in tense situations.
- Handle confrontations assertively, not aggressively.
- If you lose control, apologise without excuses and learn.
- Practise your self-control in the small things.
- Recognise tendencies to over-indulge and become accountable.

The change catalysts I aim to practice in order to develop the characteristic of self-control are:

_____
_____

Signed _____ Date _____ Review Date _____

Ask a good friend to monitor your progress and encourage you.

! Caution   Self-control, when over-extended, creates an appearance of aloofness and disinterest. It suppresses emotions and hides genuine feelings. This leads to a dependency upon set procedures and routines.

Achieving Personal Growth

DECISIVENESS – a dynamic attribute of character

Choose any 2 or 3 of the change catalysts you are currently exercising but wish to develop further. Then choose 1 or 2 in which you recognise a need to grow and strengthen.

Change Catalyst

- Note any times when fear has held up decision making.
- Plan the decision making process; list all the options.
- Set deadlines and target dates for all achievements and to do lists.
- Develop a ruthlessness with data, paper, and unused information.
- Do not put off till tomorrow what can be done today.
- Attempt unpleasant and difficult tasks first – make easy ones your reward.
- Learn to distinguish between urgent and important.
- Be positive, proactive, and stand firm.
- Build inner confidence by focusing on your strengths.
- Take stock of all your good points

The change catalysts I aim to practice in order to develop the characteristic of decisiveness are:

_____
_____

Signed _____ Date _____ Review Date _____

Ask a good friend to monitor your progress and encourage you.

! Caution An over-extended decisiveness can appear brutal and harsh to colleagues who feel they too should engage in the decision making process. Decisions taken too quickly will have unforeseen circumstances.

PERSEVERANCE – a dynamic attribute of character

Choose any 2 or 3 of the change catalysts you are currently exercising but wish to develop further. Then choose 1 or 2 in which you recognise a need to grow and strengthen.

Change Catalyst

- Portion tasks into smaller, manageable units of activity.
- Reward your achievements and successes.
- Examine your stamina and work within it.
- Break the habit of complaining.
- Use the energy derived from legitimate anger to achieve your visions.
- Set realistic goals using deadlines and timetables.
- Enlist people who share your objectives and can help fulfil them.
- Thoroughly examine everything you delegate and never abdicate.
- Practice forgiving your own failures.
- Always ensure that the big picture sets the agenda.

The change catalysts I aim to practice in order to develop the characteristic of perseverance are:

_____
_____

Signed _____ Date _____ Review Date _____

Ask a good friend to monitor your progress and encourage you.

! Caution Over-extended perseverance will become an unattractive stubbornness. Such people are poor listeners, ignore wise counsel and appear arrogant about their own opinions and judgements.

WISDOM – a passive attribute of character

Choose any 2 or 3 of the change catalysts you are currently exercising but wish to develop further. Then choose 1 or 2 in which you recognise a need to grow and strengthen.

Change Catalyst

- Regularly seek out and keep wise company.
- Examine why you prefer to make snap decisions – it might be laziness.
- Plan to honestly reflect on failures and failings.
- Ask yourself; 'In what ways do others perceive me to lack wisdom?'.
- Consider whether you have caused frustration by not admitting responsibility.
- Evaluate those whom you respect sufficiently to make yourself accountable to.
- Check tendencies to be impulsive in meetings and conversation.
- Reflect on the style and goals of others during interactions.
- Cherish a reputation for making wise decisions.

The change catalysts I aim to practice in order to develop the characteristic of wisdom are:

_____
_____

Signed _____ Date _____ Review Date _____

Ask a good friend to monitor your progress and encourage you.

! Caution If wisdom is over-extended it will appear to be pompous and pontifical. Avoid being seen as the 'know it all' but make brief, judicious comments at opportune moments.

HONESTY – a passive attribute of character

Choose any 2 or 3 of the change catalysts you are currently exercising but wish to develop further. Then choose 1 or 2 in which you recognise a need to grow and strengthen.

Change Catalyst

- Tell yourself the truth, being alert to self-deception.
- Set realistic expectations of yourself and others.
- Understand your own strengths and weaknesses.
- Admit your shortcomings.
- Never cheat or lie – they develop into habitual reflexes.
- Do not fear or avoid confrontations.
- Be scrupulously fair in all your dealings.
- Voice your real concerns.
- Combine honesty with sensitivity and tact.
- Resist the temptation to exaggerate – it has no boundaries.

The change catalysts I aim to practice in order to develop the characteristic of honesty are:

_____
_____

Signed _____ Date _____ Review Date _____

Ask a good friend to monitor your progress and encourage you.

! Caution Indiscretion and naivety are the signs of over-extended honesty. It is vital to combine this characteristic with the ability to judge how much should be said, in what context, when, and to whom. The manner of honesty is as important as the message.

Achieving Personal Growth

OBJECTIVITY – a passive attribute of character

Choose any 2 or 3 of the change catalysts you are currently exercising but wish to develop further. Then choose 1 or 2 in which you recognise a need to grow and strengthen.

Change Catalyst

- Analyse those emotions that drive you.
- Create checks to control impulsive and automatic reactions.
- Learn to listen to all the facts.
- Seek counsel before responding to complex issues.
- Honestly face any feelings of rejection or disapproval.
- Prepare to confront unpleasant issues.
- Where possible, delay making important decisions for 24 hours.
- Suspend all bias and prejudice.
- List your new successes.

The change catalysts I aim to practice in order to develop the characteristic of objectivity are:

_____
_____

Signed _____ Date _____ Review Date _____

Ask a good friend to monitor your progress and encourage you.

! Caution Objectivity, if over-extended, slows down the decision making process. This would result in a continual search for relevant data, becoming a form of procrastination. It will ignore and stifle intuition and creativity.

DISCERNMENT – a passive attribute of character

Choose any 2 or 3 of the change catalysts you are currently exercising but wish to develop further. Then choose 1 or 2 in which you recognise a need to grow and strengthen.

Change Catalyst

- Learn to listen assertively.
- Be discriminating without judging the other person.
- Watch the body language of others.
- Sensitively develop the use of 'open' questions.
- Learn the skills of those who are discerning.
- Listen out for the feelings behind the words.
- Observe the tone of voice others use.
- Probe for further information.
- Be warm and accepting in order to encourage openness.

The change catalysts I aim to practice in order to develop the characteristic of discernment are:

_____
_____

Signed _____ Date _____ Review Date _____

Ask a good friend to monitor your progress and encourage you.

! Caution If discernment is over-extended it can be perceived as judgemental and conveying an air of superiority. Continually highlighting motives and presenting the need for change will simply irritate others.

The two change agents of honesty and willingness are just like any muscle or organ. They are faculties designed for activity. Honest self-appraisal followed by some reasonable behavioural choices enables us to set a course, review our progress, and find satisfaction through genuine success.

The amazing feature of human character is that by applying ourselves to just a few disciplines, we tend to experience benefits in a holistic way. Being kind also grows the trait of humility and demands that I be wise and discerning as well. As this process of growth is enhanced by applying the growth catalysts you have contracted to develop, there should be a substantive improvement in the effectiveness experienced in relationships, and the pursuit of your personal and professional goals.

SECTION 4

VALUES AND ATTITUDES

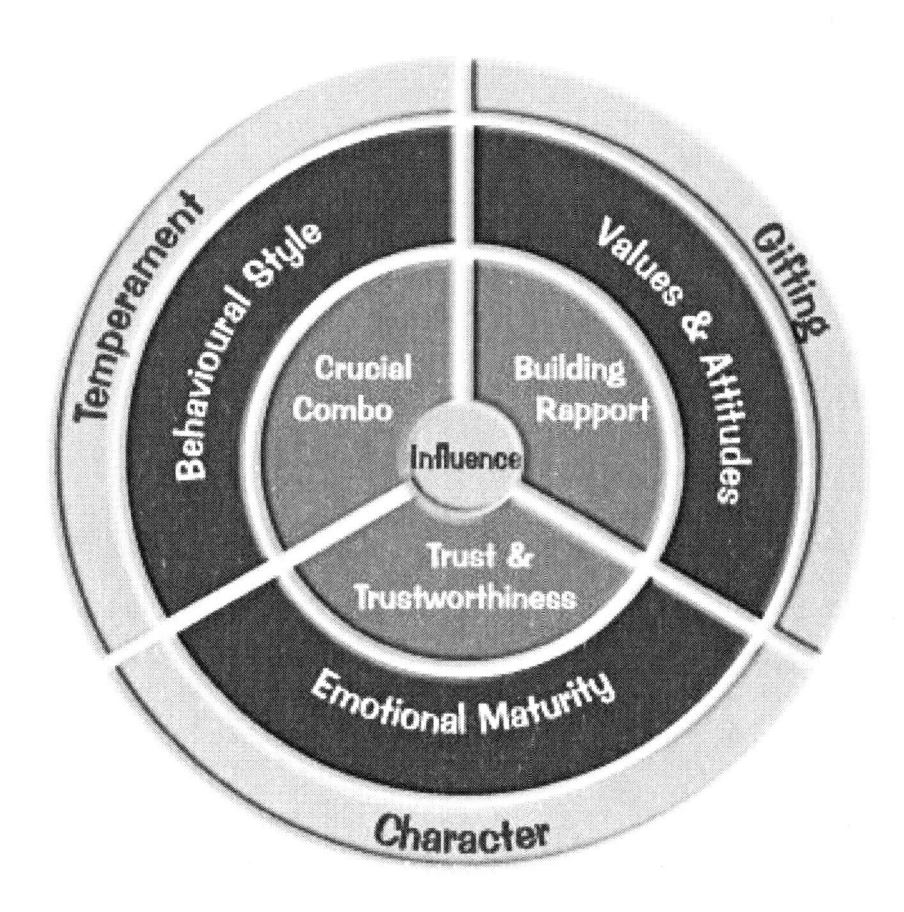

The following chapter contains the fourth element of becoming a Trustworthy Adviser. It explains those things that provide our motivation and the basis on which we make our judgements.

Values and Attitudes

> - Why do people see things so differently?
> - Exploring the sources of our values
> - The six attitudes of mankind
> - How attitudes are formed

These are the four issues we are going to examine.

In order to become Trustworthy Advisers, we have to arrive at an understanding of both ourselves, and those with whom we are dealing. Temperament, as we have seen, is a major contributor to our behaviours. Having understood its significance in our own lives, we are able to appreciate the part it plays in the lives of others. The next step is to understand how people look at us, the regard in which they hold us, and why they respond to us as they do. Hopefully that is already beginning to permeate your thoughts and observations.

Having examined how we might adapt our communication to suit the style of our clients and colleagues, we need to consider the underlying material that forms the basis of human opinion, response and reaction. We can then proceed to explain how our behaviours can be advantageously adapted as well.

11

DO YOU SEE WHAT I SEE?

A modern parable

Two men, Bob and Pete, who share the same age and nationality, are walking along a woodland path together. They are new neighbours, just getting to know one another. They talk about their children, their wives, and their parents. Both men share what they would call 'Family Values', by which they mean a belief in the nuclear family and its centrality to human society. Each one attributes their nurture and fundamental standards to the way in which they were parented. They talk about their educational background, agreeing about its crucial role in personal development and the advance of civilisation.

In the middle of this discussion, they see a large stag deer ahead of them. Its fully developed antlers have a span of five feet and look more like two small trees. A magnificent creature! Bob sighs: 'If only I had my camcorder.' Pete is oblivious to his friend's passion to immortalise the moment. Lost in another world, he lifts his right arm up to his cheek while stretching his left arm straight out in front of him. 'Wish I had my hunting rifle,' he murmurs, 'I'd have a freezer full of venison and that fantastic head over my new mantelpiece'. The two men stop, look at each other in amazement and disgust, and then walk on in total silence. They no longer feel they have anything in common!

Why does one man want to kill what another stops just short of worshipping? How is it that out of the same culture and education system, come two totally different sets of outlook? And not just different emphases or ways of looking at things, either. They each find their neighbour's attitude to be repugnant. This difference causes them to silently question each other's morality and strength of character. (Hunters often regard male conservationists as repressed, unfulfilled individuals, while their counterparts view the hunter as wasteful, moronic and destructive.)

What separates Bob from Pete? The answer is: their values. They may share more than they differ over, but the values that divide them have formed in each man a set of attitudes that govern their view of one another. These attitudes will not only affect the atmosphere during the rest of their walk, but the opinions of one another they go away with, and later relate to their families. Those attitudes will also ensure that they never take a walk together again. An exchange of Christmas cards is all that can be expected in their relationship from now on. With no reindeer on the front pictures!

The significance of values

Most businesses would want to assure their clients that they have strong corporate values. If asked to define them, a few standard words and phrases would emerge that tell us little more than the fact that we are not dealing with criminals, bigots or ruthless tyrants! 'Integrity, honesty, diligence, customer care, equality, environmentalism, inclusiveness, respect, professionalism', will all be expressed. Added to this vaguely moral sounding list will be some assurances that gender, age, ethnicity, sexual orientation and physical disability are all respected and their dignity upheld. Yet doing what you must in order to operate within the law, or appeal to the market, is not an expression of values. It says nothing about what you regard as worthy. It therefore says nothing about how you might act if the restraints were removed, or if you begin to operate in an environment where they are not obligatory.

The Oxford English Dictionary describes value as: 'the regard something is held to deserve'. In other words, it is about its significance, not its cost. When we talk about 'Values' we are speaking of principles that guide, or even dictate, our thoughts, words and actions. These form a set of beliefs to which our behaviour conforms and by which we judge ourselves, the things with which we are associated, what we allow to influence us, and even the behaviour of others.

Bob has values related to the living world. He may eat meat from properly farmed animals but he always chooses free-range eggs because he believes animals should be respected and treated well. He will eat venison on the assumption that the deer was humanely slaughtered and none of it wasted.

The act of killing is accepted as necessary but he would take no pleasure in it. A wild stag is to him an object of beauty, even grandeur. Killing it, even to feed people, offends him because he wants to admire natural beauty, protect and preserve it, help others to appreciate it as well. These are his values. Pete would dispute the logic about eating meat but refraining from killing it, because he is essentially more pragmatic. Hunting, however, is one of his values. He believes in taking pleasure from the skills involved, providing you consume what you kill, or better still, share it with your neighbours. A deer head on the wall is his idea of beauty because it represents those things he esteems. Both men have values. Irreconcilable values!

The source of our values

Experience
Every day, we face experiences requiring us to behave in certain appropriate ways. This applies particularly in our working environment. These experiences cause us to think, to make decisions and to act. Consciously or unconsciously, every decision, reaction or response arises from our beliefs, our values, our habits and our attitudes.

Some authors have said we are the sum total of our experiences, and that multiple experiences lead to our beliefs. The intensity of each experience, therefore, leads to varying degrees of conviction. In addition, repeated experience strengthens those beliefs.

Beliefs
Where experiences lead to beliefs, a number of beliefs cluster together to form our values. Conversely, you may have a cluster of beliefs that tell you what you do not value. Bob does not value hunting!

However, not all our beliefs derive directly from an experience. Bob's beliefs may not be due to good experiences of animals, or bad experiences of guns. Our beliefs are often worked out intellectually, even though they arouse strong feelings. They are frequently the result of teaching by others. Significant people, whom we respect, help form our beliefs even without explaining them to us.

Some of our beliefs derive from aspirations. Bob may never have had a pet, but he aspired to do so. He grew up in the inner city and never visited the countryside until well after his love for nature had begun to grow in a purely theoretical, non-experiential way. His friends may not have had pets either, so his experience of animals was confined to visits to the zoo, or watching nature programmes on TV. What developed in this vacuum of direct animal experience was a set of aspirations about enjoying nature and experiencing its beauty first hand. These became his beliefs.

Habits

Habits tend to be thought of as either good or bad. The obvious negative example is racial prejudice. If I have chosen to believe the worst about anyone of a particular nationality, this decision will inform every experience and behaviour. I will automatically categorise Italians as lazy, Greeks as dishonest, and the Japanese as cruel, because I associate those characteristics with everyone belonging to those nationalities. I am thinking habitually. This becomes so strong that if I join a team consisting of an industrious Italian, a scrupulous Greek, and a kind Japanese, I will contrive ways to justify my views that enforce opinions which the evidence is clearly refuting. I will say things like: 'The exception that proves the rule', (a logical absurdity!), or 'They do this to deceive you and then their real character comes through'. Bad habits enforce bad values.

The same is true in reverse. The belief that disciplined hard work leads to fulfilment and success produces a set of values to live by. In so doing I find myself feeling fulfilled and satisfied. It becomes my habit to get up early, arrive punctually, keep focused, avoid waste, and set high personal standards. My values have directed my behaviours and my habits now reinforce and validate the values. Habits can be as constructive as they are destructive. Steven Covey's 'Seven Habits of Highly successful People' makes that case profoundly.

The significance of attitudes

Attitudes are also regarded as either bad or good. However in 1927, Eduard Spranger wrote a book called 'Types of Man'. His thesis was that he had observed six attitudes through which we value the world. These attitudes define the 'why' of our behaviour. Spranger's six attitudes were:

Theoretical	**Utilitarian**	**Aesthetic**	**Social**
Individualistic	**Religious**		
	(to apply this commercially, we will refer to it as 'Traditional')		

We tend to pursue what we value. We will get on well with people who have the same values and a lot less well with those who have different, or opposing, values. Your valuing of life is your attitude. Of the six attitudes observed by Spranger, it is your top two that will explain your behaviour and the views you hold. In applying this, our understanding of others, being open-minded and prepared to adapt, will lead to better personal connections.

Spranger believed that our attitudes were predetermined by nature and evident by the age of eighteen. This author would part company with him at that point. Although this may in part be true, personal as well as professional experience would indicate that life's experiences and difficulties, parenting, and what are called 'Significant Others' (those who have profoundly influenced us), all play a part in forming our attitudes. What is beyond doubt is that understanding your attitude greatly helps you to understand yourself.

How are our attitudes formed?

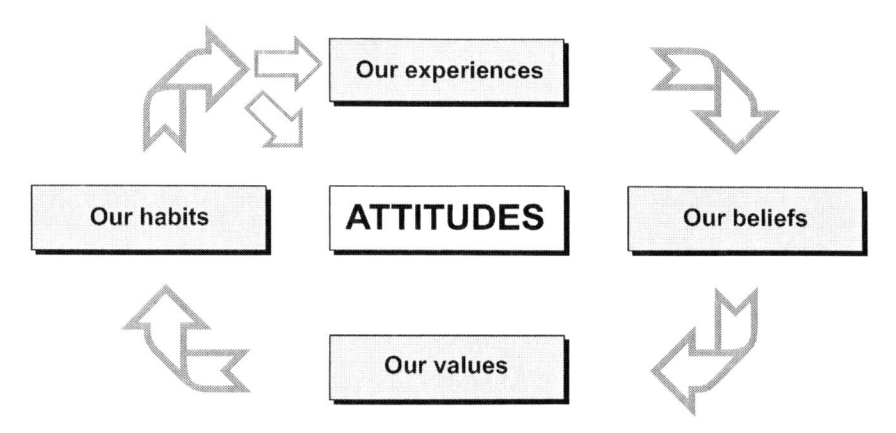

```
                    Our experiences
                    
   Our habits       ATTITUDES       Our beliefs
   
                    Our values
```

To pull all this together, what we can say is that there are factors contributing to our personality and behaviours over which we have had no control and that cannot be changed. Temperament is a major factor, but so too are our experiences, which play a major role in the development of our beliefs, which in turn contribute to the forming of our values. Equally, there are other aspects, which can be subject to change if we so choose. Beliefs are not fixed, nor are values or attitudes. We can choose to adapt them, or even make major changes in the light of new information or experience. The following diagram sums this up.

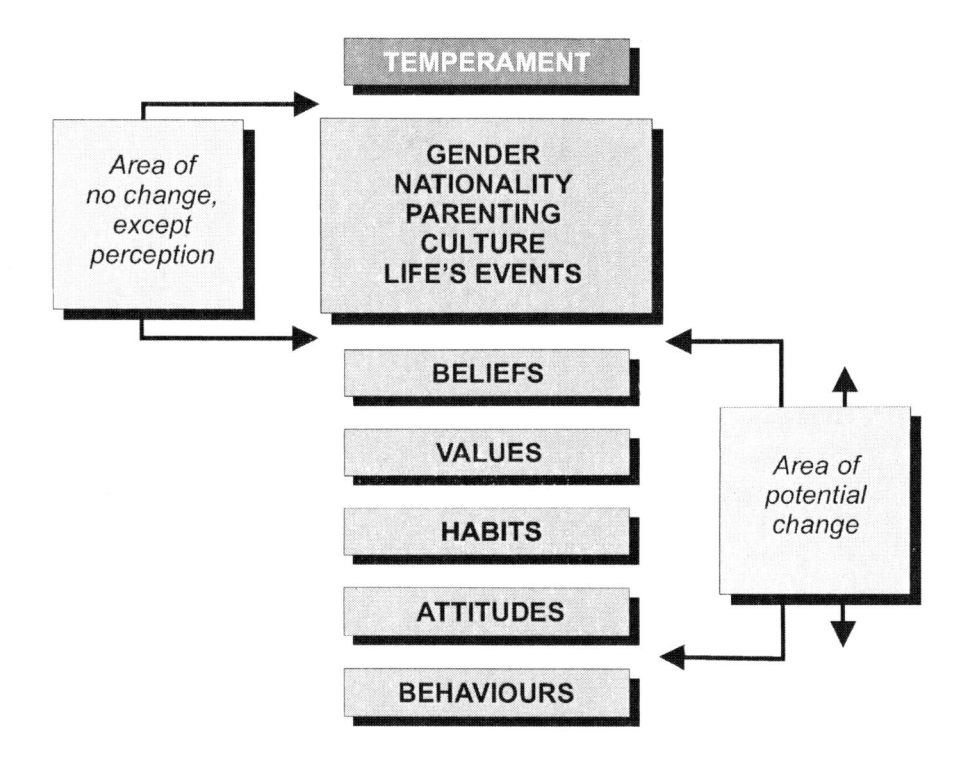

```
                    ┌─────────────────┐
                    │   TEMPERAMENT   │
                    └─────────────────┘
  ┌──────────┐      ┌─────────────────┐
  │ Area of  │────▶ │     GENDER      │
  │no change,│      │   NATIONALITY   │
  │  except  │      │    PARENTING    │
  │perception│      │     CULTURE     │
  │          │────▶ │  LIFE'S EVENTS  │
  └──────────┘      └─────────────────┘

                    ┌─────────────────┐
                    │     BELIEFS     │◀──┐
                    └─────────────────┘   │
                    ┌─────────────────┐   │   ┌──────────┐
                    │     VALUES      │   │   │ Area of  │
                    └─────────────────┘   │   │potential │
                    ┌─────────────────┐   │   │  change  │
                    │     HABITS      │   │   └──────────┘
                    └─────────────────┘   │
                    ┌─────────────────┐   │
                    │    ATTITUDES    │◀──┘
                    └─────────────────┘
                    ┌─────────────────┐
                    │   BEHAVIOURS    │
                    └─────────────────┘
```

The formation of attitudes and the behaviours that result from this process, has two direct applications to becoming a Trustworthy Adviser. Firstly, we have a duty to ourselves to examine the attitudes, which fuel our behaviours. If, for example, I hold strong prejudices, they will be likely to find expression under less guarded moments, despite my attempts to keep them hidden from a client I want to win, rather than offend. Equally, my attitudes could simply prevent me from seeing the needs of another person simply because I never experience those needs. Highly confident D. type temperaments, can be oblivious to the need for affirmation and encouragement of a S. type, for example.

    Secondly, we are largely responsible for the attitudes others develop towards us. Because experience is the starting point of the equation, I can exercise a degree of control in regard to whether a clients' experience of me is perceived by them to be positive and constructive, or negative and unhelpful. Knowing their attitudinal type will greatly enhance my ability to present myself wisely.

Experience
"I speak with A.B. to benefit from his business insights on a regular basis"

Habit
"I always include A.B. in the early stages of strategic business planning because I want his advice at the start of a project"

ATTITUDES

Belief
"I believe A.B. is highly professional and thoroughly reliable"

Values
"I value A.B. for his commitment and understanding. He is my preferred choice of consultant"

The variety of perceptions

Because of the different attitude categories that Spranger observed, we can look at the same world and see it entirely differently. Hence Pete sees a target where Bob sees a photograph. This is what we mean when we speak of someone 'seeing it through their own eyes'. The general assumption is that *our* eyes see best! If we aren't careful with this attitude we will feel that every opportunity must be taken to correct the viewpoint of others because it is somehow deficient.

However, if we can appreciate that in addition to temperament, we also differ in attitudes, which are the expression of our beliefs and values, then we are in a good place to grow into Trustworthy Advisers. We have begun to gain insight into both ourselves, and others, which will stimulate us to make the changes that can result in being more effective. All temperaments have strengths and weaknesses. All attitudinal grouping have strengths and weaknesses. Building on that which is strong, while modifying that which is weak, enables us to mature, and thus offer a far greater degree of competence and assurance to those we aim to influence and serve.

Do You See What I See?

The following fresco is a well-known masterpiece. To explain the different perceptions of attitudinal groups, I have given a summary of the way in which six individuals, one from each group, would consider this painting if he or she were able to buy it.

'The Last Supper' – Leonardo Da Vinci

Each person has the funds to purchase the painting at auction. What we need to appreciate is the thought processes of each person, which derive from their specific 'attitude'. All six see the same fresco. All six want to buy it. However, each one has a very different reason for wanting to possess it. What we are looking at now are the **attitudes** that shape our motives. To understand the source of the motive is to have an insight into human behaviour that equips us to achieve far more than predict likely behaviours. It offers us the ability to communicate the significance and worth of a particular course of action. It provides us with the 'Emotional colouring' that each person puts on things. It also gives us rational and reasonable opportunities for persuasion and influence.

Theoretical

Look at the expressions on all of the faces. Before I buy this I want to find out when it was painted and any other information about it.

Utilitarian

If I buy this now, it will increase in value over the next several years. It's a good investment.

Aesthetic

What a beautiful work of art. It speaks to me of a very important event, and seems to come alive as I look at it.

Social

Important works like this should be shared. If I were to buy this, I would put it in a gallery for everyone to enjoy.

Individualistic

I need to own this. With this as the central piece, mine will be considered one of the most prestigious private collections.

Traditional

This painting makes me think of my priorities. It speaks to me of the divine and what is important in life.

Information or insight?

You have probably identified yourself within Spranger's analysis. Some of your closest colleagues, family members, friends and clients will also be quite obvious to you. As you read the simple comments listed above, you may even be able to hear the accents and vocal inflections of people you know, as they look at such a painting with their perspectives.

Try visualising some of your clients at this imaginary auction. Now put yourself into their shoes and listen to the inner whirring of their thought processes. You are looking at this painting through their eyes, not your own. This is what empathy really means. Identifying with the thoughts and feelings of another person. To see things as they see them and hear things as they hear them.

It may be interesting, even useful, to gain information about the attitudes that drive human motivations. Such information helps us to make sense of, even occasionally predict, the resultant behaviours. But what is of serious value is the insight it offers. Insight into what really matters to another person. This, in addition to understanding temperament, provides us with the tools for finding ways in which we can genuinely influence and persuade others.

- **Knowing just how to communicate in terms that are meaningful and significant to our clients.**
- **Appreciating the essence of how they see and value things.**
- **Providing ideas, proposals, and strategies in the language most acceptable and accessible to their way of viewing things.**

This is not about manipulation. Nor is it about becoming commercial chameleons that change their colour or character, in order to gain an advantage or close a deal. It is about recognising that those to whom we provide the service of Trustworthy Adviser need to be confident that we understand them and instinctively appreciate what it is they want, and why they want it.

Margaret Thatcher had her favourites within government during her lengthy tenure as Prime Minister from 1979 to 1990. One of these was Peter Carrington. Her comments were instructive. 'Others come to me with the problems,' she explained, 'Peter always comes with solutions'. He knew that she would make up her own mind about what to do. She was a politician who worked by instinct and trusted those instincts. She also had a sharp mind and valued thorough analysis and research. Lord Carrington's skill was that he understood both her temperament and her attitude. She was decisive and determined. She valued results and success. She therefore appreciated options; proposed courses of action that gave her opportunities to make decisions, take steps, determine events, and effect change. Peter Carrington was a Trustworthy Adviser to Mrs Thatcher because he had insight into her nature and knew how to adapt his skills and behaviour to best effect.

SECTION 5

BUILDING RAPPORT

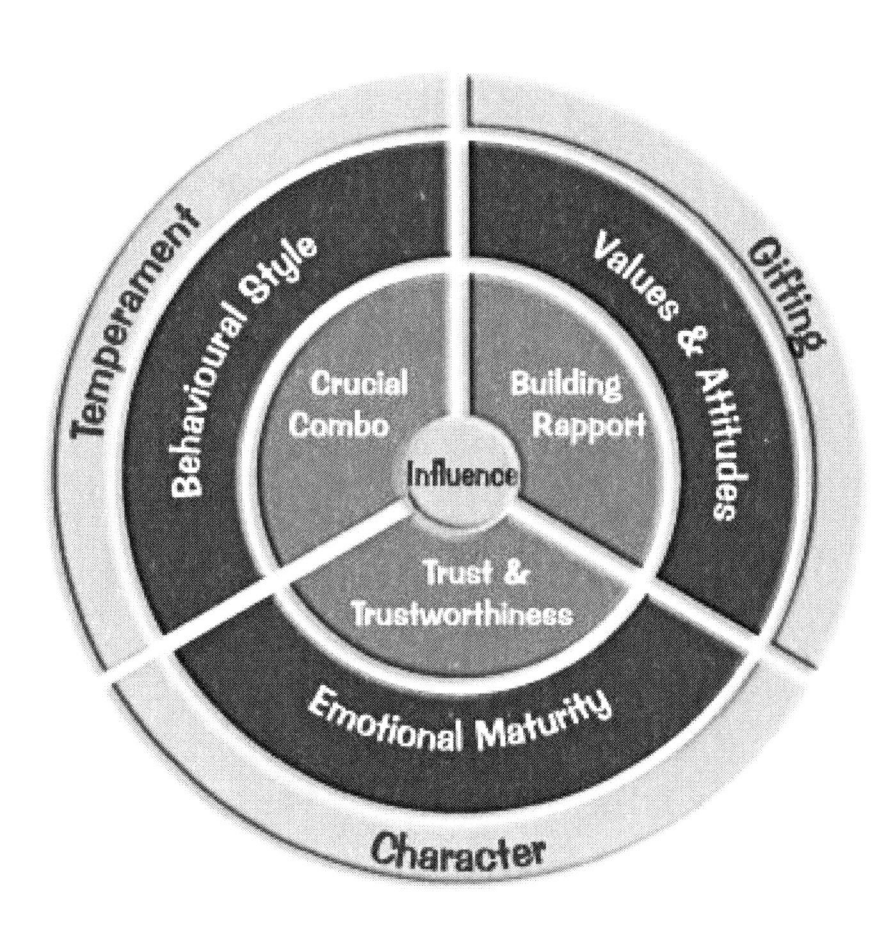

12

PERCEPTUAL PREFERENCES

- Senses and perceptions
- Different but not wrong
- Score your learning style
- Better connections
- Building Rapport

When Harry told a story to Kate, Tim and Zoë

Harry's stories are worth hearing. He packs them with colourful detail, imitates his characters perfectly, and gets to the point. Sitting in the pub with him were his wife Kate and their two friends, Tim and Zoë. Harry was relating his recent frustrating experiences with a builder they had contracted to install a new kitchen.

Zoë punctuated his tale of woe with sympathetic noises and some of her signature phrases. 'I'd feel dreadful' she interjected. 'What an absolute pain' she said more than once. She watched Harry's hands and facial expressions, she enjoyed the builder's accent and his heavy shrugs, so accurately mimicked. At the end, her mind was made up: 'Quite right, give him the elbow, tell him to push off'. Zoë has what is known as a **kinaesthetic learning style**.

Tim listened thoughtfully. He seemed oblivious to Harry's copious gesticulation. He analysed the words of 'Bob the builder', filtering out the accent and tones. Even the body language was irrelevant. Songs on the sound system kept seizing his attention and he tried to engage Harry in a discussion. 'That sounds appalling, did he try to justify it?' Harry just shook his head and continued. Tim asked if the builder 'actually verbalised that' and hoped to follow up with his own viewpoint. He quickly followed Zoë's conclusion by adding: 'From what I hear, this man is dangerous'. Tim possesses what is known as an **auditory learning style**.

Kate knew the story – it was her kitchen! She pictured that absurd confrontation which Harry was describing, recalling exactly where everybody was standing and the builder's unshaved face, dirty clothes, and wide-eyed sincerity. She also saw the mess in which her kitchen had been left for two weeks before another contractor put things right. Turning to Zoë she said: 'Can you imagine the chaos? I can still see it now, you know.' She affirmed Harry's account by adding: 'From my viewpoint, the man was utterly inept and it painted a very bleak picture of one-man building firms'. Kate has what we call a **visual learning style**.

Life is for learning

Our bodies are designed to observe, evaluate, process, memorise and learn. Sensory organs and neurological processes combine to ensure that our experiences are also lessons, helping us to make life easier, more successful, happier, and safer, as we encounter the familiar within each new event. The process of our learning is often instinctive, our five senses constantly observing, triggering memories, making comparisons, and prompting appropriate responses. We never need to tell our noses to start smelling things!

As we see, hear, smell, taste and touch, the miracles of recognition, emotional responses and cognitive reasoning take place without our needing to press buttons or move levers – we just start learning and using what we have already learned. The sunset is either disappointingly hidden, average, pleasing or majestic. We label it without too much deliberation. The same goes for that glass of wine: we declare it to be sour, cheap, palatable or excellent. That perfume is sickly, too strong, acceptable or tantalising. Similar judgements arise with equal speed in relation to music, movements and touch.

Each sense has its own dedicated body part, or organ. The learning process to which it is attributed is known as a learning modality. Psychologists often refer to this realm as 'Sensory Perception'. However, due to the confusion that arises with regard to what is sometimes called 'Extra-Sensory Perception', I prefer to speak about perceptual preferences.

SENSE	ORGAN/BODY	PERCEPTUAL PREFERENCE
seeing	eyes	visual
hearing	ears	auditory
feeling	fingers/touch & movement	kinaesthetic
smelling	nose	olfactory
tasting	mouth	gustatory

Perceptual Preferences

Human beings have not developed the last two skills to anything like the sophistication they possess with the other three. Many mammals use their sense of smell far more than their sight, but rely very little on touch. For us humans, however, seeing, hearing and feeling are the sensing priorities and it is therefore through these mediums that we do most of our learning and communicating.

Generally, and with good health, these senses continue to function throughout our entire lives. We are, therefore, to some extent, always travelling on a road of discovery. Life is for learning: a process that occurs in every experience and all of our relationships.

Preferred not exclusive

Most of us use all three major styles to some extent. Kate didn't just sit there seeing pictures, while Zoë stretched her consciousness out into her feelings, leaving it there to see what registered. Tim managed to listen despite the distraction of pop songs and his strong impulse to make a verbal contribution. We may have a preference, but it is not watertight. For this reason, management training has undergone vast changes over the past twenty years. From a lot of talk with a little interaction and just a flip-chart to provide the odd visual stimulus, we have moved to powerpoint presentations, full of interaction with team exercises and baroque musical background sounds, which have been neurologically proven to be the best stimuli for creative thought.

Research suggests that in Western society our preferred sensory perceptions break down as follows:

- Visual   60%
- Auditory   30%
- Kinaesthetic   10%

Remember that these are preferences not exclusive choices. However, it does have significant bearing on our behaviour when trying to maximise the benefits of our connections. A Trustworthy Adviser is constantly seeking to understand their clients' motives and wishes, while at the same time attempting to ensure the best possible communication. If twice as many people favour a visual form of learning and communication as do those with a tendency towards an auditory method, we need to apply ourselves to acquiring the skills that enable us to identify people's perceptual preferences, as well as the skills entailed in making the best of our communication.

Different but not wrong

In all the material I have included in this book, it is important to remember that we are observing and adapting in order to achieve better connections. No one Temperament is better than the others, no particular Attitude is superior, and no Perceptual Preference is the right one. None of this is to make us judgemental. In fact, all these instruments for understanding others are essentially non-judgemental.

Personally, my preference is Kinaesthetic. This combines with my intuitive nature. But because that is my preferred style of learning it will not necessarily be the case for those with whom I do business. In fact, it would appear that 90% of those I meet would prefer another style! The challenge is to firstly suspend judgement, secondly to make that connection. I have to remember that I want to connect with them and build that essential rapport. If we ever think that our own style is the right one, the result will be a long and lonely wait for others to adapt to us. Especially if like me, you represent only one in ten!

The Perceptual Preference Questionnaire

This is to help you understand your own learning style. You might want to share this with a close friend, or your partner, in order to see if you are adept at assessing the perceptual preferences of others.

There are 20 items, each of which has 3 statements. You have ten points to distribute to those statements which best describe your preference. You may give 10 to one preference and nil to the other two, or spread the points over two, or even three. The aim is to award the points according to the weight you would attribute to each of the three statements when describing yourself.

This is not a test. You cannot fail, and your answers are correct if they are true to your preferences. We are all unique, and this questionnaire is simply an expression of that uniqueness.

Once you have completed the scoring, transfer the results to the next table and add up your score. You will almost certainly find that under various circumstances you favour certain sensory perception over others. However, a pattern emerges from the scoring, which reveals your general preferences and how you would ideally choose to receive information and process it within your mind.

The Perceptual Preferences Questionnaire

1 When I am reading, I often find that I:

Read out loud or hear the words inside my head ☐
Visualise what I am reading in my mind's eye ☐
Fidget and try to 'feel' the content ☐

2 When I'm focused on a conversation with someone, I often find myself saying:

That sounds right to me ☐
I was moved by what you said ☐
I see what you mean ☐

3 I learn best when I:

Watch someone show me how ☐
Hear someone tell me how ☐
Try to do it myself ☐

4 When I'm in a restaurant deciding what to order:

I discuss with myself the various options ☐
I visualise the food ☐
I choose whatever seems to be the most appealing ☐

5 When I meet up with an old friend I am likely to say:

It's good to hear your voice again ☐
I've missed you! – and give them a hug ☐
It's good to see you again ☐

6 When someone is describing something to me verbally, I tend to:

Try to visualise what they are saying ☐
Get bored if the description gets too long and detailed ☐
Enjoy listening but want to interrupt and talk myself ☐

7 If I am having to wait for something, I keep occupied by:

Walking around, manipulating things with my hands, or moving with my feet as I sit ☐
Looking around, staring at things, or reading ☐
Talking or listening to others ☐

8 When solving a problem, I:

- Write or draw diagrams to help me see it better ☐
- Talk myself through it ☐
- Use my entire body or move objects to help me think ☐

9 I can tell what other people are thinking from:

- The tone of their voice ☐
- The vibes I get from them ☐
- The look on their face ☐

10 When I'm trying to concentrate I get distracted by:

- A lot of activity around me ☐
- A lot of noise ☐
- A lot of clutter or movement around me ☐

11 I remember something better when I:

- Pace or walk around while reciting it ☐
- Write it down so that I can see it ☐
- Recite it out loud ☐

12 When given written instructions on how to build something, I:

- Read them silently and try to visualise how the parts will fit together ☐
- Try to put the parts together first and read the instructions later if I have to ☐
- Read them out loud and talk to myself as I put the parts together ☐

13 When I have a lot of things to do, I:

- Feel uncomfortable until all or most of the things are done ☐
- Keep reminding myself of what needs to be done ☐
- Make a list for myself or imagine doing them ☐

14 When I go on a course the main way I like to learn is by:

- Getting involved in practical activities and group discussions ☐
- Listening carefully to what the presenter is saying ☐
- Making lots of notes and reading them, and the handouts, afterwards ☐

15 I might suspect that people were lying to me from:

- Their tone of voice ☐
- The way they look or avoid looking at me ☐
- A feeling I get about their sincerity ☐

Perceptual Preferences

16 When trying to spell a word I like to:

Write it down to see if it looks right ☐
Speak it out loud to determine if it sounds right ☐
Write it out to check if it feels right ☐

17 Typical expressions that I use when speaking with others are:

That looks good to me ☐
I hear what you're saying ☐
That gives me a good feeling ☐

18 When I meet someone for the second time I find it easy to:

Remember his or her name and what we talked about ☐
Remember what we did together last time ☐
Remember his or her face and where we first met ☐

19 When making a decision about something important:

I must see all aspects of the situation ☐
I know when it's the right decision because my gut feelings tell me so ☐
I must be able to justify the decision to myself or somebody else ☐

20 When asked to give directions, I:

Like to point or move my body as I give them ☐
See the actual places in my mind as I say them ☐
Have no difficulty in giving them verbally ☐

Scoring

Each of the statements indicates your Visual, Auditory and Kinaesthetic perceptual preferences.

1. Transfer your points for each statement to the scoring sheet below so that you can see which statements load into each of V, A and K.
2. Add your total scores for each of V, A and K.

V - visual	
A - auditory	
K - kinaesthetic	

1 When I am reading, I often find that I:

Read out loud or hear the words inside my head — A
Visualise what I am reading in my mind's eye — V
Fidget and try to 'feel' the content — K

2 When I'm focused on a conversation with someone, I often find myself saying:

That sounds right to me — A
I was moved by what you said — K
I see what you mean — V

3 I learn best when I:

Watch someone show me how — V
Hear someone tell me how — A
Try to do it myself — K

4 When I'm in a restaurant deciding what to order:

I discuss with myself the various options — A
I visualise the food — V
I choose whatever seems to be the most appealing — K

5 When I meet up with an old friend I am likely to say:

It's good to hear your voice again — A
I've missed you! – and give them a hug — V
It's good to see you again — K

6 When someone is describing something to me verbally, I tend to:

Try to visualise what they are saying — V
Get bored if the description gets too long and detailed — K
Enjoy listening but want to interrupt and talk myself — A

7 If I am having to wait for something, I keep occupied by:

Walking around, manipulating things with my hands, or moving with my feet as I sit — K
Looking around, staring at things, or reading — V
Talking or listening to others — A

8 When solving a problem, I:

Write or draw diagrams to help me see it better — V
Talk myself through it — A
Use my entire body or move objects to help me think — K

9 I can tell what other people are thinking from:

The tone of their voice — A
The vibes I get from them — K
The look on their face — V

10 When I'm trying to concentrate I get distracted by:

A lot of activity around me — K
A lot of noise — A
A lot of clutter or movement around me — V

Perceptual Preferences

11 I remember something better when I:

Pace or walk around while reciting it — K ☐
Write it down so that I can see it — V ☐
Recite it out loud — A ☐

12 When given written instructions on how to build something, I:

Read them silently and try to visualise how the parts will fit together — V ☐
Try to put the parts together first and read the instructions later if I have to — K ☐
Read them out loud and talk to myself as I put the parts together — A ☐

13 When I have a lot of things to do, I:

Feel uncomfortable until all or most of the things are done — K ☐
Keep reminding myself of what needs to be done — A ☐
Make a list for myself or imagine doing them — V ☐

14 When I go on a course the main way I like to learn is by:

Getting involved in practical activities and group discussions — K ☐
Listening carefully to what the presenter is saying — A ☐
Making lots of notes and reading them, and the handouts, afterwards — V ☐

15 I might suspect that people were lying to me from:

Their tone of voice — A ☐
The way they look or avoid looking at me — V ☐
A feeling I get about their sincerity — K ☐

16 When trying to spell a word I like to:

Write it down to see if it looks right — V ☐
Speak it out loud to determine if it sounds right — A ☐
Write it out to check if it feels right — K ☐

17 Typical expressions that I use when speaking with others are:

That looks good to me — V ☐
I hear what you're saying — A ☐
That gives me a good feeling — K ☐

18 When I meet someone for the second time I find it easy to:

Remember his or her name and what we talked about — A ☐
Remember what we did together last time — K ☐
Remember his or her face and where we first met — V ☐

19 When making a decision about something important:

I must see all aspects of the situation — V ☐
I know when it's the right decision because my gut feelings tell me so — K ☐
I must be able to justify the decision to myself or somebody else — A ☐

20 When asked to give directions, I:

Like to point or move my body as I give them — K ☐
See the actual places in my mind as I say them — V ☐
Have no difficulty in giving them verbally — A ☐

To check that your addition is correct, add up the three totals awarded to V. A. and K. They should combine to a total score of 200. This helps you to understand just 20 of the many ways in which your own perceptual preferences operate. What we need to consider next is how this helps our commercial objectives.

Making better connections

Becoming a Trustworthy Adviser involves learning how to listen. Listening, however, is more than just evaluating the content of someone's communication. It includes listening to their style.

The phrases we use to make comments about what we hear tend to reveal our own preferred learning styles. Remember our three listeners in the pub as Harry told his tale of woe: Zoe talked about what she felt; Tim wanted to talk about what was said; Kate focused on what she could see. Three people with three different learning styles.

Once we have started to listen to the way in which others speak, we can proceed to modify our own communication to suit theirs. This is called 'mirroring'. Quite simply, it means that we express our ideas, and our questions, in ways that are more accessible to our clients. Let's examine the style indicators that reveal our perceptual preferences. These are the kind of statements and questions frequently used by those preferring each particular style. Obviously everyone has their own manner of speaking, so you may need to adjust the syntax of each phrase in order to match it to your clients. What these indicators reveal, is the general manner in which information is processed by the person concerned.

Visual people

Visual style indicators

>I see what you're saying
>But can you see the larger picture?
>Now in my view
>The way I look at it
>Is your perspective on this reasonable?
>Yes, I can see that quite clearly
>What I had pictured was

Am I looking at this right?
We need to reflect on this one
I'll go and look into that
It looks to me as though
Do you see this being successful?
He'll come round when he sees the light

Visual people:
- use visual words and phrases
- would rather do a demonstration than give a talk
- prefer things on paper
- like to use written language
- favour tasks involving reading and writing
- remember what they write down
- like to take notes
- appreciate handouts at presentations
- want to see things on screens, charts, diagrams, and tables
- value colourful data
- enjoy finding information on the Internet
- read instructions before they attempt to use new equipment
- rarely get lost, even in new surroundings.

Visual people tend to:
- be good at spelling – seeing the words in their minds
- be strong, fast readers
- prefer to read than be read to
- be observant of details
- exercise caution until they are mentally clear about issues or projects
- find remembering verbal instructions difficult
- like asking for things to be repeated
- often know what they want to say but struggle to find the right words.
- visualise faces and places
- think in pictures
- have rich imaginations
- doodle and draw pictures, even on handouts
- look for illustrations of equipment to explain the instructions
- usually prefer art to music.

> **Making better connections with visual style people**
> - Use their kind of visual language.
> - Accept that they might need to interrupt in order to clarify things.
> - Maintain good eye contact to hold their attention.
> - Use plenty of examples and analogies to illustrate your points.
> - Never interrupt them because it ruins their train of thought.

Auditory people

Auditory Style Indicators

I hear what you say
We seem to be in tune on this one
According to my understanding
Am I beating the drum on this one?
It sounds as though
Listen to this
I need to talk this through
Is this sounding clear to you?
Yes, so to speak
It's helpful to discuss
What this told me was
That was well said
Shall we crank up the volume on this one?

Auditory people:
- listen carefully to words and phrases
- appreciate interaction with lots of questions
- value structured presentations
- expect clear introductions to verbal material
- want summaries of what they heard
- like to give presentations
- believe their knowledge is worth sharing
- hear the way something is written
- learn best by verbal interaction
- prefer to be talked through equipment operating instructions.

Perceptual Preferences

Auditory people tend to:
- talk themselves through complex issues
- think out loud
- be easily distracted by noise
- be better at telling than writing
- spell better as they verbalise rather than as they write or type
- enjoy reading aloud
- appreciate things being read to them, if done well
- learn by listening
- remember what is discussed rather than seen
- be talkative and quite eloquent
- engage in lengthy descriptions
- have the ability to repeat others and sometimes mimic them well
- like jokes better than comic books
- enjoy music more than art.

Making better connections with auditory style people
- Employ body language that displays interest in what they say.
- Fold your arms.
- Keep your chin in one hand.
- Tilt your head to one side.
- Nod frequently but slowly.
- Tell them that what they say sounds good, reasonable, wise etc.
- Speak clearly, enthusiastically, and fairly loudly.
- Make sure your information is concise and clear.
- Provide plenty of feedback on progress and developments.

Kinaesthetic people

Kinaesthetic Style Indicators

This feels good
Can you grasp what he's saying?
I'm worried about that

Yes, I warm to that
I can handle this one
He's very pushy
Let's get to grips with it
Am I muscling in on this?
I suggest we sleep on it
She's a pain in the neck
Is he going to shoulder the blame for this?
I'd like to touch their pocket once more
Are you comfortable with this approach?

Kinaesthetic people:
- process information through what they experience
- obtain data through talking
- move about as they speak
- enjoy touching objects
- require external stimulation to aid concentration
- gesticulate a lot
- scan material for the big picture before reading the detail
- draw and doodle when listening to presentations
- appreciate changes in communication mediums
- value concentration breaks
- learn by doing things
- like colourfully presented data.

Kinaesthetic people tend to:
- start using new equipment before reading instructions
- manipulate things in order to stimulate memory
- speak slowly
- touch others to get their attention
- stand close up during conversations
- use a finger or marker when reading
- find geographical data difficult unless they have been there
- use action words more than concept ones
- like involved games
- dislike prolonged periods of sitting down
- fiddle with objects
- enjoy fixing things
- value physical skills in others.

> **Making better connections with kinaesthetic style people**
> - Employ words and phrases that express emotions.
> - Ask lots of appropriately phrased questions and expect them to reciprocate.
> - Do not be offended if they seem easily distracted during conversation.
> - Occasionally touch their arm to show reassurance.
> - In Western society, they value close physical proximity.

Conclusion

So many aspects of human nature combine to make us individually different. Perceptual Preferences are one of these factors. However, because they have patterns of behaviour and observable features, we are able to recognise these traits and allow for them.

If Zoe, an Estate Agent, wants to make a better connection with her client Tim, she has to adapt her normal Kinaesthetic style to his Auditory one. That means not talking in terms of how she feels but what she thinks. Tim, in turn, will need to adopt a Visual style when he talks with his colleague Kate, by referring not to how he thinks about a subject but how he sees it. Each one will fulfil their business objectives and be able to tick off their agenda points but the way in which this is expedited will vary according to the other party.

As for Harry, the difficulty will be getting a word in edgeways!

13

ESTABLISHING RAPPORT

The incumbent United States President usually gets to choose most of the issues upon which the presidential election will be fought, after his first term of office. He can act presidentially, appearing on the world stage with other leaders, point to his successes, demonstrate the governing skills of his team, and subtly hint at the lack of experience his opponent will bring to the job. Yet for George Bush Snr, it all seemed to go wrong.

There were economic issues working against him in the early 1990s. There was also a bad military operation in Africa, with too many film cameras and too little operational intelligence. 'Watch my lips: no more taxes,' had become a haunting phrase he wished had never been said. Yet after the success of the Gulf War, and with a strong team and no scandals, he stood to win his second term against an unknown candidate from a small Southern state.

Then Bush made his sad admission about not having 'the vision thing'. The very strength and appeal of Clinton became a factor that divided the two men and yielded the higher ground to the challenger. This was the very issue upon which Clinton was building rapport with the electorate and the President was admitting to being without this vital ingredient!

Next came the TV debate. Clinton was relaxed, charming and able to engage both his live audience as well as the watching millions. He became approachable, vulnerable, persuasive, charming – and believable. Bush, on the other hand, was defensive, nervous, aggressive, edgy and very unpresidential. He scored nil for his audience rapport while Clinton got the maximum votes the judges could award. The election outcome was now sealed. The man with rapport won, despite doubts about his character and competence. The man with the competence and unblemished character lost decisively. Rapport was the defining issue on all levels.

Establishing Rapport

<u>Rapport:</u> 'a close and harmonious relationship, characterised by affinity, empathy, and liking, in which there is a clear and common understanding'

You win some, you lose some

We all have varying degrees of success in establishing rapport. On a good day I find it occurs almost instantly. Everything works smoothly, whether one-to-one coaching sessions, or speaking to a thousand conference delegates. When I have the right mindset, it seems to happen naturally and intuitively.

I attribute this to my 'I' temperament, (the people one), having a Social Attitude (people again) and my Kinaesthetic preference; I learn by feeling and therefore find it easy to enter another person's world.

But there are bad days! On a bad day all the wrong attributes combine and I can easily end up with a disconnect. The impatience of my 'D' temperament, coupled with my other attitudinal strength, which is Utilitarian, can work against my objectives. Add to that the fact that I am an Iconoclast, (one who attacks cherished beliefs or institutions) and you can understand why sometimes rapport is less sweet.

> **'I have become a reformer, and, like all reformers, an iconoclast. I shatter creeds and demolish idols.'**
> (George Bernard Shaw)

Rapport is both a process and an outcome. Probably the greatest opportunity for excellent rapport is with one's partner (assuming that you like each other to start with!). It is also the greatest opportunity for non-rapport. After the initial romantic love begins to fade that 'close and harmonious relationship' will either begin to develop, or its absence will define the vacuum that needs to be filled. It has been said that everything we do is motivated by love: either the love of others or the love of self. Love of others facilitates rapport whilst love of self destroys it.

Personal rapport

Take a look at couples in a restaurant who literally 'Only have eyes for one another', Their eye contact is excellent. Their facial expressions will often be the same and so will their body language. If you were able to listen to their conversation, they would probably be speaking in the same tone of voice and with the same pace of speech. When you see two people who are really getting along well together, they literally do become one.

Conversely, have you noticed the couples that perhaps have been married rather longer and are struggling to establish rapport? There is usually not a lot of joy in their expressions and eye contact is often rare as they look around for something more interesting to occupy their attention. The body language will be fairly closed and eavesdropping their conversation might be difficult as neither one is talking to the other!

Personally, the person I have the best rapport with is Susi, my wife. Achieving this took a great deal of patience, grace and application on both our parts, with the odd door slamming incident along the way. Not all our connections were ideal! Hardly surprising, when one considers that we are such opposites. My temperament is D and I, hers is C and S. In these respects you could not get two people less alike. It makes decorating a house from top to bottom an interesting exercise, full of growth opportunities. If we manage to find something on which we agree, we go with it, rather than hunt for lots of options.

For people like us who understand the psychology, we manage to explore the issues together; there are huge benefits to understanding temperament, attitudes and personality. Appreciating that Susi is wired differently from me, I have learned to understand and value that difference, adapt to improve rapport, and take advantage of our different strengths. I would get frustrated when instead of saying; 'Yes' to my impulsive suggestions, she would search for information and seek to clarify the issues. I'd say: 'Let's go and look at a new car', hoping for a 'Yes!' response, only to be met with questions. Now I have come to value that check on my impulsiveness and the opportunity to think through exactly what I am looking for. (This is generally true, if not entirely!)

> **'Everything we do is motivated by love: either the love of others or the love of ourselve.'**

Our relationship has developed rapport to a stage where I have moved from a position of being self-centred; 'Let's go and do what I want to do', to a position of being other-centred; 'What is it you need to know to help you make a decision you would be comfortable with?' I am meeting her needs, not just my own.

Professional rapport

In order to achieve long-term business success, it is essential to develop the skills of establishing rapport. Political commentators have observed that Margaret Thatcher's dominatrix style was largely to blame for her downfall. She failed to build rapport with her colleagues. On a bad day, her focus was exclusively on her own needs, as defined by political projects and policies, the needs and aspirations of others failed to even appear on the horizon.

Those with a 'D' and 'C' temperament, find it easier to build professional rapport in the first instance. The 'I' and 'S' temperaments are wiser to start with personal rapport and build from there, if possible. What needs to be borne in mind by all parties is that the best way to get what you want is to give people what they want. This should be the first rule of persuasion. Whatever our personal style, professional rapport is vital.

A team with strong rapport is one in which individuals are not marginalised because their pace is slower than others, or their voices are quieter. Everyone contributes and everyone is respected. The team that takes into account the disciplines and professional responsibilities of its members, is high on rapport and usually very successful. The loss of energy and time generated by poor rapport is incalculable. Rapport makes a team competitive, rather than a pool of competing individuals.

Strong business partnerships thrive on professional rapport. There is an intuitive understanding and a deep level of commitment to one another's success. This is why entire teams transfer organisations when the team leader takes a new position. They know the loyalty of their colleagues, the skills each one brings to the task, and the chemistry between all the players. Rapport is priceless, but where it exists the rewards are measurable in both financial and emotional ways.

There is a magic that comes with rapport which many people take for granted. This is unfortunate because we need to see it as something that has to be worked at. When we make a connection, rapport is the bonding or feeling between two or more people that signals they like, and can relate, to each other. This ability to relate is a fundamental principle of rapport, which leads to a deepening of relationship and a more meaningful connection.

Throughout my business career, I have had a natural ability to develop rapport with key influencers, colleagues or staff. When things have not gone well, it has usually been when rapport has broken down, or hardly been established in the first place.

Welcome to my world

In order to achieve rapport, it is essential that one be prepared to 'enter their world'. If approached correctly, you will be made welcome and thus gain their perspective. This may turn out to be a new experience. You will appreciate their needs, expectations, apprehensions and aspirations. You will acquire the capacity to think as they do, which in turn will allow you to feel as they feel.

To some, this is natural and intuitive, while to others it is something they have been taught for a specific reason. Personally, I trained as a counsellor to understand the importance of entering another's world. If someone has been damaged, they need to know they are understood. Once that is established, a relationship of trust can be developed.

For others, this process has been learned over the years. We all need to deal with certain types of people in business; the difficult boss, the reluctant employee, the obnoxious customer. It all starts with establishing rapport. Not learning these lessons is a serious hindrance to career progress.

Mirroring and matching

Mirroring and matching are the labels NLP (neuro-linguistic programming) practitioners use to describe how best to establish rapport by entering another person's world. It is a subtle art that requires mature application and much practice if one is going to succeed. If you are a 'people watcher', you will have observed the process during natural social interaction.

We tend to be drawn to, and build rapport easier, with people we like and who tend to be like us. Managers for example, often employ people with similar traits to themselves. What takes place between people is that they become a 'Mirror Image' of others by matching various behaviours of the person whose world they want to enter. For example, children moving to another part of the country very quickly adopt a local dialect along with regionalised slang. The same applies to adult speech patterns, forms of dress, mannerisms and interests.

Body Language is the biggest single contributor to communication breakdown. This would seem to be the ideal place to start applying this principle! Try to align your body language with that of the other person. If their posture is fairly laid back and relaxed, adopt the same position. If their head is tilted to one side, make an adjustment to mirror their style. Equally important, note their facial expression and make a connection by responding to their visible mood.

This needs to be a gradual process and should not be attempted all at once. Subtlety is crucial when attempting to achieve this, and if you are successful there is no doubt it can enhance communication.

Unfortunately the opposite can also happen. I was recently talking to someone who was clearly applying these principles but in a programmed and obvious fashion. When I crossed my legs so did he. As I put my hand up to my face, he did the same. In the end it became a game! I got more and more outrageous to see how far he would go. For me it was fun, but for someone else this attempt at mirroring might have appeared more like mocking.

Tone of Voice is the second highest contributor to effective communication. Again, it is helpful to match the other's tone. If they are speaking softly, join them by softening your own. If they use lots of pauses and inflections, do the same. But beware of mimicking their style – people notice this. The aim is to help them to gain confidence in you, not to be so focused on this method of achieving rapport that you fail to take in what they are saying!

Words are also important to match. As we discussed in the previous chapter, matching perceptual preferences can do a great deal to help the other person understand, feel understood, and consequently improve rapport.

Detect the **pace** used to deliver the words and try to communicate at the same pace. This helps the other person feel you are on the right wavelength. Closely linked to this is breathing, which is an important clue to their emotions.

In Summary

If there is an obvious mismatch in any of the above, particularly in the area of body language, it may indicate that there is disagreement over an issue and rapport has started to break down. People begin to change their tone, their posture, their gestures and their vocabulary, when they feel offended, misunderstood, undervalued or ignored. Look for the signs and respond appropriately.

An important exception to this is when you are coaching someone. If they start to indulge in a 'Poor me – pity party' that is not a world you want to enter. It is important not to offer sympathy, but instead to empathise, offering hope through challenging them to see things differently, and to offer direction to change an outcome. Coaching is meant to lead a person to success and maturity, not to allow them to wallow indulgently in negative feelings. If we mirror wrong attitudes we are endorsing them and failing to be of genuine service.

Mirroring and matching, if done well, will allow you to enter the other person's world and greatly enhance rapport to the benefit of all concerned.

Three Crucial Needs

When I speak and am passionate about something, I tend to gesticulate a lot. One young lady who does a lot of graphics work for me finds this mesmerising. The end result is that I feel I am not being listened to and our communication has broken down.

This leads me to a vitally important element of rapport that has to do with our most crucial of needs. I call them the three Ss. **Security**, **Significance** and **Self-worth**. Understanding and seeking to help others to have these needs met will enormously facilitate the establishment of rapport.

Security

Security means different things to different people. Accumulating wealth is regarded by many as the best form of security. The lessons of wisdom and history teach us that wealth can disappear overnight, however. Even those with vast amounts of money never seem to regard it as sufficient. Paul Getty when asked, 'How much is enough?', replied, 'just a little bit more'.

Being in control is another means by which people seek security. In the 'Friends' sit-com, Monica is driven to absurd lengths in order to gain and maintain control of every situation. We laugh at her because we see so many people we know, possibly ourselves included, in that one character.

Very often fear is at the root of the need to control. It produces an inability to trust and a need to hold onto the reins of life. Then along comes redundancy, the death of a loved one, a stock market crash, or a hundred and one others things that are beyond human control and one is faced with the nightmare that all one's efforts have been trying to avoid: a loss of control.

Whatever mechanisms people use to seek security, I believe the only time we truly feel secure is when we experience 'unconditional love'. My colleagues sometimes cringe when I use this terminology in seminars or conferences, and would prefer me to use terms like 'respect', but that is not quite what I mean. If I communicate that I love someone, it doesn't mean a sexual attraction or a sentimental foolishness. It simply means that I have a desire for their greater good. It involves laying aside selfish motives, and

Establishing Rapport

being prepared to sacrifice what I want, in order to achieve that.

Imagine how rapport would soar when the other person realised that this was your sincere goal? We all need to feel loved in this way, and by being prepared to initiate this attitude, the other person will be more inclined to reciprocate. The result would be an upward spiral of rapport. If you are both male and British, you may feel uncomfortable with this concept, even as you read this, but I would challenge you to ignore this at you peril.

Significance

Significance is the second crucial need. Titles, status, and power, all provide a temporary source of significance but if removed the effect can be shattering. The reality is that we all need to feel important. Knowing that our lives count for something and that our efforts are appreciated is part of our humanity.

3 Crucial Needs

Security ... Loved
Significance ... Important
Self-worth ... Valued

I recently spent time with a young woman who was experiencing depression. She was in her mid-thirties, had two young children and felt taken for granted by both her husband and to a lesser extent her children. In her words, she 'Was continually doing everything for everyone'. The root of this was very revealing.

The youngest of three children, Lorna (not the real name) and her entire family had lived in a commune during her early childhood. All her parents' time was taken up with attending meetings and Lorna was left to play with her older brother. Craving the attention of her mother, which she rarely received, Lorna grew up feeling unimportant and unloved. Children spell love: T-I-M-E. When she reached the age of seven they came out of the commune and Lorna anticipated a time of receiving her mother's attention. Then the unthinkable happened; her mother became pregnant and all her attention was given to the baby sister. Lorna's beliefs were now confirmed; she felt she had no personal significance whatsoever.

This wrong thinking had taken a firm root and become the means of interpreting all events. If her husband failed to show appreciation over anything she felt ignored. She was convinced that her mother fussed over her sister's children more than her own, and this served to confirm that even her children were not important to their grandmother.

Had one tried to establish rapport with Lorna over business issues, the potential for bad connections would have been enormous. A loss of eye contact, an occasional misinterpretation, perhaps cutting across her to make a point, all these would inevitably have touched the pain inside. She would have felt ignored, unimportant and rapport would have been lost. It would not have been possible to know her background and be prepared for the issues. However, proper attention to the principles of rapport would help avoid such difficulties.

During any connection, one must ensure that the other person is left to feel that they are important. Your role is not to help someone find their sense of purpose but to help them retain their sense of significance. For Lorna, this began with the revelation that bad experiences had created wrong thinking about herself. She was then able to deal with the pain, forgive her mother, and choose to think correctly about how significant she was to so many other people.

Self-worth

Self-worth is the third of our crucial needs. This is not the same as significance. Mikhail Gorbachev was regarded as significant even after relinquishing his role as Russia's President. However, his usefulness within the nation he had led into a bloodless revolution had come to an abrupt end. A former colleague, Boris Yeltsin, whom he had sacked as Mayor of Moscow for his bombastic style of management, had taken his role and was regarded by the West as a pair of safe and radical hands. Gorbachev had survived a treasonous plot only to be deposed by a showman. His cabinet showed no loyal support at this point. It is this loss of being valued by others that impacts our sense of self-worth. To experience self-worth is to feel valued, irrespective of one's social significance.

We all need to sense that not only what we do adds value, but that who we are is valued. After all we are human beings and not human doings. It is a basic human desire to believe that we are personally regarded as worthwhile. No one would want to build rapport with those who regard their contributions as worthless, or their presence as unnecessary. In order to build rapport, we need to ensure the message we convey is that the other party is valued as a person. We do this by making sure we listen more than we talk, make eye contact, and demonstrate that we understand their point of view.

It is a recognised psychological truth that if we genuinely try to understand another person's point of view, with sincerity and empathy, they become psychologically obligated to try to understand ours.

Establishing Rapport

We all need to have a sense of feeling loved, important and valued – there are no exceptions. Most of my coaching sessions that require bringing resolution to deep personal issues require that one or more of these needs be addressed. After role-playing whilst holding Trusted Adviser workshops, an important question I ask those delegates adopting the role of clients is: 'Did the Trusted Adviser make you feel loved, important and valued?' Frequently the answer is no, which simply says the rapport was not what it could have been. Paying attention to the three crucial needs will increase the likelihood of establishing rapport. Remember, ultimately you get back what you give out.

Summary for establishing rapport

- Plan to establish rapport to build trust.
- Be aware of the behavioural styles.
- Prepare appropriate open questions.
- Practise Exemplary Listening™.
- Aim to enter the other person's world.
- Determine hearer's preferred attitude.
- Adopt a selfless mindset.
- Mirror and Match with subtlety.
- Adapt body language, tone of voice.
- Engage Perceptual Preferences™.
- Observe breathing, tempo and pace.
- Watch for evidence of mismatch.
- Suspend ego and judgemental attitude.
- Like who you are with.
- Be involved, interested and interesting.
- Allow appropriate emotion and empathy.
- Cater for the 3 crucial needs.
- Always aim to be authentic.

SECTION 6

CRUCIAL COMBO

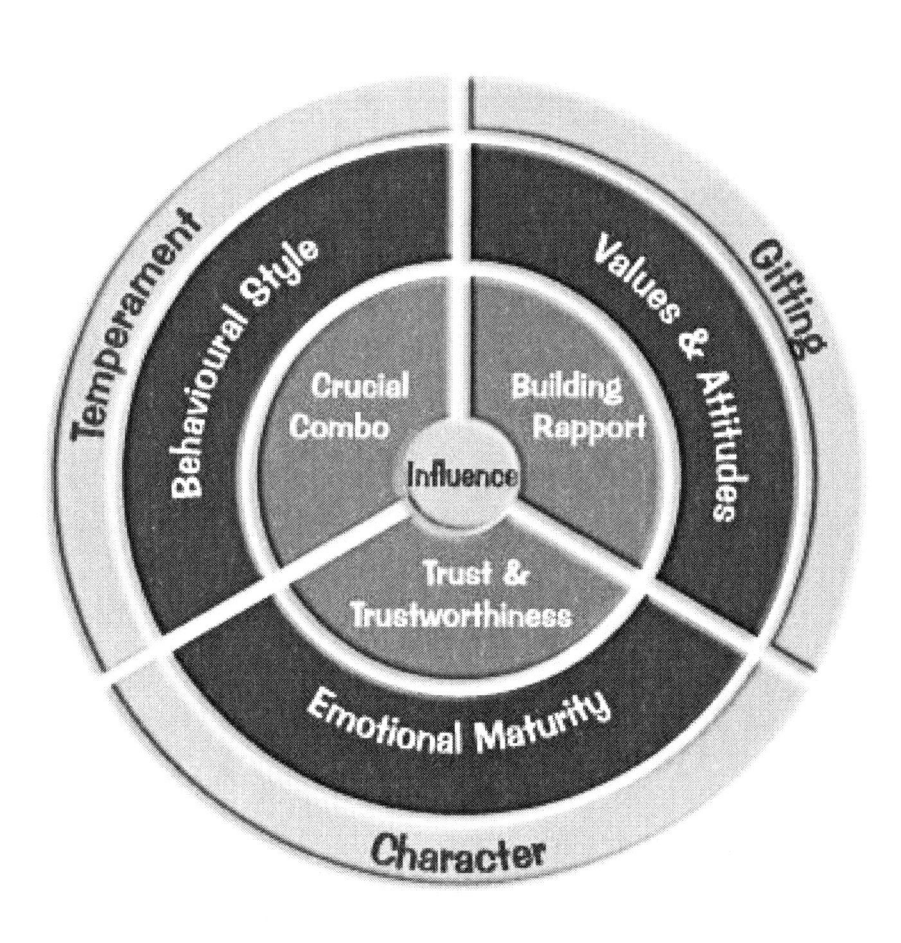

14

THE CRUCIAL COMBINATION

Neuro-Linguistic Programming (NLP) is a fascinating sphere of learning that enables our unconscious skills to become understood and developed in order to enhance our credibility, communication and interpersonal skills. An NLP principle states that 'representation is not reality'. In other words, our generalisations only represent the reality. Reality itself is different. What we believe to be real may differ significantly from the way in which other people represent the same thing. If our representation is real, then everyone else would be wrong!

Another way NLP practitioners express this is to say 'the map is not the territory'. In other words, the territory is reality but we all have our own maps, or perception, of that reality. Because I enjoy cooking, I tend to prefer saying 'the menu is not the meal', because a menu simply represents a meal in a verbal form.

> **The menu is not the meal.**

We perceive the world through our five senses, what we hear, see, smell, taste and feel. This information is not reality (the meal), it is merely how we have re-presented it in our mind (the menu).

Whilst living in Borneo, I acquired a passion for the local dish, Nasi Goreng. I have cooked it many times since, but it has never come up to the expectations forged by my memory. My wife also loves Nasi Goreng, but she prefers it mild with thin slices of omelet and coriander leaves. (I have to go easy on the Sambu Oleck for her.) Personally, I only enjoy it if topped with lots of sliced chilli, garnished with parsley, and the heat covers my forehead in beads of sweat. We both have our ideal Nasi Goreng and it is so different!

Events and conversations have ingredients too. Yet even though one event has only one set of ingredients, we manage to see it quite differently. Why is this?

Having taken information in via our senses, the input is then subject to filtration. It must pass through our:

- **values** (what is worthwhile and important)
- **attitude** (e.g. half full or half empty)
- **beliefs** (that which is possible)
- **habits** (that which we do automatically)
- **temperament** (the nature we were born with).

We then use our vocabulary, tone of voice, mood and body language to communicate back to the outside world. When one considers the process, it is small wonder that communication often breaks down and two people see things differently!

> **'The degree to which you are prepared to be flexible will determine the degree of your success.'**

To gain knowledge and understanding of another person and their situation, we need to understand what their menu looks like. With that insight we can better enter into their world. Once we are in their world, seeing and feeling as they do, the degree to which we are prepared to be flexible will determine the degree of our success.

The vehicle for delivering that success is communication. All communication requires the **'crucial combination'** if it is to be effective. That combination is the simple disciplines of asking questions and listening to the answers. We all know how to do it, but the mass of wasted effort caused by poor communication and misunderstanding is testimony to the fact that most of our asking and listening is done poorly, with little planning, and probably no developmental training. For the Trustworthy Adviser, these skills are absolutely crucial. Getting this right unlocks the world of those with whom we deal and enables our dealings to be successful.

We all ask simple, factual questions and pay attention to the answers, such as, 'which terminal does flight no 438 leave from?', ' do you want to come to my party?' or 'how much does this shirt cost?'.

We also ask questions that are perfunctory; we are not too fussy about the answers, and therefore do not listen very intently to the reply. 'How are you?' is often a victim of this range of question. 'Do you like… ?', or 'have you ever…?' might be just polite silence fillers and nothing more. Yet in all of these scenarios, a 'connection' is taking place. The quality and outcome of that connection depends on your ability in the **'Art of Asking'** and your observations during the **'Lessons of Listening'**.

The art of asking questions

Questions drive interactive communication. Asking the appropriate questions, at the correct time, in the most effective manner, is essential in order to achieve a 'good connection'. The quality of an answer depends on the quality of the question. Questioning the other person can be one of the most effective ways of getting them involved. Once involved, they may well begin to reveal their needs, concerns, expectations and attitudes. Hence a typical management consultancy question is 'What is your pain?'

This process of enabling the other party to reveal what really matters to them also allows you the opportunity to demonstrate empathy by a careful use of **Exemplary Listening**™. It enables you to offer benefits in the most appealing way and to offer reassurance wherever necessary. If you have been aiming at securing agreement to points throughout the dialogue, then a final commitment to action is only a small step to be taken.

Reasons why we ask questions
- to obtain information
- to ascertain attitudes, habits, preferences
- to clarify points and evaluate understanding
- to arouse interest and encourage thinking
- to create opportunities and assess potential
- to get firm commitment for a way forward
- to better understand needs so as to more usefully offer benefits
- to avoid incorrect assumptions and taking wrong pathways
- to involve the other person in the connection
- to give the other person a chance to talk
- to guide the discussion towards a mutually beneficial outcome

Types of questions

We have all been taught that there are basically two types of questions – OPEN and CLOSED. OPEN questions tend to gain information, reveal opportunities, present challenges as well as highlight needs. CLOSED questions tend to focus attention and gain commitment.

Open questions are designed to explore new information. They will usually be prefaced by such words as WHO, WHAT, WHEN, WHY, WHERE, HOW and invite longer, more involved answers. e.g. 'how do you normally communicate with you customers?'

Closed questions are designed to bring conclusion and are usually prefaced by such phrases as do you, have you, will you, are you, can you and invite shorter answers, e.g. 'is it necessary for me to stay much longer?' Obviously, some people will answer a closed question with a long description and others answer an open question with the minimum of words and little or no information. Generally though, if we want someone to talk, we ask open questions.

Information-gathering questions, if asked correctly, are non-threatening. **'How'** questions often relate to process & procedures, e.g. 'how do you manage your customer's expectations?' **'Who'** questions are people centred, e.g. 'who are the different people involved in the operation?' **'What'** is a good information question, e.g. 'what are the things that if changed would help considerably?' **'Why'** questions can be both powerful and problematic if not asked and received in the appropriate fashion. 'Why do you think the campaign failed?' may provide insight into the cause and may also make the receiver feel condemned if it was his or her campaign.

> **I keep six honest serving men –**
> **They taught me all I knew.**
> **Their names are What &**
> **Why & When**
> **And How & Where & Who.**
> Rudyard Kipling

Timelines questions

Questions about the past are helpful to gain insight and understanding about the current situation and how it was arrived at. 'How would you describe what went wrong?'

Present questions address current issues and concerns. 'Where do you currently get support from?' There is a tendency at this stage for some sales people or consultants to enthusiastically leap in and offer a solution. Better to continue the dialogue, asking even more questions that may reveal further information, and perhaps opportunity.

Future questions provide an opportunity to envision the other party through allowing them to see their world as it could be. 'What would be your ideal environment?' Undoubtedly answers to questions like that will lead to subsequent questions about detail, motives and reasons, thus encouraging dialogue.

> Me: 'What would be your ideal environment?'
> You: 'One where everybody worked in harmony and was highly productive'
> Me: 'OK, it sounds like there may be a lack of collaboration and results perhaps not as good as they could be. Tell me more about … …

The Socratic method

'A method of teaching or discussion, as used by Socrates, in which one asks a series of easily answered questions that inevitably lead the answerer to a logical conclusion.'
Webster's New World Dictionary

Socrates was a master of what we call 'drawing people out'. His skills began with the judicious use of short, easily answered open questions. 'Why is this so?' would be an example. This ability to keep things simple, yet profoundly investigatory, was combined with exemplary listening. **Exemplary Listening**™ entails using our eyes as well as ears to perceive the feeling behind the words. This requires observing body language, especially facial expressions and hand gestures, plus listening to the tone of voice, and discerning the mood. A combination of wise questioning and observant listening provides the means of enabling the other party to disclose their world and thus provide a more meaningful connection.

Having got the issue or topic out on the table, there may well be a need to 'drill down' in order to gain more information. This is achieved through using Socratic Probes similar to the one in the last exchange.

> 'Explain a little more to me about the need for harmony.'
> 'What other things do I need to know about competitiveness within the team?'
> 'Give me some examples of competing agendas.'

The Socratic method treats the other party to a dialogue, deferentially. The approach is selfless and helps the answerer to feel understood, valued and important. Given this environment, the other person is more likely to engage at a deeper level, reveal truths, express their motives and aspirations, collaborate more, and ultimately buy the product or solution you have to offer.

Asking questions

Why:	To reveal business challenges and opportunities; to identify needs, to gain commitment to progress.
When:	Early on to encourage involvement and dialogue.
What sort:	Open – to get the other person involved.
	Closed – to focus on commitment.

How many: As few or as many as necessary.
How: With sincerity to demonstrate empathy.

Unfortunately there is a trap when asking questions – the interrogation trap. Sometimes the connection can degenerate into a series of questions and answers with the questioner demonstrating no empathy whatsoever. Use questions effectively and efficiently, not to the annoyance of the other person. Your goal is to find things out for mutual benefit, not to use the other person as a source of facts. Don't squander this valuable opportunity by asking inappropriate questions.

> *'It is the province of 'knowledge' to speak*
> *But it is the privilege of 'wisdom' to listen.'*
> Oliver Wendell Holmes

Exemplary Listening™

Effective communication is a connection. A connection that expresses and imparts either a thought, a feeling, an impression, a fact, or a concept. We can say there is always a transmitter and a receiver. If you are the transmitter, that connection always leaves the other person, the receiver, with an impression and an opinion. Following their response, one is left with some answers from which choices and decisions can be made. The choices made as a result of that connection could have far reaching consequences.

> US pension fund laws allow individuals to exercise their own discretion over investments. Ordinary people, not trained in economics and without financial expertise, heard a message in the late 1990s, which they failed to fully understand.
>
> Rising stock prices, a buoyant equity market, an economy growing largely due to the expanding technology sector, and a decade of peacetime all seemed to say one thing; 'Invest now, choose growth sector stocks, expect huge returns'. The dot.com sector seemed to have been created for this army of amateur, but intelligent, investors.
>
> People were not lied to, nor were the facts hidden from them. What took place were thousands of bad connections. A belief that anyone could simply make wealth out of what professional investors always say is a complex and demanding industry, took hold of many people's imaginations. Consequently the questions they asked were about how to invest and re-invest. Questions

about business cycles, how to spread a portfolio over high and low risk options, and crucially; what actual value did the companies have in which they were investing were not asked. Just those three questions, properly asked, thoroughly answered, and thoughtfully considered, would have meant no dot.com boom and crash, no dramatic losses of life savings, and a number of very real human tragedies would have been avoided. One distraught investor in Atlanta Georgia even slaughtered his fellow investors before taking his own life. Our choices, based on communication connections, can have massive personal implications.

Most business decisions will not lead to personal or corporate disasters. However, the potential for success or failure is always present. That is why I label these 'the crucial combination'.

As the receiver, it is your role to listen to what is being said. That presents you with two positive opportunities. Firstly it is an opportunity to learn something, be inspired, gain knowledge and obtain sound advice. However, there is also the opportunity to show the transmitters that you understand them, and what they have to say is worthwhile. Continuous good listening builds the confidence and self-esteem of the transmitter, which in turn improves the quality of the transmission, thus enabling and helping us to learn even more.

> 'The most basic of all human needs is the need to understand and be understood. The best way to understand people is to listen to them.'
> Ralph Nichols

There are of course many other negative opportunities that we will cover later.

Types of Listeners

There are three types of listener. Let's examine them and be honest about which kind describes us most of the time.

1. The Superficial Listener

'The lights are on but no one's at home.' Superficial listeners range from not listening at all, to continually interrupting and listening only sporadically. They often substitute real listening with paying attention to their own internal self-talk, or any welcome distractions. They are, however, very interested in what they have to say! Consequently their listening time is taken up preparing the next diatribe. They are often seen by others to be insensitive, always wanting the last word. Communication with the Superficial Listener is difficult and very hard work. They are sometimes viewed as a 'critical parent' figure, leading to a great deal of bad connections and misunderstanding.

2. The Clinical Listener

These people are concerned with dissecting and analysing the words that are spoken. They often keep their own emotions at arms length, exhibit a very clinical approach and tend to lack empathy and sensitivity. The main concern of Clinical Listeners is to persuade the transmitter to their way of thinking, rather than embracing the entire transmission, words, body language, tone of voice and mood. This cold and logical approach can lead to tense transactions, which ultimately result in functional and superficial relationships, often festering with frustrations and resentment.

3. The Exemplary Listener™

People who are able to suspend their own bias and ego, being prepared to embrace the whole of the transmission. That includes the tone of voice, mood, and body language. They hear, see, and feel the transmitters' communication with an open mind, seeing it from their point of view. The exemplary listener is prepared to lay aside cynicism and scepticism, focusing on what is being said with patient contemplation because of their desire to learn and understand. They are able to see behind the words, discerning the motives, intentions and desires. They avoid interrupting and aim to speak for only 20% of the communication time.

Exemplary listeners continually look for signals to stop talking and allow the other person to take the lead. They are skilled in the art of asking. Questions are employed to encourage clarification and to probe for further information. The aim is always a deeper level of understanding.

To become Exemplary Listeners we need to do two things:
- remove the listening blocks
- practice the principles of Exemplary Listening.

This is a process of change for most people. Just like physical exercise, it can hurt a little at first and our efforts might seem insignificant. However, regular exercise builds strong muscles and stamina. Consistent good practices also become easier and more natural as we progress.

Removing the Listening Blocks

Listed below are the 10 most common blocks to good listening.

- **Judging**: we all do it and hate it being done to us! Hasty judgments based on prejudices and strong opinions distort listening.
- **Comparing**: continually measuring everything said against the results of our own experience.
- **Filtering**: listening to hear all the things we disagree with, thus preventing us from taking on board much of the new learning.
- **Answer Preparing**: continually thinking of the next thing to say whilst looking for a lull in the dialogue in order to break in.
- **Advising**: assuming the role of wise counsellor, more interested in presenting a solution than appreciating the pain.
- **Competing**: topping the speaker's communication by coming out with statements like, 'that's nothing, let me tell you about....................'
- **Self-justifying**: whatever is said, having difficulty owning up to being wrong about something and continually arguing the case.
- **Ingratiating**: the listener wants to be liked at any price, and perpetually agrees with everything.
- **Dreaming**: something said propels the listener into their own little world where they listen to their own thoughts.
- **Ambushing**: deliberately looking to disagree with the transmitter and attempting to take them down another track.

Practicing the Principles of Exemplary Listening™

- ➢ **Be transmitter centered** rather than self-centered. Be prepared and motivated to listen rather than talk.
- ➢ **Differentiate message from messenger**: respond to what is being said rather than react to the person saying it.
- ➢ **Make eye contact** that is appropriate, gentle and at all times accompanied by affirmative body language.
- ➢ **Suspend ego and bias** and be aware of your own 'hot buttons' which may cause you to react rather than respond.
- ➢ **Ask open questions** which allow the transmitter to express more of their thoughts and feelings.
- ➢ **Observe style** and delivery, this may enable you to define the temperament type of the transmitter.

- ➢ **Use feedback** to check for understanding that your interpretation is an accurate representation of what is being said.
- ➢ **Be open minded** and remember everybody has a different map of the territory. Abandon cynicism to enable you to learn.
- ➢ **Observe feelings** behind the words by examining the mood, tone of voice, and body language.
- ➢ **Avoid distractions** by choosing a venue that is free from noise and a time when your thinking will be focused.
- ➢ **Don't ignore inner voices** of intuition that may be speaking at the same time. Heed what is said and respond accordingly.
- ➢ **Take notes** during the communication. Trusting everything to memory is unwise and may signal lack of interest.
- ➢ **Be sensitive** to the needs, concerns and expectations and perceptual preference of the person.
- ➢ **Don't interrupt or interject.** Let others go first, your turn will come. Believe it or not, you can't talk and listen at the same time.

How often have you spoken to someone, only to find his or her eyes firmly fixed on their PC or laptop screen? In fact, how often have you been that person? What does it say to you? The message is quite clear: 'What you are saying is not sufficiently important to warrant my full attention'. Perhaps the message goes even further to say: 'The reason I am not looking at you is that you are less important than what I see right here'.

All too often our diverted gaze, checking our watch, or continuous interruptions convey this same message. Trustworthy Advisers have to choose to practice Exemplary Listening. They need to give, and prove they have given, their undivided attention to their clients. As the Listening Blocks are removed, and the Principles of Exemplary Listening are practiced, you will achieve far greater understanding of others and make significantly better connections.

Temperament and the Crucial Combination

Every temperament style benefits from upgrading the skills of asking questions and listening. Indeed, the way in which we carry out both of these skills is influenced greatly by our own temperament style. As you look at the following comments be honest with yourself, about yourself! Make a commitment to improve your questioning and listening today.

The 'D' Temperament

People with 'D' type temperaments are very focused, direct and results oriented. They tend to favour short, closed questions that focus on commitment, and very often do not leave much room for manoeuvre. They are very capable of asking open questions, but these are often obscured within, or buried at the end of a diatribe extolling exactly what they think on the subject. They tend to ask the WHAT questions, 'What do you think the results will be after this investment?'

They are often selective listeners, preparing answers whilst the transmitter is speaking. They tend to interrupt when they feel they have heard enough, in order to get their point across. They are often three or four steps ahead of what is being said and wonder why they should bother to listen, when they probably know the answer anyway.

There is no doubt that if the 'D' temperament were to learn to listen more obviously and actively, they would gain greater understanding and perspective. This in turn would help them become more effective. This demonstration of empathy would also help to elevate their position of Trustworthy Adviser, by causing less offence and intimidation.

By asking open, easily answered questions, dialogue would be encouraged and the other party invited to speak about the topics they want to discuss. Much can be learned from an open question prompt where the questioner seems genuinely interested in the answer, however long it takes in coming.

The 'I' Temperament

People with 'I' type temperaments rarely have a problem either expressing what they think, or how they feel. Asking open questions is not the first thing that comes to mind, as they are usually engrossed in what they are saying. Once they are satisfied that what they want to say has been said, they are very capable of asking open questions and encouraging discussion. Their affection for people in general aids this ability. They tend to ask the WHO questions, 'Who will mainly get the recognition for a job well done?'

They are very often sporadic listeners with a definite tendency to speak much more than they listen. Driven by a need to be liked, they will often overdo the 'transmitting' at a significant cost to the 'receiving'. An 'I' temperament person once said, 'That's enough of me talking about myself, now tell me, what do you think about me?'

Of all the types, this is the one that talks too much, very often thinking out loud. By becoming more receiver-centered, they would learn far more about the other party's issues and circumstances. This would lead to a much deeper and more meaningful connection, as well as increase the respect others have for them.

The 'S' Temperament
Far less assertive than the previous two types, the 'S' people will focus on maintaining harmony and therefore ask questions that are non-threatening and avoid conflict. They circumnavigate questions that could 'open a can of worms' but are very capable of asking open questions around people issues. They tend to ask the HOW questions, 'How do you think I should be involved?'

They are the best natural listeners of the four types. Along with their natural empathy for people, they possess a powerful combination that enables them to rapidly put the transmitter at ease, and encourage them to talk. Having a diplomatic and kind disposition, they tend to find that people will naturally open up to them and reveal many things they would withhold from others who listen less well.

Asking questions in a bold and confident fashion, plus probing for answers to 'bigger' questions would greatly enhance the effectiveness of this type. Coupled with their excellent listening skills, this would form a powerful combination that would rapidly propel them to the status of Trustworthy Adviser.

The 'C' Temperament
People with 'C' type temperaments will not automatically ask questions. They do not like to participate in small talk and therefore require a very good reason for asking question that relate personally. Being very interested in facts and detail, they will pursue a line of questioning until they obtain the qualified answer they require. The receiver may in the end feel interrogated, as the focus will be on facts and detail rather then on people and feelings. They tend to ask the WHY questions, 'Why did you choose to do this first, rather than that?'

Being cool and unemotional, they are sometimes seen as poor listeners often missing the 'feelings' that go along with the spoken word. Focused solely on the task in hand, they share little of themselves and can be seen as indifferent, unapproachable, and poor listeners. This causes some people to be wary of them.

The Crucial Combination

A more optimistic and positive questioning style would encourage dialogue and a more open connection. By developing an ability to see beyond the words to the tone of voice, the pace and emotion being expressed, the 'C' temperament can create deeper and more lasting relationships. Coupled with their inert need to get things right, they could over time develop a valued and long-lasting status of Trustworthy Adviser.

15

KNOW THE WAVELENGTH

The satisfying sound of applause filled the conference hall and I gratefully acknowledged the delegates' appreciation. My three-day session had come to a close. Taking my seat as the final clapping faded away, I waited for that extra layer of affirmation; the CEO's concluding remarks. My smile of response to his welcome accolades began to tighten around the corners of my mouth, threatening to twist out of shape. This was the moment of adrenalin starvation.

All that stimulation; the interactive presentation, the anxious energy generated by groundless fears of equipment malfunction, the effort to carry off trans-cultural humour, projecting my ideas and enthusiasm to every participant, handling the Q & A sessions deftly and with confidence, one-to-one clinics during the break periods, and negotiating two more contracts over hastily consumed lunches. It was now all draining away. The inner resources were depleted but the tasks were all completed, I deserved a well-earned rest.

Espresso coffee helped me to complete the business proposal on the return flight and ignore my very confused body clock, which was incorrectly demanding that I eat heavily and then sleep soundly. On the drive home, I felt the tension knots in my shoulder muscles but the thought of a work-free, gentle and pampered weekend kept me awake, alert and grateful.

'Shattered,' was how I answered Susi's inquiry. 'But glad to be home,' I added.

'Take your shoes off, put your feet up on the sofa, and I'll get you a large, single malt,' she said.

Perfect. Gentle, relaxing, pampered. I mentioned the shoulders.

'Finish your drink while I run you a hot bath and then I'll give you a massage.'

More pampering, more affection. The stresses of the past five days were already a distant memory. I no longer needed the solutions to other people's interpersonal problems, or the intuition to discern the real issues behind the guarded disclosures. I could be myself, drop my defences, and become a middle-aged child in need of a little maternal indulgence. Susi knew me inside out.

By the morning, I was ready to start giving something to our relationship again. There were a few minor chores that needed attending to, a holiday difficulty to resolve, and a capable mole-catcher to be hired. And as my energy levels went up, so my needs changed, my focus sharpened onto external matters and we continued to operate on the same wavelength.

Let's suppose Susi had responded differently. Instead of the large whisky I received a litany of household jobs requiring my immediate attention. As I waved my hand to signify that I couldn't be bothered with them right now, she explained why my choice of holiday was impractical, the need to make different arrangements and the absolute necessity of listening when she advises me that my proposed dates may not fit with the decorator's schedule. So much for the hot bath!

As for the massage, my complaint about stiff shoulders led to her complaint about the elusive mole whose mission in life was to ruin our lawn. The mole catcher I hired through Yellow Pages had been unsuccessful.

Now, if all this instruction and information seemed to have an edge that implied that the problems were either entirely my fault, or my responsibility to resolve, we would have been heading for serious conflict. Especially if my hope and expectation had been to receive a sympathetic homecoming and five star pampering. I might have sulked like a spoiled child, or defended myself with counter-aggression and taken us into a full-blown row. The potential for inter-personal damage is very high when we are tired, stressed, or feeling unappreciated. Even between business colleagues, matters can get very personal as small issues spiral out of all proportion.

Most of us can look back to arguments and conflict with the ability to clearly identify just when, where and how the other party missed our mood, made a poor interpretation of our viewpoint, or failed to respond reasonably and rationally. Many of us can go one step further; we can identify our own wrong responses as well. The questions we need to be able to answer in order to improve communication and reduce conflict and misunderstanding to a minimum are:

> ➢ Why do reasonable and intelligent people sometimes struggle to engage in constructive communication?

- How can those who know one another so well, misunderstand one another so badly?
- What exactly breaks down when a response is so different from that which was expected?

A communication model

Transactional Analysis (TA) provides us with an insight into how communication takes place, what we are each looking for in the responses of others, why it can all go so wrong, and how to make it successful and effective. The first time I read and understood this methodology, was one of those exciting moments of revelation. The light bulb was turned on!

I use an adaptation of TA in many of my workshops and combine it with NLP, or cognitive therapy, during many one-to-one coaching sessions. I have lost count of how many times I have seen those light bulbs go on for other people. Apologies in advance to all the purist students of TA, who may see my approach as rather simplistic. However, my approach derives from the way in which it impacted me personally, and has greatly helped many others.

The International Transactional Analysis Association defines TA as follows, *'Transactional Analysis is a theory of personality and a systematic psychotherapy for personal growth and personal change'*. I believe it is not sufficient as a theory of personality; however, it as an excellent model of communication, enabling personal growth and change, along with profound insights into human interaction. TA also adds value by contributing to our understanding of internal dialogue, in other words self-talk.

Dr Eric Berne, 1910-1970, was a Canadian psychiatrist who first reported on TA. After his first two articles on the ego state theory – which we will examine later – his third article, entitled *'Transactional Analysis: A New and Effective Method of Group Therapy'*, was presented by invitation at the 1957 Western Regional Meeting of the American Group Psychotherapy Association of Los Angeles. With the publication of this paper in the 1958 issue of the American Journal of Psychotherapy, transactional analysis became a permanent part of psychotherapeutic literature.

Berne was not trying to develop a new form of therapy. Instead he offered a new theory of communication that even his lay clients could understand. It is not surrounded in psychobabble but does require us to learn a few new phrases in which familiar words take on specific psychological meaning. This theory makes complex interpersonal transactions more easily understandable. In the mid sixties with the launch of Berne's book 'Games People Play', T.A. gained wide public interest. Since then many others have contributed to the initial theory set out below. As you study these next few pages I believe you will see how this helps to answer the question posed earlier and appreciate how our 'connections' can be enhanced and all our communications made more effective. This is highly practical psychology. It is about not just getting on the same wavelength but both parties being on the right one as well!

The three ego states

Who am I now?
Berne's central theory, propounded in his first two papers, is that each person exists within, and communicates from, one of three parts which he called 'ego states'. Ego, in psychology is 'Self', normally denoted by the words 'I' 'Me' and 'Myself'. Ego denotes who we are as unique individuals. Freud first used the term ego to define our conscious personality: that which controls thought and behaviour, and is in touch with external reality.

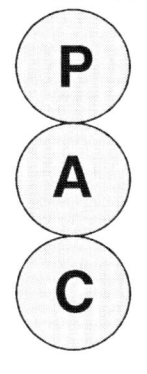

Berne defined an 'ego state' as a consistent pattern of thinking, feeling and behaving. His theory was that each of us possesses three ego states, which he referred to as PARENT, ADULT and CHILD. These terms are not used to define specific relationship. We each have a Parent ego state even if we are have no children, and a child ego state no matter how old we might be. The terms define the way in which we are thinking, feeling and behaving. Each state has its own characteristics, as we shall see later.

Parent:	**the taught concepts of life**
Adult:	**the thought concepts of life**
Child:	**the felt concepts of life**

So at any point in time, you and I exist within, and communicate from, one of these three ego states. When I came home from the overseas conference, I was clearly in the Child ego state.

The parent ego state

(P)

This ego state represents all the taught concepts of life
Most parents of teenagers cringe inwardly when they hear themselves repeating to their kids those self-same words of wisdom, which their own parents used to reiterate ad nauseam! Even knowing the reaction they will cause, we still trot out those moralising platitudes and well-worn clichés. We are not only speaking as physical parents, but it is our Parent ego state that is doing the talking. It repeats that which it has been taught. And repeats it, despite our awareness that it has no power to affect teenagers' behaviour!

The Parent ego state is a recording of the things our parents, or those who were in authority over us when we were young, have instilled into us. It is a collection of pre-judged, prejudiced rules for living. Much of how we view the world reflects how our parents viewed it. Hence much of what we teach our children is the same material.

In the Parent ego state we decide, without reasoning, what people should be like, how we should react in certain situations, and what is right or wrong.

Who is the parent?
Just as we have two biological parents, we also have two Parent ego states. The first is known as the Nurturing Parent, the second is the Critical Parent. The style of speech and behaviour we exhibit when functioning in either mode is obvious from the title. The former is supportive, accepting and unconditional in its love and affection. The latter is judgemental, often fault finding, and shows love and affection on conditional terms. Both are valid, depending on the context. This is not a moral competition.

(NP | CP)

Most of us have experienced parents or guardians who were both nurturing and critical. Neither approach is wholly right or wholly wrong. There are positives and negatives in both parent ego states. There is a right time to be a nurturing parent, and a right time to be a critical parent. Getting it right is fundamental to good communication.

The adult ego state:

	Positive attributes	Negative attributes
CRITICAL PARENT	Establishes rules	Controlling
	Warns of danger	Dominating
	Stands alongside	Demanding
	Creates boundaries	Hypercritical
NURTURING PARENT	Loving	Smothering
	Supportive	Sentimental
	Empathetic	Stifles feelings
	Protective	Holds grudges

The adult ego state

This ego state is concerned with the thought concepts of life

The Adult within us is like a computer. It receives and imparts information, unemotionally. It solves problems and checks out reality, continually on the look out for facts. After receiving and processing the facts it will then make decisions. It also decides probabilities. The Adult is central in personal and professional growth. However, even when acting in the Adult ego state our behaviour is not necessarily mature! You are presently using the Adult ego state to learn about Transactional Analysis.

The Adult acts as a reality check. It continually monitors and updates the Parent tapes, whilst at the same time protecting the Child. It also looks at the outside world and assesses the appropriateness of our responses. Whereas the Parent is concerned with our values, the Adult is concerned with our thinking.

The Adult is a data gatherer. It takes into account all the information from the Parent, along with all the feelings from the Child. The Adult ego state will review your history, consider processes, evaluate past decisions and results stored in the memory, check out new information received from the outside world, analyse it all, and arrive at decisions, options, and action plans. Sometimes it will happen in less time than it has taken you to read this paragraph!

The adult ego state:

	Positive attributes	Negative attributes
	Thinker	Cool
	Action Oriented	Calculating
	Assertive	Distant
	Chooser	Unsympathetic

The child ego state

This ego state is concerned with the felt concepts of life.
The Child is emotional, creative, fun loving and spontaneous. It is the part of your personality that loves life. This represents the real you, before anyone started to shape your thoughts and values.

Our mind not only records all the events of our lives, it also records the feelings that accompanied them. This is why you can be in a situation that reminds you of one twenty years ago, and suddenly all the old feelings come rushing back. When this happens the Child within us is to the fore.

Which Child?

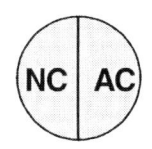

Like the Parent, there are two aspects to the Child. The **Natural Child** is free, spontaneous and expressive, whereas the **Adapted Child** is obedient and compliant.

The **Natural Child** enjoys life to the full, is not bound by any rules, and is free to have fun and enjoyment. Think of a six year old in the school playground at break time unconcerned about the reactions of others. He can be a train, a ghost, a soldier, or a prehistoric monster; the choice is his! The Natural Child is a very important aspect of the total person. However, it is not a state we could remain in permanently. There is a need for boundaries, and adaptation, which is where we meet ...

The **Adapted Child**, who is submissive, seeking gratification by doing what is expected.

The child is a very important ego state: many of us can testify to being controlled at times by our feelings. If we are to make any change in our behaviour, we must learn to act independently of our Child ego state at times.

The child ego state:

The Child ego state is usually viewed as fixed from the time we are about 5 or 6 years old.

	Positive attributes	Negative attributes
NATURAL CHILD	Free	Selfish
	Fun loving	Hurtful
	Creative	Stubborn
	Authentic	Disobedient
ADAPTED CHILD	Polite	Overly compliant
	Well mannered	Fearful
	Self- controlled	Suppressed
	Obedient	Bound up

Strokes for folks

Strokes can be defined as any act implying the recognition of another person's presence.

Some friends come round for dinner. As the door opens, everyone smiles.
– stroke one; non-verbal.

The entrance is filled with friendly phrases: 'Good to see you'; 'So glad you could come'; 'Hey, you look great'; 'I like your haircut'.
– stroke two; verbal.

Once the flowers and wine have changed hands, gratitude and friendship is expressed physically; the guys hug, the girls kiss, the guys kiss the girls.
– stroke three; physical.

Rene Spitz, 1887-1974, was a medical consultant working with young institutionalised children in 1945. Spitz observed that although physically well cared for they suffered a much higher incidence of physical and emotional difficulties than their non-institutionalised contemporaries. His research concluded that the lack of sensory stimulation, normally given by parents, was the cause. Effectively, they suffered from a form of emotional deficiency, or deprivation.

Spitz demonstrated that physical and non-physical forms of recognition are essential building blocks of human development. Other researchers affirmed his initial findings, and that strokes are a fundamental need within us all. Berne referred to this as 'recognition hunger'.

'Stroke me!'

TA is built on the conclusion that strokes are vital. Although positive strokes are best, negative strokes are better than no strokes at all. If there are no strokes, our communication fails to accomplish a 'Transaction' and consequently breaks down. What is more significant, without strokes, a person will feel lonely, isolated and rejected. Besides the obvious disadvantage of one's mental health being damaged, the effect, as Spitz demonstrated, can also be physical.

In the commercial world, the implications are enormous. People will lack rapport, motivation, emotional energy, creativity, and any sense of reward beyond fiscal remuneration. There will also be a higher incidence of sickness, job mobility due to dissatisfaction, and negative behaviour. Let's create a scenario.

> On Monday, you arrive at work and greet your neighbour: 'Hi, John, how are you?' He replies: 'Great, good to see you.' These positive verbal strokes make communication good, and the pair of you are both happy.
>
> On Tuesday, you repeat the greeting – same words, tone, body language. This time John looks up, frowns, and looks down again. This is a negative non-verbal stroke.
>
> On Wednesday, John ignores you completely, not even bothering to look up. You have received no strokes. Now, because we all need them, you may end up feeling deprived.

Each day's response will produce certain feelings in you. Because the event first passes through our thought process, which is influenced by our temperament, we may all interpret the event differently, arriving at various conclusions. What would be your conclusion from each of the different responses?

Positive strokes

These are the best! We like them a lot, but they have to be within the protocols of our culture and Temperament preferences. (An Englishman with a high C temperament may well struggle with a triple kiss greeting from a Russian, whose high I Temperament causes him to add back-slapping and cheek-pinching into the encounter!)

Smiling is a powerful positive stroke. All salespeople are well aware of this. Three thousand years ago, King Solomon advised his citizens to use smiling as a means of making contact and creating well being during social interactions.

Handshakes, in non-oriental cultures, should be far more than either knuckle-crushing experiences or cold, dead fish encounters. Firm, friendly, and positive, they communicate acknowledgement, acceptance, sometimes agreement, and a measure of equality. Barristers in Britain will never be seen to shake hands in public for fear of sending a message that they are doing deals in the matter of justice – it is a taboo of their profession. Handshakes can and should be significant positive strokes.

Hugs and embraces are, thankfully, becoming commonplace within British culture. The very language of opening one's arms signifies acceptance and the embrace communicates warmth and intimacy. It implies trust, too. Some psychologists have calculated that for the best emotional health we all need up to seven hugs per day.

Simple words of affirmation, support, recognition, acclaim, compliments and gratitude are all positive verbal strokes. Just pausing to think how much pleasure, security and motivation we derive from these inexpensive but valuable recognitions should inspire us to show greater generosity to others through these means.

Positive strokes provide us with significance and self-worth. They take two forms.

Unconditional positive strokes

'I think you're fantastic!'
'I so enjoy your company.'
'I appreciate you for who you are.'

These kinds of strokes emanate from our experience of nurturing parents; those who show unconditional love and acceptance.

Conditional positive strokes

'You played that piano piece so well, I really enjoyed it.'
'You hit your target, you deserve your bonus.'
'You tell those jokes with immaculate timing.'

These tend to emanate from the Critical Parent. Note that such communications have their validity in our lives. The idea that the Critical Parent is a bad ego state should be firmly rejected. Each ego state has its value and contribution.

Negative strokes

How can negative strokes be better than none at all? Think of the child deprived of strokes. They often display bad behaviour because, although not as good as pleasure, pain is better than no recognition at all. Parents sometimes remark that their child misbehaves simply to attract attention. What the child instinctively wants is the significance that comes from recognition.

During my childhood, my parents owned a hotel. Everybody was so busy running it that I was left to my own devices. I quickly learned how to get their attention in order to generate my own strokes! The balance of strokes we received in childhood is the one with which we feel most comfortable in adulthood because it is familiar. That same naughty child might be quite happy to have his boss shout at him. At least he is being noticed.

Negative strokes also have two forms.

Unconditional negative strokes

'I hate you.'
'No matter how hard you try, you will never be accepted in this organisation – your face just doesn't fit.'

These are the worst of all because their pain has no purpose except to motivate forgiveness and tell us to move on. I mention them because the impact they have on someone's life often programmes them to inflict this sort of abuse on others. As Trustworthy Advisers, there is no place for them at all within our repertoire.

Conditional Negative Strokes

'You failed to play as I asked, so you're off the team.'
'You missed the quota, that means no bonus this quarter.'
'You were late. That doesn't impress me.'

We may not like these kinds of strokes but they are essential for our personal development and career improvement. We will all have experienced them in our childhood and provided they were mixed with a good measure of unconditional nurturing, they will have been valuable.

We all need strokes and we all ensure that we receive them. The quality and the quantity required by our ego are dependent not just on childhood conditioning but also Temperament. The high 'I' temperament thrives on recognition and fears rejection, no matter what their family background.

Transactions

I smile, you smile back – that's a transaction. I ask a question, you reply – that's another transaction.

Transactions occur when I communicate and you respond. Those actions are termed 'Stimulus' and 'Response'. The transaction is only completed when the stimulus has evoked a response.

'What is the biggest challenge you face right now?' Stimulus.
'How to reduce costs.' Response. Transaction completed.
'How do you plan to do that?' Stimulus.
'By outsourcing our design work.' Response. Transaction completed.

A transaction can be defined as a unit of social discourse consisting of a stimulus and a response. Each transaction contains two opportunities for giving recognition i.e. strokes. 'Communication' is therefore a series of 'transactions'.

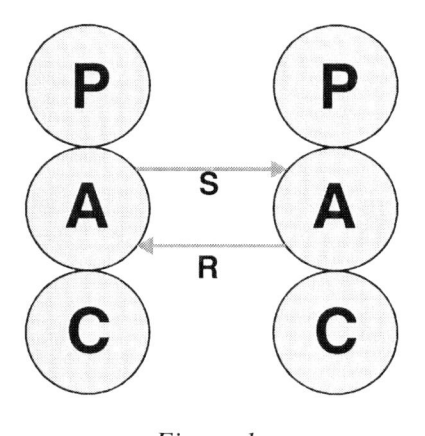

Figure 1

Figure 1 depicts each of the transactions described above. We are both communicating from our Adult ego state. These transactions are therefore successful. Cognitively and emotionally the two parties connect. They are on the same wavelength. Wavelength is the key to effective communication.

In each of the following diagrams, the person on the left makes the initial communication i.e. stimulus. Before looking at them, let's familiarise ourselves with the terminology.

Ego State:	Parent, Adult, Child.
Positive Stroke:	Word or action acknowledging a person in a positive manner.
Negative Stroke:	Word or action acknowledging a person in a negative manner.
Transaction:	Word or action that evokes a response.
Transactional Vectors:	Lines between ego states that represent stimulus and response.

Complimentary Transactions

These exist when the transactional vectors (the S and R lines) are parallel. This means the ego state that responds is the one that was addressed. There are nine potential complementary transactions. Another example can be seen in figure 2.

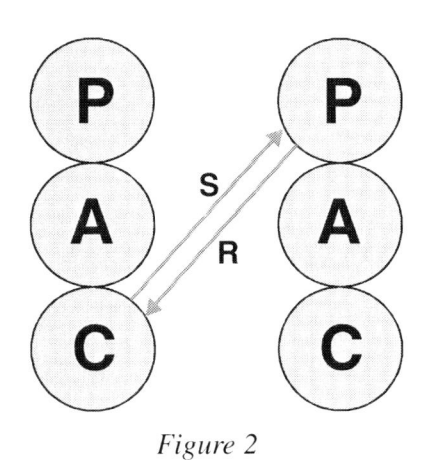

Stimulus: sad face, looking for sympathy. 'I'm shattered. That was such a demanding itinerary.' Child to Parent.

Response: arm around shoulder and led over to the sofa, 'There there, put your feet up while I bring you a large whisky.' Parent to Child.

Good communication will continue as long as the transaction vectors remain parallel. The critical issue is that the correct ego-state responds.

Figure 2

Crossed Transactions

This is where the problem arises! A crossed transaction is when the vectors are not parallel or when the ego-state that responds is not the one that was addressed.

In figure 3 'have you seen my car keys?' is the Adult to Adult stimulus.

'Why can you never remember where you put things?' is the Parent to Child response. This forces me into the Child ego state. That response equalled, 'You silly little boy!'

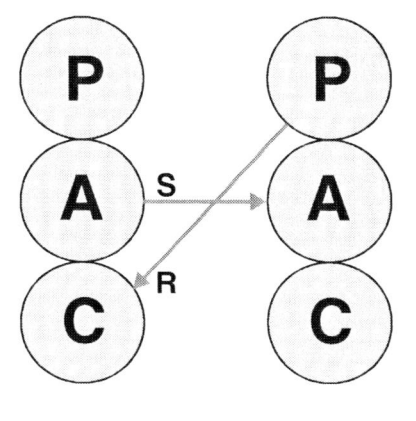

Figure 3

The vectors have crossed and now I'm cross!

There are 72 potential crossed transactions; the most common is where an Adult to Adult stimulus experiences a Parent to Child or a Child to Parent response.

Muddled Transactions

This is a non-technical term to describe a problem we often encounter. The Transactions can appear crossed between the Parent and Child ego states because each state has two dimensions.

I drink my whiskey, take a hot bath and return with a sad face, registering a bit of pain. I flop onto the sofa. 'My shoulders are really knotted up. Any chance of a massage?'

Susi looks down, gives me a pitying smile, and in a mocking tone says, 'You must be joking, I've got my horticultural course. Dinner's in the oven.'

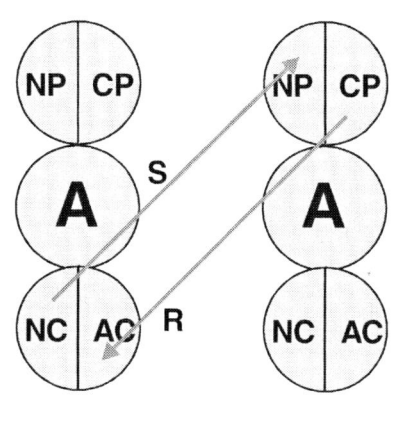

Figure 4

This is fig 4. My stimulus was Natural

Child to Susi's Nurturing Parent. Her response was Critical Parent to my Adaptive Child. The unspoken words still come out as: 'You silly little boy!'

The Transactional Vectors are clearly parallel but the Transaction is muddled. The wrong half of the appropriate ego state responded to the wrong half of the one that made the stimulus. This is common when the party receiving the stimulus makes a judgment about the other party. In this case, I appeared self-pitying and was over-milking her sympathy.

So what happens as a Trustworthy Adviser when you get a client who is in Critical Parent ego state, forcing you into your Child where you don't want to go? This is where 'open questions' come in. If the adult asks the questions carefully, it will help to bring the client from the Critical Parent into the Adult ego state, which is where you want them to be. Avoid responding from the Adapted Child. This may well be the reason for the Critical Parent stimulus.

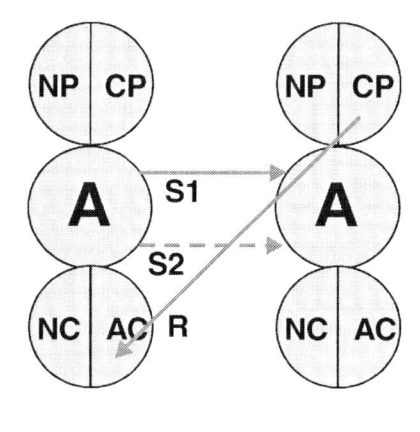

Figure 5

Remember that not only words, but tone of voice, body language, and mood will all communicate your response. Whenever a crossed transaction occurs, one or both people have to change ego-state for communication to resume.

> In Figure 5, Stimulus 1: 'Whom do you partner with at the moment to deliver your solutions?'
>
> Response: 'You have no right to ask me who my partner is, besides they have just let me down and it is none of your business.'
>
> Stimulus 2: 'I am sorry, you obviously feel very strongly about that. My question was because we currently work with several of your partners. What do you suggest is the best way forward?'

This open question calls for a thought through answer rather than a knee jerk reaction. As long as the body language, tone and mood are congruous with the Adult ego state, you have delivered strokes and you will get the desired result.

Know the Wavelength

I was recently talking to a very successful 65-year young chairman of a global group of companies. During a discussion on the value of understanding the different temperament styles, he said, 'You know, you really irritated me. You know I have a big ego, and yet you gave me no credit for the in-depth knowledge and understanding I have on this topic. Had it been someone else, I would have switched off.'

During our transaction, I had communicated from the wrong ego state, not giving him the positive strokes he was seeking. I managed to retrieve the situation but that transaction taught me a great deal about the two of us. As a Trustworthy Adviser, it is still easy to make these mistakes and we need to learn the art of communication recovery.

All three-ego states are important to a healthy well-balanced person. It is the job of the Adult ego state to keep the other two in balance but wouldn't it be boring if we were stuck in the Adult forever?

If we are to be successful as Trustworthy Advisers, much of our time will need to be spent in the Adult state, with excursions into the other two at the correct time and in the appropriate way. Many people grow up spending too much of their time in one particular ego state. Others frequently respond from the wrong one to the wrong one. This is what makes us both different and interesting. It is also a feature of what can cause us to be attracted to some people and repulsed by others. A Trustworthy Adviser has to overcome these superficial judgments and seek to be consistent, wise and thoughtful in their responses, and constructive in their communication stimuli.

Hopefully, this brief introduction to Transactional Analysis will enable you to get on the same wavelength as your clients and ensure that you both spend most of your commercial encounters enjoying effective communication.

SECTION 7

INFLUENCE

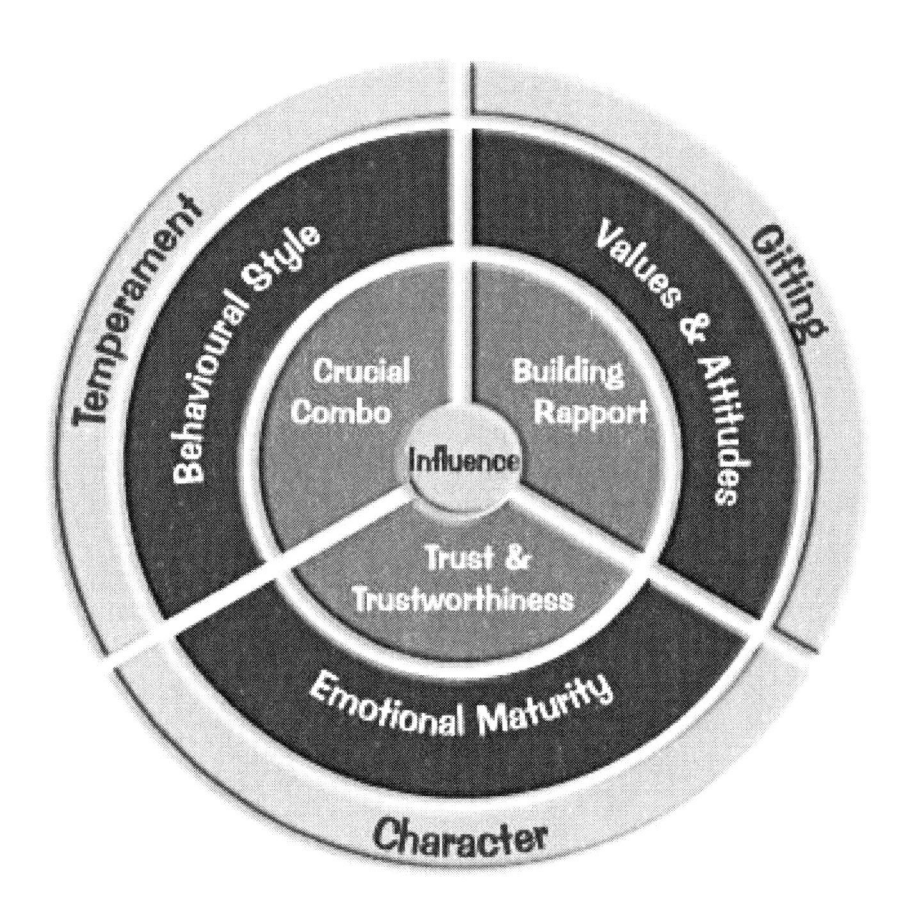

It seemed that from day one, Charlie just had that special something. He had an influence over others, that extra edge of persuasion. It manifested itself first at his nursery school and later in the infants' school. If Charlie said: 'Let's build a Lego giant', it was an appealing project. When others said it, the idea seemed to lack vision; if it did get started, it would certainly never be finished.

If Charlie suggested behaving like dogs, within minutes the entire room would soon be full of canine noise and behaviour; everyone spontaneously joining in, as though they were programmed to participate once a behavioural prompt had been triggered.

Charlie wasn't the most dramatic, or imaginative child. Neither was he the biggest, or the brightest. At times he seemed to lead, at others he just wanted a single comrade to play along with. Yet somehow, whatever he wanted others to do, he found someone who felt it was an enormous privilege to do it with him. He had no need to bully, demand, shout, threaten, or bribe. Charlie just plain had influence, even before he could spell the word. He could effectively persuade without seeming to even try. His mild suggestions seemed to work like 'Jedi mind tricks' on those with lesser mental strength. Charlie had high impact skills without knowing it. What he subsequently did with them would be a matter of choice.

- What do we mean by influence?
- Can we acquire the aspects of influence?
- Is it all just a matter of charisma?
- Defining the skills of personal persuasion.

Whether we are managing or motivating, selling or strategising, merging or marketing, we need to influence everyone with whom we interact. What we are seeking is not hierarchical obedience to leadership, nor is it blind agreement to wacky ideas, but fully cognitive and emotionally energised commitment. Gaining that agreement is the **process of persuasion**; achieving the emotional 'Buy in' is the **effect of influence**.

What do we mean by 'Influence'?

The Oxford English Dictionary defines Influence as; *'The capacity to have an effect on the character or behaviour of someone or something'*.

Daniel Goleman in his excellent book; *'Working With Emotional Intelligence'*, rightly refers to 'The Arts of Influence' and demonstrates conclusively that without the emotional competencies associated with influence we cannot possibly hope to achieve our objectives whenever they involve human interaction.

Robert B. Cialdini's textbook work *'Influence'* develops six fundamental forms of influence, scientifically and practically demonstrating their power and method. I am indebted to both these authors for their insights and thorough analysis of this subject.

Influence could be described as: *'The ability to get people to do what you want'*. That sounds appealing to some and appalling to others! The essential difference between domination and service lies in your attitudes. The difference between manipulation and collaboration lies in your motives. A right attitude will be expressed through humility and a right motive through co-dependency.

Niccolo Machiavelli, 1469-1527, gave his name to the dubious political art of using absolute power to cleverly ensure that people always did what you wanted. He started from the premise that people were wicked and therefore needed powerful, even ruthless, leaders to protect them from themselves. He was the original political theorist and probably the inspiration for what later came to be known as Fascism. His systems of government were devoid of morality, lacking any respect for others. Today we call all forms of deceitful, manipulative scheming: 'Machiavellian'. However, getting others to do what we want need not imply the forming of a Machiavellian plot. We should no more be afraid of attempting to influence others than we should be seeking to control them.

Can we acquire the skills of influence?

Clearly some individuals are more persuasive than others. Landslide political victories are often won by leaders capable of inspiring complete strangers to believe that their lives will be made better, and their aspirations achieved, simply by voting for them. They exercise greater powers of persuasion. Some salespeople communicate a sense of privilege to their customers when they buy the product or service on offer.

From the standpoint of an observer, we can see those who have charm, good looks, an easy manner, who speak lucidly, smile naturally and ooze charisma. Such people may well accomplish quick results and generally leave a good impression, yet it is often the case that a persuasive individual exercises very little real influence, whereas one who is influential will also be persuasive, although perhaps less dynamic in their style.

This definition, which is a composite of several dictionaries, reveals four things.

Persuasion: the process of providing sound reasons for others to believe or do something.

1. Persuasion is not a command/obey mechanism.
2. Persuasion must require some degree of patience and perseverance.
3. Persuasion is essentially cerebral; an intellectual exercise.
4. Persuasion need not involve relationship, or lead anywhere else.

What we see here is the different nature of influence and how it affects those seeking to become Trustworthy Advisers.

Influence: having an effect, impact or sway over the thoughts and actions of others. Providing guidance, leadership, and agency.

1. Influence is persuasive, but not simply through cogent argument.
2. Influence has a broader remit than dealing with a single issue.
3. Influence has continuity.
4. Influence need not require the initiator's presence in order to be effective.
5. Influence connects with the motives and feelings, as well as the intellect.

In social terms, it would be true to say that European civilisation has been influenced by Christianity for the past two millennia, for example, but clearly not all Europeans have been persuaded to accept Christian beliefs. The same is true of many corporations in which the influence of the leader, or founder, is felt in their absence or even after their departure. Virgin has a value of enjoyment and fun derived from the personality of their founder, Richard Branson. British Airways, by contrast, is sober and staid. Branson's influence is likely to continue for decades after his retirement; it is now a part of the corporate identity.

The good news is that you do not have to be the founder or leader in order to exercise influence. Nor is it essential to have a dynamic personality. Social scientists have identified various forms of influence, all of which can be learned and judiciously applied.

There are seven aspects of influence that are invaluable in facilitating the mature relationship that a Trustworthy Adviser enjoys with their clients.

The seven aspects of influence

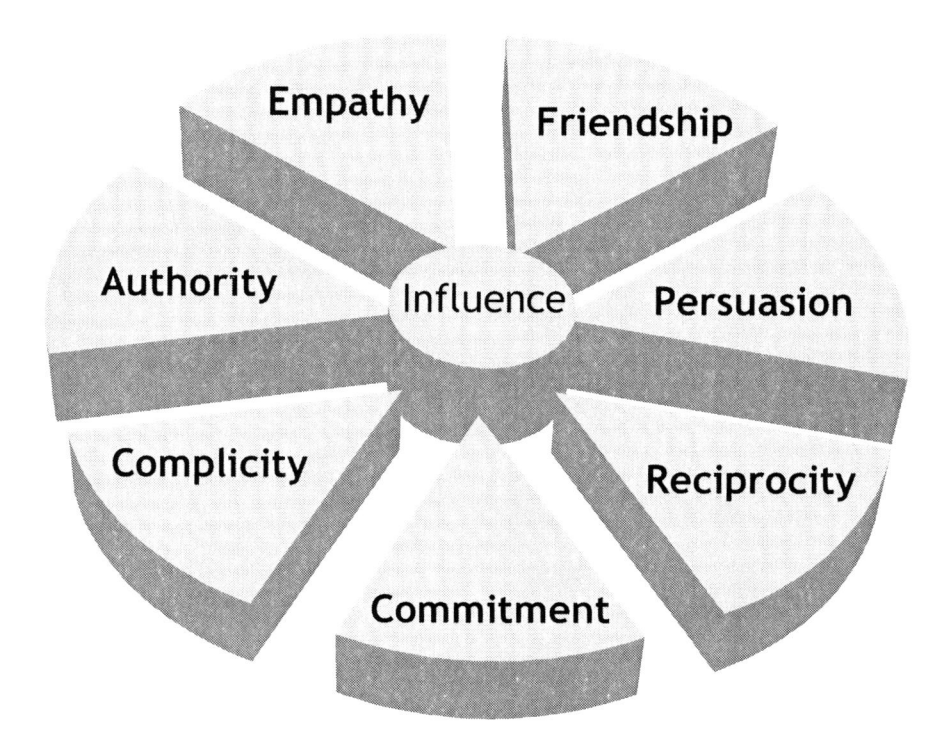

- Empathy
- Friendship
- Authority
- Influence
- Persuasion
- Complicity
- Reciprocity
- Commitment

16

EMPATHY, EMPATHY, EMPATHY

- The 1st and most crucial element of influence
- How to lose by winning
- Diverse definitions
- Demystifying this skill
- A practical exercise
- Everyone a client

In ancient architecture, the cornerstone was the vital part of a building. It ensured that the whole construction was true and would hold strong. If the cornerstone were made of inferior material, the stresses would ultimately pull the structure apart. Properly in place, however, the cornerstone guaranteed that the building was robust and would remain upright.

Empathy is the cornerstone of influence. Without it, we are left with a derelict group of practices that consist of either domination, or manipulation. These would yield only short-term results, and are no basis for winning and maintaining trust. Besides any moral considerations, they fail to produce long-term success. Empathy builds people together. It also ensures that when employing the aspects of influence, we use that which is appropriate. Inappropriate influence will actually have the reverse effect.

Winning the points, losing the deal

Let's suppose that a client already views you as their 'Preferential supplier'. Whether you sell equipment, ideas, your professional time – whatever the field – you are his first choice. However, his initial thinking about any new development is done without you.

Your goal is to raise your status to that of Trustworthy Adviser. This unique business relationship will enable your client to think broader and more deeply, make better strategic plans, and benefit from your exclusive attention and creative input. You have his respect and in some measure his trust. What you are looking to do is grow your influence.

An opportunity for business arises at the client's request. You thoroughly research his needs, obtain some insightful advice from other sources, and feel sure of your ground. This could well prove to be the watershed that achieves the paradigm shift in attitude towards the nature of your service.

You feel confident that you know this client's Temperament, the beliefs that shape his values and attitudes, and how the individual is wired. You have good rapport; usually getting just the right balance of friendship and facts, vision and agenda. However, at this meeting things are different.

The client seems unsure, uncharacteristically vacillating between the sound advice you offer, and his own original thoughts, which have become muddled with anxieties. The conversation starts to follow a loop.

You patiently examine all his objections, systematically demolishing each one of them in the nicest possible way! Respectfully, you explore the ramifications of his ideas, leading him to conclude that they are second best. You invite the client to take ownership of your advice, consider its likely outcome and judge for himself the benefits to be derived. You draw out his contributions, generously acknowledge them, show appreciation and build to a conclusion. Not as you expected, but a result nevertheless.

Later you receive a terse email (not uncommon!) to say they will not be proceeding. Later still, you hear they have engaged a competitor. Why?

You won all the points but lost the deal. You also lost that opportunity to advance your status to that of Trustworthy Adviser. The research was thorough, the presentation first class, your knowledge of the client and his business was commendable. Yet you still failed to influence him. When it really counted, your skills lacked impact.

On that day, almost uniquely for him, your client did not need closure on anything. What he required was a sounding board, without prejudice and without agenda. It was that rare moment when rational thought, goal setting, and visionary foresight held no appeal. Success, for once, was not on the client's horizon. The highest impact skill he needed on that day was the acceptance of his right to a temporary paralysis of decisiveness. A commitment that allowed him to just be below par for twenty-four hours.

One could speculate as to the causes of his problem. Sometimes, even those we know intimately, prefer to keep personal things to themselves until they feel we have demonstrated sufficient interest in them to deserve a candid disclosure of their feelings and difficulties. In other words: we have to earn it. Crucial in this scenario, was the ability to discern the immediate need of the client. Failure to do so meant you won all the points but lost the deal. You also lost the client. He was simply aggravated by your persistence. The crucial skill required was not persuasion, but *empathy*.

Diverse definitions

Empathy has been described as *'understanding and entering into the feelings of another'*. I prefer not to attribute that definition because I would argue that it is inadequate. Empathy is far more than feelings and it is highly practical besides. One could argue that it is as 'hard' a skill as numeracy and as evidential as the ability to read. Because it has so many applications, it is capable of a diversity of definitions. The following analysis of 12 facets of empathy, and what it means to empathise, is limited to commercial applications, especially those with relevance to becoming a Trustworthy Adviser. It is not presented as an exhaustive examination of this skill.

1. Sensing the feelings of others

Having the competency to be in touch with the feelings of another person through one's own feelings. This is often achieved intuitively but that does not mean it is an emotional equivalent of clairvoyancy. We sense people's feelings by having registered in our lives that certain vocal tones, facial expressions, body language and mannerisms indicate particular feelings. As we observe them in those with whom we interact, there is a neurological short cut that puts us in touch, without having to go through the laborious routine of questioning, analysing, and remembering.

Very small signs can indicate a great deal to those with highly attuned empathetic skills. Even variations in the length of time between questions and answers can reveal feelings. Empathy is about sensing what is being transmitted without being vocalised.

2. Taking the emotional temperature

We all have feelings about things. Empathy includes the skill of recognising if others are cool towards an idea, or hot about it. The same is true of news they receive, or the way in which a new person is introduced to a team or meeting.

We may not know the reason for the feelings, or even be too sure exactly what those feelings are, but we have taken the temperature. We discern a change and can tell if it is of a positive or negative nature. This informs us to be watchful, discreet, cautious, but not timid.

3. Showing tact

Empathetic people recognise discomfort and sensitivity within others over issues and situations. They respond accordingly and show thoughtfulness about what they say, how their remarks are framed, and the degree of gravity or humour that is appropriate.

This is more than simply wanting to avoid offence: it is based on a true assessment of the feelings, values and attitudes of another, leading to deliberate choices and behaviours.

4. Being genuinely interested

Politicians do not kiss babies because they are tender hearted towards infants! Their interest is in the adult vote and the public impression they give. Genuine interest in others is expressed through being totally focused on them during interactions, making a point of remembering their issues, asking questions about what keeps them awake and where the pain is in their working day.

Empathetic people display a concern that goes beyond simply providing a solution. The client is a person with issues, not a prospect in need of a product. The empathetic leave people feeling valued, not just another project.

5. Discerning another's perspectives

By listening carefully, observing thoroughly, and remembering accurately, the empathiser will go beyond recording the client's ideas and preferences, to the place of 'seeing where they are coming from'. This is one of those highly empathetic phrases that has entered and enriched the English language in recent years. It reflects a growing desire and ability to appreciate that we each have our own perspectives on almost every subject.

To discern another's perspectives does not mean that we share, or even understand, them. It means that we recognise the impact those perspectives have on the issue at hand and are therefore able to take them into account.

6. Demonstrating support for ideas

Generally speaking, empathy is expressed by being supportive, encouraging, affirming, inclusive and upbuilding. It involves us in taking the time and trouble to comment favourably and show appreciation. The crux of this is the person, not the value of their contribution.

Self-worth is built up by showing the significance of the individual through the recognition of his or her thoughts. Even when we profoundly disagree, there is an empathetic way of doing so that will provide other people with a dignified way of giving up their viewpoint.

7. Recognition of motives

Empathy takes us behind the plans and schemes to the underlying forces that drive people. The chapter on Values and Attitudes is designed to enable you to identify those aspects of human makeup that are responsible for shaping our motives. To develop this skill, there is no substitute for asking questions like 'Besides making a profit on this, what other objectives do you want to fulfil?'

Reasonable, gently probing inquiries enable us to check their responses against what we feel to be the case. Obviously there is no guarantee we will always be told the entire truth, or even that the other parties are entirely in touch with their own motives. However, time will out, and we learn to use this gift by observing its effectiveness. One note of caution is appropriate here – we must never use our skill at recognising motives to become accusative or suspicious. The client must always be honoured.

8. Serving their objectives

Empathetic individuals will not content themselves with knowing the motives, but are concerned to enable their clients to achieve their goals. Success is measured in the fulfilment of the plans of others. Empathetic people therefore do not force their agenda onto others but draw out the dreams and wishes, offering ideas that enable the other party to develop a strategy. This is more than just agreeing to help. Empathizers embrace the motivational drive and personal perspective of their clients and add those to the overall mix of objectives.

When NASA set out to put an American on the moon, it was more than a technological project. The NASA leadership knew that there were political and emotional agendas connected with the national pride of their masters. Keeping in tune with it all was essential if the vast investment in research and development were to be maintained.

9. Intuiting the thoughts of others

Empathy involves getting inside the other persons' shoes. It is about their feelings, motives, longings and thinking. We need to know if someone's thoughts are anxious, muddled, selfish, desperate, clear, constructive, principled, and everything else! This is about listening for consistency as much as logic. It requires observing the manner of communication as well as the content. It demands our attention and analysis, as well as tuning into our gut feelings.

This is not about mind games but about that which is communicated between people every day without any attention to the process. It is largely about watching for reactions and responses to what is said and done. The slightest movements of eyes and mouths can deliver more eloquent expressions of inner thoughts than many carefully worded statements.

10. Empathizers anticipate problems

Being empathetic is more than inter-personal. It includes interacting with groups, organisations and the future. Those with empathetic skills are able to consider the impact of issues on others and identify the difficulties. This is not about pessimism but about exploring the effects of events yet to occur, by reference to one's knowledge of people.

When the British government awarded an annual increase in the state pension of 75pence per week, it led to a national outcry. It appeared that no one in the cabinet had been able to predict the likely response. The nation was astounded that the government expected to escape severe criticism. We will have to wait the statutory 30 years before we will know if the entire cabinet was without an empathetic voice!

11. Sensitive to the needs of others

Empathetic people feel what others need. This may mean reassurance, or encouragement, direction, or a friendly ear. There is no 'one-size-fits-all' for those with empathetic dispositions. Each person is an individual and their lives are complex, therefore needs vary according to situations, seasons and personal circumstances. Empathy expresses itself in recognising particular needs and seeking to fulfil them.

12. Empathetic people are considerate
This is especially true when individuals are struggling and encountering difficulty, or opposition. Encouragement is more than the proverbial kick up the backside; it has to have persuasive and rational elements. General Custer encouraged his troops to believe they were invincible under his command. His degree of influence was based on authority and his reasoning proved to be fatally irrational. Empathy is considerate. This means it weighs up the issues a person faces and evaluates the reasonableness of their concerns.

Empathy is far more than feeling what another feels, because this skill is not about the abandonment of the thought processes. It is about the full deployment of cognitive reasoning allied to emotional intelligence and good observational skills.

Empathy is not mystical!

Half the list of empathetic characteristics detailed above are practical. Empathy cannot simply be regarded as 'useful if you have it'. It is the core skill for exercising influence. Unfortunately, there are those who prefer to believe that any form of emotional intelligence is outside their realm. Usually this is just an excuse for being lazy!

It is true that empathy is a skill used more frequently by women. However, recent reports on the performance of senior female managers show as great a lack of empathy as that displayed by the previous generation of only-male executives. The evidence tends to suggest that the sheer effort of achieving equality, plus the stress experienced at the top level of leadership, have caused some female executives to deny, or neglect, their emotional skills. Both sexes are equally capable of this error.

Although empirical evidence suggests that women use empathy more than men, the reasons are unclear. Social history indicates that emotional, especially intuitive, skills are developed more among those groups experiencing various forms of deprivation, prejudice and disadvantage.

Research shows that men's empathy increases as the feelings of others become more evident. There is nothing to support the idea that men are either lacking in empathy, or unable to express it. The greatest barrier to the development of this skill is fear – fear of vulnerability and appearing weak.

Yet all the evidence points to empathy in men bringing about popularity, especially with women, increased success, and inner strength.

Unfortunately, some men who recognise their own deficiency in this competency assert that it is primarily a feminine characteristic. They even go so far as to defend their own deficiency by turning it into a virtue. How often do we hear the statement: 'I can't be bothered with all that touchy-feely stuff. What I believe in is straight talking and plain facts.' However, when we enter the inner world of another person's feelings, we become far more able to talk straight and present facts in a way that is persuasive, inoffensive and influential. We get the job done with minimum conflict.

Empathy is not a mysterious science. It is a skill that can be developed. By practicing the principles of this competency we can develop the inner responses that lead to the outer behaviours. This might mean a rather wooden, or mechanistic start, as you shed the taboos of a lifetime, which have prevented this competency from being allowed to develop. For some it means allowing your feelings to exercise a little more authority within your responses and relationships. Adjusting to a more people-oriented perspective is a skill that becoming a Trustworthy Adviser entails.

What went wrong?

Let's return to that client who went to a competitor. His decision was not due to a complete failure to show empathy. Understanding his business needs and motives, the meticulous efforts of research, and patience with his prevaricating mood, all showed an empathetic approach. The weakness was caused by your personal agenda, which obscured your vision of his emotional need. You failed to get on his wavelength.

The passion for presenting our own creative thoughts, the pleasure at having all the winning arguments, and the satisfaction of business success can often prevent asking simple, unobtrusive questions that will tell us how to behave. In the face of someone acting out of character, it is not inappropriate to ask: 'You obviously have a good reason for not wanting to make a decision about this. Have I missed something here, or is there an issue I need to take into account?'

A demanding question, allowing the possibility that you may be at fault, combined with empathetically showing that your attention is focused on the client, not the project, enables them to respond. In fact, they have no alternative! Perhaps a family pet died the night before, or their daughter received bad exam results that morning, or they need to let go some staff. Whatever the cause for being below par, they are likely to give you the reason because they see by your empathy that it affects you too. They also feel secure about doing so because there is no impatience, bluster, hostility or accusation in your manner. The deal is still there for the winning, but on another day. What should take place is the deepening of your relationship and the bonding of mutual trust, not the loss of it.

An exercise in developing empathetic skills

- Think of a person you find difficult.
- Think about how they spend their time and money.
- Why do you suppose they make those choices?
- Now visualise them doing something they enjoy.
- Suspend your judgements of that activity.
- Begin to see it from their perspective.
- Try to actually feel the pleasure they derive.
- Consciously put yourself into their clothes, their car, their home.
- Remember their pet phrases and facial expressions. How do these help them relate to their world?
- Visualise their gestures and body language, asking what it is they aim to communicate by them.
- Now explore how they might feel about your style and manner.

During this exercise you may well experience annoyance, even anger, if this person really gets under your skin. Stick with it! The aim is not to identify that which offends you and why, but to momentarily put yourself into that person's shoes and become that person.

If you can begin to do this with someone you don't love, possibly don't even like, you can quite easily begin to do it with those you respect, admire and appreciate. It works like athletes in training. They put on extra clothing, heavier shoes, and sometimes take a backpack with weights in it. As they build muscle and stamina by training in false conditions of hardship, it becomes easy and joyful to exert themselves in the conditions of an event.

You may think of other exercises you wish to add to this list. The value of regularly putting yourself into the shoes of another person is that quite soon it starts to become easier – just like physical exercises.

Empathy is seeing things from the other person's perspective, feeling what they would feel, thinking their thoughts, and entering into their motives and aspirations through understanding their values and attitudes. Empathy leads to connection. Connection grants you influence.

Everyone a client

If you believe that competitive behaviour is the route to success, you will never become a Trustworthy Adviser. Practicing empathy in every commercial situation is crucial – it cannot just be turned on to impress. Any discerning individual will see that veneer and penetrate it with devastating results. Many of us will have witnessed corporate heads talking graciously about the environment, the developing world, youth employment, safety at work, and various other egalitarian themes, only to react angrily when an informed shareholder challenges the ethics of company policy. The world is always looking out for those who 'walk the walk' and is quick to pass judgement on the one who simply 'talks the talk'.

Everyone whose working day involves interacting with others is faced with a set of relational choices.

1. Do I use these people to advance my personal goals?
2. Shall I keep my distance and remain aloof?
3. Am I able to win by competing?
4. How much truth shall I tell?
5. Can I find ways of asserting my superiority?

6. Are we team-workers with common objectives?
7. What can I do to build friendship and co-operation?
8. Is there something we can all work to overcome or achieve?
9. Why should I keep any useful information to myself?
10. In which ways can I serve others and help meet their goals?

These ten questions show two vastly differing approaches to the working environment. You could easily double them from just last weeks' experiences, no doubt. The point we need to recognise is that if we regard every colleague, team-worker, employee, supplier and service provider as a client, we will practice empathy throughout the day. We will also apply all the other principles of a Trustworthy Adviser and thereby grow in our character and commercial stature.

It is not possible to reflect the first five questions during the in-house part of our day, and adopt the latter five when dealing with external clients. Besides, for many of us, being a Trustworthy Adviser is primarily, if not exclusively, about our role within the organisation. If I adopt an approach to those whose business I want to win, which differs from my behaviours towards colleagues, the tension will become stressful. I will develop a two-style personality. The longer the empathetic nature is exposed, the more likely I am to make a sudden reversal in order to protect myself when I perceive a threat to this pretence. The solution is consistency.

Your colleague who requires information is a client. Your boss who wants a report is a client. The account department analyst who wants some statistics is a client. The more we appreciate that everyone is a client, the more easily we can practice the skill of empathy and become adroit in its usage.

Empathy is the cornerstone of influence.

It is the primary skill that facilitates the effectiveness of the other six.

Constant practice of the principles along with regular exercises to visualise the inner world of others will enable this competency to develop, grow, and serve you well as a Trustworthy Adviser.

17

PUSHING THE BUTTONS

- Friendship
- Persuasion
- Reciprocity
- Commitment
- Complicity
- Authority

Each of the six aspects of influence listed above is a high impact skill, when appropriately applied. They also have significance to complete strangers whom we meet for the first time because these are proven factors when it comes to the social science of influence.

> '**You cannot antagonise and influence at the same time.**'
> John Knox

We all know that different things work differently for differing people. Each **aspect of influence** is a powerful tool when applied empathetically. For example, someone with an 'I' or 'S' behavioural style is likely to be influenced by those who display friendship and show personal interest in them. Conversely, a strongly individualistic and independent minded 'D' style temperament will not easily be impacted by the fact that lots of other people are employing the same methods. They will probably dismiss that as 'herd mentality' and decide to invent their own unique approach. However, knowing their behavioural style provides insights that, empathetically employed, will enable us to push their buttons.

The second aspect of influence: FRIENDSHIP

Many of our decisions, purchases and plans are made because we feel we like the proposer. A lot of our actions are more to do with who we know than who we are. There are those we want to please and whose approval and acknowledgement mean a lot to us, even though we may have very little in common. This human proclivity for community and belonging is one that drives much of what we do and the way in which we do it.

Being hospitable, warm, generous, smiling a lot, and showing interest in another's welfare, are all aspects of friendship, which is a key element in influencing others. Generally speaking, these actions and attitudes cost us very little, or nothing at all. Yet they are sought after, appreciated, remembered and acclaimed. Their actual value is incalculable; their cost is minimal.

Anyone with a social disposition responds quickly to behaviours that display acceptance, a sense of fun, and genuine warmth. Those who tend to use friendship as their strongest suit in influencing others are themselves more susceptible to this particular art than any other. This is especially so, if it enhances their sense of significance and self-worth.

People need reasons to like others. Some are self-driven, like loneliness, most are responses to what they experience. The same is true of respect. It can be purely hierarchical but generally it derives from inner qualities and skills that we can observe and measure. A Trustworthy Adviser is obliged to provide reasons for being respected and being liked. Being a genuine friend fulfils both of these goals without needing to compromise or become a social chameleon.

Consider the characteristics of a true friend:

- ✓ a person who is not offended by your weaknesses
- ✓ someone who does not need you for your strengths
- ✓ one who is loyal, faithful and consistent
- ✓ a reliable support in times of trouble, difficulty, even crisis
- ✓ one who will not refrain from telling you the truth, even when it hurts
- ✓ someone who is always accepting of you, yet never compromises
- ✓ a person who delights to see you happy and successful
- ✓ one who takes an interest in that which interests you

- ✓ someone who can feel your pain and knows your vulnerabilities
- ✓ a caring, warm and easy manner, never rushing you to deadlines
- ✓ someone with whom there is a chemistry, even after long gaps in contact.

If these attitudes and behaviours are cultivated in your business relationships, you are exercising the second aspect of influence: friendship. Something everyone looks for in those they trust to advise them.

The third aspect of influence: PERSUASION

As has already been stated, persuasion involves our reasoning. Yet we are often persuaded because something about another person just seems to click with us. The ability to persuade may depend on calculated and structured methodology, it may also be an emotional ability to connect with the aspirations of others at a deeper level and engage with them emotionally.

Passion is persuasive

> During their 1997-2001 period of office, the Labour Party of Great Britain worked hard at appearing plausible, economic managers. The press often enjoyed putting the speeches of John Prescott under scrutiny because he not only represented 'Old Labour' but he was renowned for his ungrammatical style and sometimes meaningless syntax. Yet he always got his point across. Prescott could persuade in spite of his muddled language. Some would say it added to his ability to communicate because it conveyed the feeling of his ideas, rather than the mere description of them. Certainly he is a persuader. Prescott's powers of persuasion lie in his passion even though they relate directly to political ideas and practical realities.

It is particularly in the realm of body language and tone of voice that passion comes into play. I am not referring to an inability to control ones feelings, or simply an expression of strong feelings when I speak of passion. Passion is about conviction. A softly spoken and mildly mannered individual like Ghandi exhibited passion through his determination, his dignity, and his self-denial. Yet he was not noted for raising his voice, pounding the table, or abusing his opponents. Passion demonstrates and communicates conviction without being offensive, or unnecessarily confrontational.

People who are totally convinced about the justice of their cause, the superiority of their product, the soundness of their argument, or the value of their service, will influence others by their passion. It may be a light in their eyes or the feeling expressed in their gestures, whatever the means – it will come across. These things add to the logic of their case and give life to the data supporting it.

Passion is vital if we are to carry others with us during a presentation being given after lunch! We call it the graveyard shift because it feels so often like a funeral. That is the best time to introduce a lively speaker, absolutely convinced about the value of his or her material, and devoted to telling the world about it. Passion is also a vital tool of persuasive influence for those whose task it is to convince others that their solutions must be considered thoughtfully. Passion is not impatient – Martin Luther King did not expect full integration overnight – but its conviction gives staying power to the one who possesses it.

Persuasion requires a vision

People need more than a cogent argument in order to be persuaded. Passion alone will vaporise if it has no substance. Persuasion depends on the existence of a vision: something that makes a person's life better in some way. It could be a set of beliefs, a lifestyle change, fresh opportunities, new solutions, or different circumstances. Whatever the subject, it needs to take the form of a vision if it is to gain someone's commitment. People take risks for visions because they are persuaded that on offer is a better alternative than the present reality.

An individual with a vision will usually be passionate and therefore persuasive. The vision of a railway system traversing the nation has inspired investors on many continents and in vastly differing cultures to risk their capital. They required hard facts and sound business projections. They demanded information and systems of accountability and management. Yet their intellectual processes were ultimately swayed by the vision of shrinking a nation and connecting people. There was an emotional connection under-girding the financial implications.

Persuasion involves an appeal

The high achieving 'D' type individual finds new ideas and dynamic solutions appealing. The 'I' type favours that which is impressive and fun. The person with a steady outlook is looking to see other people benefit from new ideas and the 'C' type individual favours that which has clear guidelines and strong disciplines. In order to persuade we have to appeal.

The most significant area of appeal for persuaders is to demonstrate that what is on offer is in the best interests of the party to whom it is offered. That means the best interest from their perspective, which may have nothing whatever to do with selfish motives. For one person, the best interest is satisfied if his or her colleagues feel secure and fulfilled. For another it is the bottom line and for some, performance bonus. The hot buttons will, as we have seen, be determined by behavioural styles, value systems, and perceptual preferences. In order to influence through effective persuasion, we should look to employ genuine passion for our material, offer a vision that speaks of better circumstances for our clients, and to make our rational appeal to their deeper needs for significance, self-esteem, self-worth and lasting value.

The fourth aspect of influence: RECIPROCITY

Studies by anthropologists and sociologist have concluded that this is a rule of human behaviour. People rarely refuse to return favours when asked.

Crudely put, it amounts to 'You scratch my back and I'll scratch yours'. Another phrase we have coined to express this response is 'One good turn deserves another'. Our language expresses our culture and different ethnic groups have these catch phrases to communicate the dynamic of this equation.

We are not simply taught the principle of reciprocity. We actually feel it inside. We have a sense of obligation to those who do us favours. It takes on a moral tone. We also feel there is a deep injustice if our good deeds are not reciprocated when the opportunity is there for the other party to do so. We feel used, even though the idea of a payback was not in our thinking at the time of doing the favour. It feels as though a code has been violated when the traffic of good turns is all one way.

Even when a service is provided freely, there is a tendency for most of us to take the opportunity to reciprocate if one arises. The idea of getting something for nothing is far too simple for us complex human beings! Countless experiments between groups and with total strangers have confirmed that reciprocity is almost a moral obligation to us, and for some people it is so great that they have to outdo the favour, gift or act of kindness. A bizarre form of guilt comes into play with the less secure individual.

By being service-minded, empathetic, responsive to the needs and wishes of others, it is possible to persuade them to take you seriously without specifically asking that they do so. This is the influential power of reciprocity. Some respond because they see it pragmatically as a way of gaining success. Others reciprocate because it seems the right thing to do. One person will respond because they see a chance to build an effective relationship, while another just loves the dynamic of human interaction. Whatever the nature of the motive to reciprocate, it is a proven fact that nearly all of us believe we should. That is why going the second mile for your clients, seeking their benefit first, and not setting limits on your personal investment in their welfare will ultimately be to your benefit as well as theirs. What goes around comes around, in life, in commerce, and in relationships.

> **When I am influenced I am still in control.**
>
> **If I am persuaded, I have made a free-will choice.**
>
> **To do, or become, or accept something, is my decision.**
>
> **My decisions rest on what I believe serves my best interest.**
>
> **To exercise influence is to be wise.**

The fifth aspect of influence: COMMITMENT

Most of us like to be seen as consistent. Once we have made even minor commitments to people or products, the tendency is to take that further, unless strongly deterred from doing so. We also tend to repeat our commitments, whether buying a new car of the same make, choosing the same holiday company, or returning to our solicitor. We feel secure about being consistent.

Many business leaders have schedules that demand quick decisions. Like everyone else, they use shortcuts to make those decisions. One of those shortcuts is to repeat past commitments. It works like this.

> Bill has used Ian's firm as an outside resource. He made no promises to do so again, but the parting words included a non-specific commitment.
>
> Bill: 'That went quite well, I thought.'
>
> Ian: 'Me too. Perhaps we could repeat this, or maybe look at one of our other packages that would fit your organisation.'

Bill: 'That's possible.'
Ian: 'I'll wait to hear from you.'
Bill: 'Fine. I'll be in touch. Many thanks.'

He is neither bound nor obligated: not legally, morally, or relationally. He was just being polite! Nevertheless he feels committed, and that puts Ian ahead of the competition.

A commitment in the present often takes the form of agreeing to allocate time in order to listen to ideas and proposals. Highly motivated individuals like to think they are in control of their time. Therefore, allowing another person to use up some of this valuable resource requires a decision about the likely outcome. In other words, they want to say yes because it justifies their consultation. Those with a 'D' type temperament use previous commitments as a shortcut to making decisions in the present and about the future. Consistency is seen as a wise repetition of a successful decision. Gaining a small commitment from such a person is a major aspect of influence.

When dealing with those who build personal relationships (the 'I' and 'S' temperaments), commitments are of the highest currency. For these people, relationships are the priority. Just a small commitment to make a phone call (they tend to find emails impersonal and lacking in the chemistry to which they normally respond), will often carry through to a larger one about reviewing business or having lunch together.

Brief, simple presentations, totally free of commitments to do business, can lead to gaining the commitment to give feedback. This puts you in the position of being able to reciprocate and offer your assistance without any formal engagement in that role. By going the second mile with your clients, or prospects, you have given them a reason to repeat their earlier commitments and start to employ you. The Trustworthy Adviser role has begun through the fifth aspect of influence: personal commitment.

The sixth aspect of influence: COMPLICITY

School children follow crazes that aren't always programmed by the seasons or expensive advertising campaigns. Even if a campaign costs millions, it will fail if it cannot catch the imagination of the market. Children comply with what they perceive the smart kids are doing, playing and getting their parents to buy.

Teenagers may not dress or talk like their parents, but they do follow closely observed social rules which define their personal interests, and which they want to be associated with. No one who listens to hip-hop would wear Gothic fashions; the two are incompatible and would draw contempt from both camps.

This simple principle is known as compliance. It influences tastes, purchases, fashion, design and leisure spending. By learning how to identify a person's values, attitudes and temperament, one gains insight into the sort of behaviours that they find helpful, and those that are obstructive to doing good business. However, when it comes to influence there is an added bonus to this evaluative skill.

We often learn how to employ these insights by concentrating on those we know. We basically carry a portrait gallery in our minds and subconsciously relate these characteristics to real people. By taking this one step further, we can think in networks. Those networks will exercise powerful influence when they create compliance. And without people even needing to meet one another!

By enabling others to be aware that those they admire and respect are engaging in a particular business activity, you are causing them to be influenced by third parties. When they see, or hear, about people with very similar values, temperaments, attitudes, and personalities to their own, buying specific products and programmes they are impressed by the weight of the testimony. Name-dropping can be crude and arrogant but handled appropriately it effects the influence of complicity.

This is not to suggest that people are essentially shallow, or manipulable. Trustworthy Advisers have to turn their backs on that sort of thinking and behaviour. However, it is an observable phenomenon of adult behaviour that we often think seriously about something if the person engaging with that activity or purchase is one we regard as similar to ourselves. This is complicity at work. However, it does not imply mindless conformity. We do it out of choice, and choices, as we have seen, are made on the basis of what we believe to be in our best interest.

We all have different drives and motives. It might be to succeed, to obtain happiness through relationships, to feel secure about things being right and predictable, to build something lasting, or to live out our ethical code. Whatever the driver or motive, we are inspired when we see someone we respect in that particular sphere acting in a way that we can imitate and embrace.

Compliance to the behaviour of others is the sixth aspect of influence. We do it all the time, quite deliberately, yet often not admitting to ourselves that it really is compliance. Because this is so human a behaviour, and so powerful a motive, it can be employed to guide others into beneficial decisions and actions without in any way denying their personal choices.

The seventh aspect of influence: AUTHORITY

Receiving instruction and showing obedience are expressions of respect. From an early age, we are taught to respect the authority of people in uniforms, those with qualifications, a person with the right looking toolkit, anyone claiming knowledge, experience, learning and a licence.

Trustworthy Advisers need to convey an authority to speak, counsel, and participate in conference. They must show that they are at ease with the subject matter. Their body language has to say; 'I am confident, but not cocky'. Their tone of voice needs to be measured and certain. These are the hallmarks of one who has authority. Handling questions, even hostile ones, has to be done with calm assurance, thoughtfulness, respect, and professionalism. These are the signs of genuine, non-presumptuous, authority.

The impression of individualism can lead to mistrust. It speaks of being a maverick. However, demonstrating a strong-minded rationality engenders confidence. This is particularly helpful for those of a formal disposition, the 'D' and 'C' Temperaments explained in chapter 4.

A steady voice, good eye contact, and a business-like posture with gestures that directly relate to what is being said, all help to communicate authority. None of this is a substitute, however, for knowing one's subject matter!

Concluding Thoughts

Well done! You made it to the end! What now? Put the book on the shelf and carry on as normal? Or choose to think and act differently?

Although now in my fifties, I would attribute most of my important learning to the past fifteen years. It was then that I began to be honest with myself about Ken Buist and his need to do things differently.

Up until then, I always viewed myself as an expert on behaviour. After all, I had already gone through one marriage, and a divorce, which, of course, was entirely my ex-wife's fault. I then went through a long-term relationship, which ended very acrimoniously, but that was all her fault. I had a group of managers who felt intimidated by me and just didn't understand me, and obviously they were at fault. My managing director would not promote me into his position, because he lacked wisdom and discernment. Just how unlucky can one guy get?

Then it hit me. One person was a common factor in all these situations. It occurred to me that perhaps I needed to do something different. Maybe I should change my behaviour. The question was how?

At that time, I discovered the subject of 'temperament'. It caught my imagination and I developed a vision for how this insight, if handled correctly, had the potential to change lives. I immersed myself thoroughly in the topic, reading everything available. Tim LaHaye and Florence Littauer opened up this field of learning for me and were quickly followed by many other authors. I combined these ideas with the Myers Briggs Type Indicators and William Marston's DISC Behavioural Patterns. Eventually my personal quest led me to develop a career in personal development, as a behavioural analyst.

It would not be overstating the case to say a thorough understanding of this topic has been a major contributor to the success of our marriage. This knowledge has taught us to understand and value the diversity between us, helping us improve our communication and deepen our relationship. I have actively taught my children how our natures are different, but not wrong.

Rosie, my eleven year-old daughter, prides her competence at being able to describe the different children in her class. She has learnt to value their diversity and how best to relate with those of different behavioural styles. Looking back on my own childhood, I wish I had understood just a little of this long ago.

Psychologists estimate that temperament is the biggest single influencer of our behaviour. Yet there are many other factors. My experience as a counsellor has privileged me to participate in life-changing events where people have been released from wrong thinking and destructive habits. Counselling is a powerful tool when used properly and effectively.

Each, and every behaviour is preceded by a thought. To simply change behaviour without changing the thinking is to invite frustration and failure. This observation led me to study Cognitive Therapy, Neuro Linguistic Programming, and Gestalt therapy.

The conclusion I reached is that there is no 'magic bullet', which is going to transform your life. Each different system is fascinating and valuable, but individuals need an individual approach. What works well for one, may not necessarily work for others. What I have included in the seven essentials model, are methodologies, which we at TPI and Personal Transformation have consistently observed to offer profound insights and achieve far-reaching results.

Some irrefutable laws

Postmodernism insists that there are no absolute truths. I beg to differ. Both through my personal faith and my observations as a behavioural analyst and counsellor, I have found agreement with those who throughout the centuries have identified and expounded the irrefutable laws of human behaviour. Here are a few worth considering in the quest to become a trustworthy adviser.

1.The major influence on becoming a success is you!
Many things can affect your success. However, personal responsibility is the priority that determines how you develop as a person.

Working for a powerful company with excellent products will make a difference. If sales, profit, and market share improve, that too has an influence. A corporation that believes in developing their people will also have an effect. So can government, the economic climate, and one's immediate colleagues. A good relationship with one's partner and children is another positive influence on personal success. However, nothing and no one compares to the significance **YOU** personally have on your **OWN** success.

By success, I mean having a life in which you feel at peace, contented, fulfilled in what you do, making a difference and an important contribution to that which matters to you, and having quality connections in every sphere of your life. The biggest single influence is **YOU**. Working harder on yourself than on anything else will lead to measurable success.

2. Change your thinking and you will change your life

Ancient scripture states 'as a man thinks in his heart, so he is'. What you think about determines your behaviour and comes to define who you are. If we allow ourselves to become prisoners of negative thinking, we participate in our own downfall. Harbouring thoughts of unforgiveness, bitterness, hatred, revenge and fear will rob us of peace and contentment. They propel us towards a life of constant irritation and frustration.

James Allen's timeless classic *'As A Man Thinketh'* puts it like this:

> 'Man is made or unmade by himself. In the armoury of thought he forges the weapons by which he destroys himself. He also fashions the tools with which he builds for himself heavenly mansions of joy and strength and peace. As a being of power, intelligence, and love, and the lord of his own thoughts, man holds the key to every situation, and contains within himself that transforming and regenerative agency by which he may make himself what he wills.'
>
> (www. Asamanthinketh.net)

Allen wrote in a time when 'man' was used generically and would nowadays be rendered 'people'.

3. Attitude, not circumstances, determines destiny

'Circumstance does not make the man; it reveals him to himself' – James Allen. Two different people can experience the same event and react in a totally different manner due to their attitudes. Every day of our lives we choose those attitudes.

Suppose two people are made redundant. One views it as the end of the world. Their thoughts are dominated by anxieties over the future, their finances, their age, the disloyalty of their employers after so many years of faithful service. Fear of facing their friends isolates them. Resentments build up and produce a paralysis of action.

The other person regards it as a force for good; providing the impetus they needed to finally go and determine their own future. The redundancy settlement provides a cushion to start a new venture. They see opportunities. Life opens up before them.

What is the difference between these two people? Attitude! Now, whose company would you prefer to keep, and which one would you put your money on to earn a living first?

I was on holiday with Susi and my daughter Rosie at Disneyland, Florida. In order to fulfil a speaking engagement, I had to interrupt the holiday and fly from Orlando to Charlotte, South Carolina. I spoke in the morning and in the afternoon listened to W Mitchell.

Mitchell had been a former mayor of Crested Butte, Colorado, a congressional nominee, and had co-founded a $65 million company. He had suffered 65% burns to his face and body in a motorcycle accident. He was now in a wheelchair resulting from a subsequent aeroplane accident. He propelled the chair with the stumps that now served instead of hands. If any man qualified to run all-day self-pity sessions, this was the man.

Yet he was one of the most positive people I have come across. As I listened to him speak, I felt ashamed of my complaining thoughts about my holiday interruption. Mitchell complained about nothing. Quite the opposite, he had written a book entitled: *'Its not what happens to you, it's what you do about it.'* He now devotes his time talking to audiences about taking responsibility for change, and the importance of attitude.

4. Every choice and decision has consequences

These consequences can have far reaching impact. What about the choice of a lifetime partner? Today in the UK, nearly 50% of marriages will fail. The pain for the couple, their children, plus the wider families and friends can last a lifetime. As I write this today, I have just learned of a friend whose wife wants a divorce as they and their fourteen-year-old son cannot get on.

I continually speak to people in coaching sessions who do not enjoy their work. We spend over 40% of our waking lives at work! What a tragedy if we do not enjoy what we do. One friend became an accountant because his father predicted that accountants in the future would run everything. He hated it, and after 15 years decided to change career into something he enjoyed.

Avoid hasty decisions. Seek wise counsel. Our personal bias, even prejudices, can form habitual ways of looking at things, which may not serve our decision-making.

> **'The way of a fool seems right to him but a wise man listens to counsel.'**

One Final Thought

The difference between where you are today and where you will be in five years time is dependent upon 'the relationships you keep, the attitudes you adopt and the books you read'. I hope this book will prove to be a major contributor to you becoming a very successful **'Trustworthy Adviser'**.

Other Services

Lots more:

If you would like more information about

- other personal or organisational development programmes & solutions, a range of unique personal assessments, personal coaching or coach training visit:

  www.personal-transformation.com

- the 'Trusted Adviser Programme' visit:

  www.thetrustedadviser.com

- how to rapidly build trust & rapport - how to assess your perceptual preferences, Visual, Auditory or Kinaesthetic visit:

  www.therapportbuilder.com

Index

Accountability, 35
Accuracy, 42
Acknowledgement, 108, 150
Action, 72
Adapting behaviour, 74
Adapted child, 222
Adapting behaviour, 48, 90
Adult ego state, 221
Anger, 124
Art of asking, 204
Asking questions, 207
Aspirations, 168
Attitudes, 99, 169
Auditory people, 188
Authority, 256
Avoiding greed, 141

'Bad day' traits, 75
Behavioural preferences, 90
  style, 49, 51
Behavioural Style Grid, 53, 75, 101
Behavioural transformation, 51
Being genuinely interested, 240
Beliefs, 168
Benefits of becoming a Trusted Adviser, 30
Berne, Eric, 218
Better connections, 84, 186
Body language, 83, 196
Broken trust, 23

Can we really change? 102
Change catalysts, 145
Change your thinking, 259
Changes in behaviour, 100
Character, 99
  traits, 94, 103
Characteristics of a true friend, 249
Child ego state, 222
Cleese, John, 76
Commitment, 253
Communication, 83, 85, 204
  dos and don'ts, 86
Compliant case history, 81

Compliant temperament, 61
Complicity, 254
Complimentary transactions, 228
Conditional negative strokes, 227
  positive strokes, 226
Consistency, 44
Contractual obligations, 27
Controlling fears, 132
Core set of behaviours, 51
Courage, 113, 155
Credibility, 42
Critical Parent, 220
Crossed transactions, 229
Crucial combination, 212

Daily routines, 25
Day of two halves, 77
Dealing with anger, 124, 127
Decisiveness, 115, 157
Dependability, 39
Destiny, 259
Developing empathetic skills, 245
Discernment, 120, 162
Do you see what I see? 166
Dominant case history, 77
Dominant temperament, 55
Dynamic attributes, 103

Effect of influence, 233
Ego states, 219
Elements of trust, 71
Emotion, 21
Emotional maturity, 93, 94, 101, 121
  temperature, 240
Empathy, 43, 237
Empathy is not mystical! 243
Essence and knowledge, 202
Establishing rapport, 192, 201
Event and process, 69
Everyone a client, 246
Exemplary Listening™, 208
Experience, 168, 171
Extrovert and introvert, 52

263

Fear, 129
  filter, 131
Flexibility, 28
Forgiveness, 106, 148
Formal agreements, 27
Formal and sociable, 52
Fragility, 23
Friendship, 249
Frustrated plans, 126

Gifting, 99
'Good day' traits, 75
Good habits, 145
Greed, 46, 141
Growth agents, 123

Habits, 99, 169
Handshakes, 225
High impact skills, 232
Hippocrates, 50
Honesty, 42, 123, 118, 160
Hostile anger, 125
How are our attitudes formed? 170
Hugs and embraces, 225
Humility, 110, 152
'Humility pill', 139

Imagination, 133
Impact, 238
In-consistency, 44
Individual trust, 22
Influence, 233, 235
  of temperament, 65
Influential case history, 79
Influential temperament, 57
Information or insight? 174
Integrity, 41
Interdependency, 36
Interest in others, 43
Inward expressions, 103
Irrefutable laws, 258

Jealousy, 127
Jung, Carl, 51
Key to good communication, 85
Kinaesthetic people, 189
Kindness, 105, 147

Knowing the wavelength, 216

Learned fear, 129
Leonardo Da Vinci, 173
Lessons of listening, 204
Life is for learning, 178
Listeners, 209
Listening blocks, 211

Marriage, 22
Maturity, 50, 94, 100, 145
Mellowing, 100
Mirroring and matching, 196
Mistrust, 65
Montgomery, Field Marshall, 43
Motives, 241
Muddled transactions, 229
Mutual trust, 21
My world, 196

Natural child, 222
Negative strokes, 226
Neuro-linguistic programming, 196, 203
Nurture, 29
Nurturing parent, 220

Objective element of trust, 71
Objectivity, 119, 161
Obstacles to personal growth, 95
Outgoing and Reserved, 52
Outward expressions, 103
Overcoming fears, 129

Parent ego state, 220
Passion, 250
  and rapport, 176
Passive anger, 125
  attributes, 103
Patience, 111, 153
Peace, 151
Perceptions, 70, 172
Perceptual Preference Questionnaire, 180
Perceptual preferences, 177
Perseverance, 109, 116, 158
Personal development, 33, 94
  growth, 144
  investment, 31
  rapport, 193

Index

Personality, 50, 64, 99
Perspectives, 240
Persuasion, 235, 250
Positive strokes, 225
Pride, 137
Process of persuasion, 233
Professional rapport, 195
Promises, 27

Qualities of successful trusted advisers, 34
Questioning, 205
Quotient, 47

Rapport, 193
Reciprocity, 252
Recognising the temperament of others, 84
Reflection, 72
Relationships, 23, 29, 58
Reputations, 142
Resolving unforgiveness, 134

Security, 198
Self-control, 114, 156
Self-esteem, 139
Self-forgiveness, 38
Self-interest, 45
Selflessness, 45, 112, 154
Self-worth, 200
Senses, 178
Sensing the feelings of others, 239
Sensory Perception, 178
Seven essentials, 17
Shedding the snakeskin, 122
Significance, 199
Skills of influence, 234
Smiling, 225
Socrates, 207
Source of our values, 168
Spranger, Eduard, 169
Steady case history, 80
Steady temperament, 59
Stroke me! 224
Strokes, 225
Subjective element of trust, 71
Success, 258
Superstitions, 130

Tact, 240

Taming pride, 137
Temperament, 50, 76, 170, 212
 - definition, 51
Temperament and behaviour, 98
Temperament and temperaments, 64
Territory of trust, 26
Tone of voice, 83, 197
Transactional Analysis, 218
Transactions, 227
Trust, 19, 27
Trust and the compliant temperament, 68
Trust and the dominant temperament, 66
Trust and the influential temperament, 67
Trust and the steady temperament, 68
Trust is organic, 73
Trustworthiness, 107, 149
 - definition, 39
Trustworthiness Quotient, 38
Trustworthy Adviser, 17, 31, 38, 54, 92, 165
Types of questions, 205

Unconditional negative strokes, 226
 positive strokes, 226
Unforgiveness, 134
Unmet expectations, 126

Values 167
Values and attitudes, 164
Vision, 251
Visual people, 186
Vulnerability, 37

Ways to decrease in-consistency, 45
 self-interest, 46
Ways to increase credibility, 42
 dependability, 40
Ways to increase empathy, 44
 integrity, 41
Whiskey story, 96
Willingness, 123
'Win-win' attitude, 22
Wisdom, 117, 159
Words, 197
Working environment, 36